W9-BUZ-867

# THE TREASURY OF SAINT FRANCIS OF ASSISI

# THE TREASURY
# OF SAINT FRANCIS OF ASSISI

*Edited by*
Giovanni Morello
Laurence B. Kanter

DISCARDED

DOMINICAN COLLEGE LIBRARY
Blauvelt, New York 10913

**Electa**

131923

*Cover Illustration*
Giotto, *Innocent III's Dream
of Saint Francis Holding Up the Church,*
detail.
Assisi, Basilica of Saint Francis,
Upper Church

*Translations*
Christopher Evans
Richard Sadleir

© 1999 by Electa, Milan
Elemond Editori Associati
All rights reserved

**The Treasury of Saint Francis of Assisi**
The Metropolitan Museum of Art,
New York
March 16–June 27, 1999

**Honorary Committee**

This exhibition was organized
by The Metropolitan Museum of Art,
the Sacro Convento di San Fancesco
di Assisi, and the Ministero per i Beni
e le Attività Culturali, with
the cooperation of the Biblioteca
Apostolica Vaticana

The exhibition in New York is made
possible by Robert Lehman
Foundation Inc.

Support for the international tour has
been provided by

**BANCA MONTE DEI
PASCHI DI SIENA** S.p.A.

Transportation assistance
has been provided by

**Alitalia**

This exhibition originated in Paris
at the Petit Palais from November 16,
1998 to February 14, 1999. After the
current showing it will travel to the
Fine Arts Museums of San Francisco

Giovanna Melandri
*Ministro per i Beni e le Attività Culturali*

Lamberto Dini
*Ministro per gli Affari Esteri*

Carlo Azeglio Ciampi
*Ministro del Tesoro*

Ferdinando Salleo
*Ambasciatore d'Italia in U.S.A.*

Francesco Paolo Fulci
*Ambasciatore d'Italia presso l'O.N.U.*

Giorgio Radicati
*Console d'Italia a New York*

Mario Serio
*Direttore Generale Ministero
per i Beni e le Attività Culturali*

Francesco Sicilia
*Direttore Generale Ministero
per i Beni e le Attività Culturali*

Pier Luigi Fabrizi
*Presidente della Banca Monte dei Paschi
di Siena S.p.A.*

Fausto Cereti
*Presidente di Alitalia*

John O'Connor
*Cardinal Archbishop of New York*

Agostino Gardin
*Ministro Generale dei Frati Minori
Conventuali*

Giovanbattista Re
*Sostituto alla Segreteria di Stato di S.S.*

Jorge M. Mejia
*Bibliotecario Archivista di S.R.C.*

Gabriel Montalvo
*Nunzio Apostolico in U.S.A.*

Raffaele Martino
*Rappresentante della Santa Sede
presso l'O.N.U.*

Raffaele Farina S.D.B.
*Prefetto della Biblioteca Apostolica
Vaticana*

Philippe de Montebello
*Director, The Metropolitan Museum of Art*

Philip H. Isles
*President, Robert Lehman Foundation Inc.*

**Scientific Committee**

*Chairman*
Antonio Paolucci, *Soprintendente per i Beni A.S. di Firenze Pistoia e Prato*

Costantino Centroni, *Soprintendente per i Beni A.A.A.S. di Perugia*
Giovanni Morello, *Conservatore dei Musei della Biblioteca Apostolica Vaticana*
Pasquale Magro, *Direttore del Museo-Tesoro della Basilica di San Francesco*
Gilles Chazal, *Directeur du Musée du Petit Palais*
Laurence B. Kanter, *Curator, Robert Lehman Collection, The Metropolitan Museum of Art*
Francesca Cristoferi, *Soprintendenza per i Beni A.A.A.S. di Perugia*
Pia Palladino, *Robert Lehman Collection, The Metropolitan Museum of Art*

**Organizing Committee**

Jorge M. Mejia, *Bibliotecario Archivista di S.R.C.*
Mario Serio, *Direttore Generale Ministero per i BB.CC.AA.*
Giulio Berrettoni, *Custode del Sacro Convento di San Francesco di Assisi*
Antonio Paolucci, *Soprintendente per i Beni A.S. di Firenze*
Raffaele Farina S.D.B., *Prefetto della Biblioteca Apostolica Vaticana*
Nicola Giandomenico, *Sacro Convento di San Francesco di Assisi*
Pasquale Magro, *Direttore del Museo-Tesoro della Basilica di San Francesco*
Giovanni Morello, *Conservatore dei Musei della Biblioteca Apostolica Vaticana*
Marcello Bedeschi, *Presidente della Fondazione Gioventù Chiesa Speranza*
Pier Paolo Saleri, *Retablo Cultura Arte Immagine*
Giancarlo Moretti, *Retablo Cultura Arte Immagine*

*Committee Assistant*
Paolo Bedeschi, *Retablo Cultura Arte Immagine*

*Commissioners for the Exhibition*
Pasquale Magro
Giovanni Morello

*Organizing Secretariat*
Retablo Cultura Arte Immagine srl, Rome

*Press and Public Relations*
Giacomo Galeazzi
Electa, Milan

*Restorations*
Rosaria Varoli Piazza, Istituto Centrale per il Restauro
Giuseppe Basile, Istituto Centrale per il Restauro
Bartoli Restauri srl
Cooperativa Beni Culturali, Spoleto
Maria Giorgi and Graziella Palei, Neith Restauri Opere Tessili, Siena

*Editorial Project*
Retablo Cultura Arte Immagine srl, Rome

*Photographs*
Studio Quattrone

*The entries were written by*
Laurence B. Kanter [LBK]
Patricia Lurati [PL]
Giovanni Morello [GM]
Pia Palladino [PP]
Alessandro Tomei [AT]
Umberto Utro [UU]

*Special thanks go to*
Giuseppe Borgia, *Provveditore Generale dello Stato*
Ennio Troili, *Ministero degli Affari Esteri*
Maria Grazia Benini, *Ministero per i Beni Culturali e Ambientali*
Franca Mataldi, *Ministero per i Beni Culturali e Ambientali*

*List of Lenders*
Assisi, Biblioteca Conventuale-Comunale
Assisi, Museo-Tesoro della Basilica
Città del Vaticano, Musei Vaticani
Cleveland, Cleveland Museum of Art
Kevelaer, Priesterhaus
New Haven, Yale University Art Gallery
New York, The Metropolitan Museum of Art, Robert Lehman Collection
Northampton (Mass.), Smith College Museum of Art
Nuremberg, Germanisches Nationalmuseum
Perugia, Galleria Nazionale dell'Umbria
Washington, D.C., National Gallery of Art

T. Robert and Katherine States Burke Collection

*"The Treasury of Saint Francis of Assisi," an exhibition that will travel around the world, is the message that Brother Francis is sending out today, with love and humility, to all men and women of good will.*

*A "mission" that is being received with even greater generosity since it is coming from the blessed city of Assisi, a city that we love as it is part of ourselves. Thus the "marks of veneration" offered to the saint down the centuries and now kept at the sanctuary in Assisi are coming back into the world, bringing with them an invitation to prayer, forgiveness and peace; to fraternity and poverty; to an intelligent dialogue among the different faiths; to joy and hope for all people, and especially for the young. For art is at the service of the revelation of God and conversion to the Gospels.*

*The whole exhibition speaks to us of values that resist the passage of time and that no earth tremor can destroy.*

*It is of particular importance to us, the Franciscans of Assisi, to greet all those who will visit the exhibition, representatives of "every tribe, tongue, people and nation."*

*In 1996 a total of 6,500,000 brothers and sisters from eighty-six countries came to this "hill of Paradise." Now it is Brother Francis, in his poverty and bearing his stigmata, who is journeying with a message of peace and goodwill, peace and joy, peace and hope.*

*I would like to thank all those who have had the generosity, passion and intelligence to conceive and realize "The Treasury of Saint Francis of Assisi" traveling exhibition. Our gratitude also goes to the Italian Ministry of Cultural Assets, the Biblioteca Apostolica Vaticana and the Museum-Treasury of the Basilica of San Francesco. In addition, we salute the religious and civil authorities of the cities that will host the exhibition.*

*The period of the exhibition will be punctuated by visits, religious meetings, cultural events, experiences of Franciscan life and opportunities to fraternize with the people. For each of these, our prayer, here, in Assisi, to Corpus Beati Francisci.*

*Finally, an invitation for you all: we are waiting for you in Assisi so that we can set off for Rome together to celebrate the great Jubilee of the year 2000, led by Brother Francis, the universal brother and missionary of peace, for Assisi is "the gateway to Rome."*

*Father Giulio Berrettoni*
Custode del Sacro Convento

*I was in the museum of the Basilica of San Francesco the day after it was struck by the earthquake of September 26, 1997. I walked through the debris of shattered glass and rubble, the dislodged and battered floors, the crumbling walls. I wasn't allowed in without a safety helmet. The firemen went ahead of me and escorted me step by step. I was accompanied by Father Pasquale Magro, librarian of the Sacro Convento and director of the museum, and by Vittorio Sgarbi, who had arrived from Rome wearing his art historian's hat, and not those of a member of parliament or television celebrity. I remember Sgarbi and I taking Guccio di Mannaia's chalice out of its repository: donated to the monastery by Pope Nicholas IV around 1290, it is a genuine masterpiece of Gothic gold work. It was as if we had gone back twenty years to the time when we—that is myself, a young superintendent and he, a very youthful inspector—had the job of looking after the works of art housed in the museums and churches of the Veneto.*

*Guccio di Mannaia's chalice was intact, as was the reliquary of the Holy Thorn, a gift from Saint Louis, king of France. Nor had the stained-glass windows of Simone Martini or the paintings of Sassetta and Masolino, Pietro Lorenzetti and Lorenzo Monaco, Fra Angelico and Giovanni di Paolo suffered any damage. The full force of the earthquake had struck the part of the monastery that houses the museum but left the works in it untouched.*

*At that moment, this came as a great relief. We had just been to see the disaster in the Upper Church (two thousand square feet of frescoes from the dawn of Italian painting, the vaults decorated by Cimabue and Giotto, which had collapsed instantly and been transformed into colored dust and fifty thousand fragments). The tympanum on the left (a thousand tons of stone laid bare and tilted out of true by the shock) threatened to fall onto the roof of the Lower Church above the chapel of San Giovanni and the frescoes of Lorenzetti, the whole system of Gothic vaults was in danger and the technicians told us that another collapse could take place at any time. Quite enough to be anxious about. However, the collections in the museum were out of danger and hadn't suffered a single scratch. The work of salvage and restoration could start right there. Within a few days of that terrible date of September 26, all the objects in the museum had been packed and stored in a safe part of the monastery. The idea of a traveling exhibition that would visit several of the world's capitals came later. The repair work on the Upper Church and the Sacro Convento had already commenced, Professors Giorgio Croci and Paolo Rocchi had already drawn up their plans for consolidation of the vaults (subsequently approved by the technical departments of the Ministry), it was already clear that the cost of restoring the building was going to exceed a hundred billion lire (sixty million dollars), and we had already made public our rash promise: Mass would be celebrated on Christmas Day 1999, on the eve of the Great Jubilee, in an Upper Church reopened for worship and restored to the admiration and affection of the entire world. So we decided, about six months later, that it would be a good idea to accompany the great effort that the country was about to make to restore the most important holy site in Italy by an exhibition that would warm the hearts and refresh the memories of people in France and the United States.*

*We have always been aware that the monastery of San Francesco belongs to the whole world, to people of all faiths and even to those who have none. After the earthquake, this has been made even clearer. I will never forget the groups of people from every country and speaking every tongue who came here last winter, when the restoration work was in full swing, driven by feelings of anxiety and solidarity. The areas where work was being carried out were closed to the public, no one could enter and yet people waited for a long time outside, in silence. From France, America, Poland, Japan, Italy and Spain, Argentina, Brazil and Australia. They stood outside the monastery and looked at the great wounded church with that sense of uneasiness and affectionate embarrassment that you experience when going to see a gravely ill relative in hospital, knowing full well that visits are not allowed. It is to thank these friends and to reassure them that the monastery of San Francesco will soon rise again that we decided to stage this exhibition.*

Antonio Paolucci
*Chairman, Scientific Committee*

*It would be no overstatement to say that the earthquakes that tore through Assisi and large parts of central Italy during the night of September 26, 1997, sent waves of shock and dismay around the world. Those of us who learned of the disaster the following morning waited anxiously for news from the Basilica of San Francesco—not only one of the holiest and most revered shrines anywhere, but also in many respects the birthplace of the Renaissance, the cradle of the Western artistic tradition. Few artistic monuments as complex, complete, or important have survived to the present century. The fear that this one might not survive into the next century was terrifying.*
*With great speed and characteristic dedication, local, regional, and national authorities in Italy set about the daunting task of securing and protecting the vast artistic treasures of Assisi. This exhibition took shape as part of their efforts: it was conceived in the hope of drawing attention to the importance of Assisi in the cultural patrimony not just of Italy, but of all mankind. It is a great privilege for us to present this wonderful survey of artistic riches from the Treasury of Saint Francis to American audiences. Presenting these treasures to the world in the wake of catastrophe, this exhibition underscores the need to preserve all aspects of our artistic legacy, wherever they may be found.*
*The Museum is fortunate to have the generous support of the Robert Lehman Foundation, whose commitment to this institution is deeply appreciated.*
*In addition, the Museum is grateful to Monte dei Paschi di Siena and Alitalia for their support and interest in this important project.*

Philippe de Montebello
*Director, The Metropolitan Museum of Art*

# CONTENTS

# INTRODUCTION

*Giovanni Morello*
Director of the Museums
of the Biblioteca Apostolica
Vaticana

On the night of October 3–4, 1226, Francesco di Pietro di Bernardone died in the bare surroundings of the Porziuncola. Having experienced the power of the love of God and his fellow creatures over the course of his brief existence (he was born in 1181), the poet of "perfect delight" rendered up his beautiful soul to God. The next day a multitude of people accompanied the body of the *poverello*, to the sound of "hymns and songs and trumpet blasts," to his birthplace, Assisi, for temporary burial in San Giorgio, a church that stood on the site where the Basilica of Santa Chiara would later be erected, a provisional tomb until such time as a special church could be built to provide a permanent home for his mortal spoils.

Less than two years later, on July 17, 1228, Pope Gregory IX, after solemnly proclaiming Francis a saint of the universal church, laid the first stone of the funeral basilica in which his body would be laid to rest. Built at the western end of the city, in the locality known as "Colle Paradisii" and on a plot of land donated to the pontiff himself by Simone Puzarelli, the church considered *caput et mater* of the Franciscan Order was ready to receive Francis's body after just two more years had passed.

Over the saint's tomb, which had quickly become a place of pilgrimage, not just one but two splendid buildings were raised within a short space of time, one on top of the other: the Lower Church and the Upper Church. Magnificently decorated by the greatest Tuscan and Roman painters of the time, from Cimabue to Giotto and Simone Martini and from Torriti to Rusuti and Pietro Cavallini, with scenes from the life of Francis and from the Old and New Testament, the Basilica of San Francesco at Assisi constitutes one of the highest peaks of Italian art. It can be said without exaggeration that it was at Assisi that the art of painting made a definitive break with the fixity of the Byzantine tradition and developed forms and stylistic features that were closer to real life. In this it was following Francis's message, so lyrically expressed in the celebrated *Canticle of the Creatures.*

On September 26, 1997, a tragic tremor shook the earth in two regions of Italy that are particularly rich in artistic and cultural treasures, Umbria and the Marches. The earthquake struck Assisi as well and the Basilica of San Francesco in particular, making it the symbol of this disaster as well as of the desire for rapid reconstruction. This exhibition, which would have been inconceivable at any other time, is in a sense the consequence of these events. Although the works of art and precious objects conserved in the Museum-Treasury of the Basilica were not significantly harmed by the earthquake, the building itself was damaged, making it necessary to dismantle the museum and store the objects displayed in it in a safe place. Many of these objects were originally donated to the Basilica by the faithful, or are offerings that have been made by popes and sovereigns to the "poor man of Assisi" ever since work commenced on the construction of his church.

A highly representative selection of the Basilica's artistic heritage is on show in this traveling exhibition, which is also intended to solicit the help of the public and all people of good will in the efforts to reconstruct the Basilica and Sacro Convento of Assisi.

Around seventy different works from Assisi are presented in the exhibition, enriched and augmented by generous loans from important museums and private collections of objects that have close links with the ones from the Basilica's treasury. This permits comparisons to be made that will be of undoubted interest not only to scholars and art lovers but to the general public as well.

In 1253 Pope Innocent IV gave the Franciscans dispensation to keep in the Basilica, notwithstanding their traditional vow of poverty, luxury articles such as "libros, calices, thuribola, cruces, sive de auro, sive de argento, tunicas" ["books, chalices, censers, crosses, whether of gold or silver, vestments," etc.]. A great deal of what remains of this treasure, having survived the adversities of nature and, at times, the rapacity of men, is now presented for the admiration of the international community in this unique exhibition.

Founding bull of the Basilica
and Sacro Convento di San Francesco
di Assisi (1228)

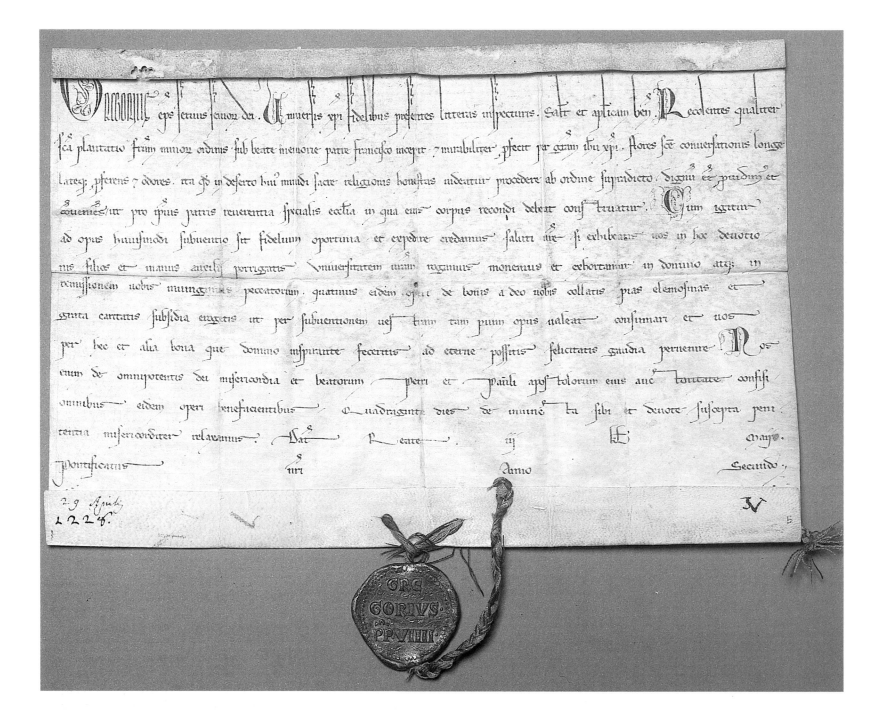

# A COLLECTION IN THE IMAGE
# OF THE FRANCISCAN SANCTUARY

*Pasquale Magro*

The Museum-Treasury of the sanctuary of Saint Francis—built in the thirteenth century—contains a collection of works of art that are an integral part of the place in which they are still housed today. These works, created with and for the sanctuary, have the same age and the same artistic and historical value as the building itself. The contents of the museum are made in the image of the place that gave rise to them, and each object reveals its votive origins and testifies to the historical development of this great center of the faith.[1] Thus these objects serve to recount the story of what is one of the most sacred and most dearly loved places in the world. And the thing that is most clearly expressed by this legacy from the past is the splendor of its origins, documented by the accurate and detailed inventories that were compiled in the thirteenth century by friars who were passionate experts on Beauty.[2]

Thus the objects that are now held up for the public's admiration should be regarded as pieces of the great mosaic that was formed during the golden age in the religious and artistic history of a sanctuary that the authorities in Rome—by permitting the creation of the Franciscan Order and thanks to contributions from the whole of Christendom—had erected in memory of Francis of Assisi. A golden thread links the pearls of the collection, and this unifying principle is none other than Francis himself. It is in him that the objects find their origin and their meaning. They are a gift made to a saint who has always been seen and celebrated by the Church and the faithful as the *alter Christus*.[3] When the author of the Perugian *Legenda* described the visit made by the Roman aristocrat Jacopa dei Settesoli to the dying Francis, he compared the offerings made to the saint with the gifts brought by the Three Wise Men in the Gospels.[4]

## A Basilican Museum

When describing it to the architects of his day as a spacious and beautiful place where it was a pleasure to go, to stay and to return, Federico Visconti—bishop of Pisa—already gave the Basilica of San Francesco the rank of number four in the hierarchy of places of pilgrimage, after Jerusalem, Rome and Compostela.[5] The majority of the panels depicting Saint Francis and scenes from his life lend particular importance to the miracles that occurred at his tomb. Dispersed throughout the Christian world, these pictures served

as true "works of propaganda," encouraging people to make the pilgrimage to Assisi, a thaumaturgic place where the presence and the power of the saint could be felt.[6]

Gregory IX, the pope who had himself laid the first stone of the Franciscan sanctuary in July 1228, wanted to make it a *specialis ecclesia. Specialis* not just for the architecture of this sepulchral "diptych" (comprising a crypt with a *cella memoriæ* and a church housing a pontifical throne), but also on the juridical and charismatic plane as was appropriate for a basilica consecrated entirely to the saint. Thus the church's dignity derives from the fact that its structural core, or *cella franciscana*, houses the relics of the founder of this *religio francescana* who had brought grace and spiritual abundance to both the ecclesiastic and civil bodies. "Recolentes qualiter Sancta plantatio Fratrum Minorum Ordinis sub Beato Francisco bonæ memoriæ incæpit et mirabiliter profecit; per gratiam Jesu Christi flores sanctæ conversationis longe, lateque proferens, et odores; ita quod in deserto hujus mundi sacræ religionis honestas videatur procedere ab Ordine supradicto; dignum providimus et conveniens, ut pro ipsius Patris reverentia specialis ædificatur ecclesia, in qua eius corpus debeat conservari."[7]

Gregory IX's desire to endow what is *par excellence* the *locus Sancti Francisci* with liturgical objects on a par with its status as a basilica is demonstrated by the gifts that he sent to Assisi at the time of the translation of the saint's body. The *Three Companions* bear witness to this: "The Pontiff has sent a gold cross studded with precious stones in which is set a relic of the wood of Christ's Cross. And with it decorative objects, liturgical objects and other objects to be used for serving at the altar, and extremely precious and magnificent sacred vestments."[8] It was at this moment that the collection in the museum of the treasury of the Basilica of San Francesco began to take shape, even though these original objects have not, alas, come down to us.

The sanctuary belonged to his Holiness the Pope, as is testified by the notarized deed recording the donation of the land on which the buildings were to be constructed.[9] Moreover, the consistorial bull *Is qui ecclesiam suam*, again issued by Gregory IX (April 22, 1230), declares the whole of the Basilica to be answerable only to the pope and to no other diocesan or regular bishop, notwithstanding its judicial-charismatic definition as *caput et mater totius Ordinis Fratrum Minorum*, rendered official by the selfsame solemn bull.[10]

The matter is not without importance: the fact is that the atmosphere of poverty that characterized the family of Francis of Assisi could have been undermined by a church that was inexorably destined to become a major shrine, possessing, by its very nature, an artistic patrimony that included frescoes and a set of sacred vessels and ornaments for the liturgy celebrated in the sacristy. By allocating to himself the ownership of the sanctuary and then giving it in usufruct to the friar-guardians, the pontiff was in reality creating a legal fiction that constituted a fundamental premise for the creation and preservation of an artistic heritage that is now fragmentary. These dispositions would be clarified by Innocent IV in the bull *Dignum existimamus* (July 16, 1253), which historians have chosen to consider the founding bull of the Basilica's Museum-Treasury.[11]

The Basilica's important collection of papal bulls testifies to the constant interest shown by popes in the church and monastery over the centuries (attending to its enlargement and restoration and to conservation of the stone and its decorations).[12] From the spiritual and juridical point of view, it was in 1754 that an event of fundamental importance for the historical evolution of the sanctuary took place: Benedict XIV raised it to the rank of patriarchal basilica and papal chapel, thereby confirming and perpetuating the intention of Gregory IX when he declared the "special nature" of this church, consecrated to God and to the memory of Francis. At the time the sanctuary was the only place of worship outside Rome to be given a title that had hitherto been reserved for the most important basilicas of the capital.[13] On average, popes were to make a pilgrimage to Assisi four times a century.

The Church historian Josef Lortz has devoted a particularly beautiful and profound essay to Francis, entitled *A Unique Saint*.[14]

In our view, what their Holinesses the Popes have done, "thanks be to God," for Francis and his sanctuary may have another significance as well: in effect, it has been a reiteration of the generous gesture made by the youthful Francis at the tomb of Peter, in Rome. "Francis," writes Thomas of Celano, "approached the altar of the Prince of Apostles and, astonished by the

miserable offerings left by the pilgrims, threw handfuls of coins onto it. By this gesture he wished to show that everyone should show particular honor to the man who God himself honors above all others."[15]

*A Monastic Museum*

According to Ludovico da Pietralunga (1570), Innocent IV consecrated—at the same time as the double church—the first nucleus of the monastery, comprising the domus or Gregorian palace: "As far as the consecration is concerned: he did not just consecrate the altar, but also the whole church and the monastery that is hence known as the sacred monastery."[16] And in fact, it is not at all common to consecrate the buildings housing the community in charge of a sanctuary. While it appears difficult to explain this move, we have to stress it for the prestige that it confers not only on the place but also on the objects used in daily life and during formal celebrations.

For over four hundred years, the evolution of the domus was systematically to presuppose a dual function: one pontifical, the other monastic. Not to take this aspect into account in our semantic and historical appraisal would prevent us from coming up with an objective explanation of the quality and value of the objects (originally in the sanctuary or monastery) that are on show in the museum. These objects, and the ordinary and extraordinary furnishings of the house used by the pope (and his entourage of cardinals and prelates), have neither the value nor the style of those usually found in a community of monks!

For over two hundred years, the popes' residence (house and garden) were situated to the north of the Basilican complex. Innocent IV made a long stay there—from May to October 1253—after his return from Lyons. At the end of the fifteenth century, the Franciscan pontiff Sixtus IV had the papal residence moved to the southwestern side of the monastery, which continued to grow through the construction of the large cloister behind the apse of the Basilica (the current location of the Museum-Treasury). When all is said and done, it was Sixtus IV who made it possible for the friars, over the course of the twentieth century, to exhibit the works of art in the rooms that he had had built and adorned with precious tapestries, objects and furniture. The memory of Sixtus IV— great patron of the Basilica of Assisi dedicated to the veneration of the saint whose thirty-seventh successor he was, in his capacity as minister general of the order—is kept alive by the presence of a statue representing him. His memory is also conjured up by the innumerable coats of arms on the outer walls of the building, as well as by the sumptuous altar frontal in the tomb and the great tapestry depicting the Franciscan tree that was woven for the salon-vestibule of the apartment: both of these works, made by Florentine and Flemish craftsmen respectively, bear at their center the effigy of a pope who was at once a devotee and a generous donor.[17]

The presence of the pontiffs in Assisi, as lords and owners of the sanctuary, and the periods spent there by cardinal delegates (or papal legates) and patrons of the order are sufficient to explain the existence of a sumptuous range of household articles. These include a precious and eclectic collection of terracotta vases and numerous antique pieces of pottery that were not all made locally.[18]

From the fourteenth century onward, the monastery was increasingly used for the education of young friars. Thus, while the institution of a general course of theology certainly represented a means of preparing the brothers for the priesthood, it also provided them with a philosophical and theological grounding imparted by the more cultivated friars. This is supported by the existence of a particularly extensive library (documented since 1265) filled with works covering the knowledge of the time. This is why the number of scholastic works in the original core of the monastery library considerably exceeds that of liturgical books (missals, anthem books and breviaries) coming from the church and the choir.[19]

*Patrons and Artists*

The civitas of Assisi would not by itself—partly for financial reasons—have been able to produce an artistic heritage of such high aesthetic quality and cosmopolitan character as to place it totally out of the common run.[20] Thus the objects of minor art in the Museum-Treasury reflect the history of the glorious art of a basilica from which they sometimes originated.

What is customarily called the major art of the sanctuary was produced by the greatest painters in Italy who, in the thirteenth and the fourteenth centuries, revolutionized Christian art. Apart from its spiritual dimension—for it is one of the greatest centers of the Christian faith—the Basilica of San Francesco is con-

sidered a melting pot where exceptional artists from all over Europe came to work on the church (an unparalleled workshop that drew architects, masons, painters, sculptors and workers in stained glass) in the fourteenth century. The Tuscans Giunta Capitini, called Pisano, Giovanni di Giuseppe, called Cimabue, Arnolfo di Cambio, Ambrogio di Bondone, called Giotto, Simone Martini and Pietro Lorenzetti; the Romans Pietro Cavallini, Filippo Rusuti and Jacopo Torriti; Umbrians like the Master of Saint Francis, Giovanni Bonino and Puccio Capanna; the Emilians Andrea dei Bartoli and Pace di Faenza: all helped to create a cycle of frescoes on the walls of the sanctuary that is considered the among the greatest of all time. As well as the wall paintings by a foreign artist (perhaps the Englishman Walter of Durham), we must also mention the stained-glass windows of the Upper Church, made by Rhenish and French masters.[21]

From the Basilica come a number of *sinopie*—detached during the work of conservation and restoration carried out over the last few decades—[22] as do the stained-glass windows visible in the rooms of the museum or kept in storage until it is possible to put them on display.[23]

We shall not dwell here on the patronage of aristocratic families (whether from Assisi, Florence or Rome) or on the gifts made by local confraternities to their side chapels in the Lower Church, major sources for the important collection of sacred objects that can now be admired in the museum.[24] All we shall mention are names linked to the major works that often mark stages in the history of art and which are borrowed from the museum for exhibitions staged all over the world.

We have already spoken of the munificence of two great patrons of the Basilica, Popes Gregory IX and Sixtus IV. The founding bull *Recolentes* was addressed to the entire body of the faithful ("Universis Christifidelibus") and offerings were requested from the whole of Christendom: the ecclesiastical and civil authorities, the people and clergy. The sainthood of Francis was declared the "grace of God for all" and the Sanctum Franciscum was supposed to be a votive symbol of this erected by the community of Christians.[25]

A couple of royal offerings are recorded: one by Henry III of England in 1245 (perhaps at the request of the English minister general Haymo of Faversham), the other from Wenceslas of Bohemia.[26]

It is believed that John of Brienne—Crusader king of Jerusalem and emperor of Constantinople who was present at the translation of the body of Saint Francis—was the donor of the magnificent vestments embroidered with gold, silver and chrome thread on yellow and red silk made by the Arab *tiraz* of Palermo.[27]

Louis IX, king of France, contributed to the realization of the work in stone and glass (Gothic rayonnant) carried out in the Basilica and treasury. The monumental Bible in seventeen volumes, part of which is conserved in the monastery library, is also attributed to the copyists in Saint Louis's extraordinary scriptoria. The royal *fleur-de-lis* of Angevin France appears on the stained-glass windows and frescoes of both the Upper and Lower Church. The royal symbol can also be seen in the chapels of Saint Martin and Saint Louis and in that of his brother, Bishop Louis of Anjou. A bust of the French king is set outside the two-light window in the south transept of the Upper Church.[28]

In 1288, the Franciscan friar Girolamo d'Ascoli Piceno was elected pope under the name of Nicholas IV. The pontiff gave the Basilica some precious vestments (now lost owing to wear-and-tear), but he remains most celebrated in Assisi for the chalice that he had made in Siena by Guccio Mannaia: this object, considered one of the finest ever examples of the goldsmith's art, bears a portrait of the pope.[29]

A French queen certainly gave the Basilica the Gothic reliquary of the Seamless Robe, a masterpiece made in a Parisian workshop by a goldsmith working for the royal house.[30]

In connection with Cardinal Egidio Albornoz, who decorated the chapel dedicated to Saint Catherine of Alexandria where he was later buried, Vincenzo Coronelli writes: "He was very useful to the sacred monastery and left it numerous gifts and various *objets d'art.*"[31]

Many centuries later, the artistic heritage of the Basilica and monastery were enriched by the bequest of the Francis Mason Perkins Collection. The American historian and art critic left the monastery fifty-six panel paintings and a marble bas-relief, in token of his gratitude to the Franciscan family and his veneration for a saint whose name he took when he underwent rebaptism in Assisi.[32]

The most recent donation to have come to Assisi is a piece of Greco-Oriental religious gold work: it is a Byzantine cross of benediction given to the museum by Monsignor Loris Capovilla, who had been invited to Assisi to commemorate the thirtieth anniversary of John XXIII's pilgrimage to the saint's tomb. The cross, made of wood with a fretwork design and decorated with precious metals, enamels, and semi-precious stones, was donated by the monks of Mount Athos to King Boris and Queen Joan of Bulgaria, who in turn offered it to the apostolic nuncio in Sophia, Giuseppe Roncalli, the future John XXIII. Finally, the pope entrusted it to his private secretary, Loris Capovilla, who, by passing it on to the Franciscan sanctuary, closed the list of great donors.[33]

*A Sometimes Difficult Transmission*

In the vast majority of cases, the collections in the museums of the treasuries of shrines and cathedrals are made up of precious objects (sacred vestments, altar frontals, reliquaries, chalices, processional crosses, sculptures or paintings) that have been rendered obsolete by cultural changes or the evolution in taste, ideas and the liturgy. At times, it was the sheer opulence of such places that, in the manner of a natural selection, led to the storage of the objects, thereby transforming them into museum pieces.

The transmission of artistic material is not always what it should be, and for a variety of reasons: frequent or injudicious use, inevitable wear-and-tear accentuated by climatic conditions that often cannot be controlled, barbarous pillages often perpetrated in the name of political ideals, thefts, corrupt practices and—in times of crisis—sales made by the community of friars.[34]

The unique involvement of the pontiff with Assisi, as is demonstrated by the presence of the papal throne in the church, has certainly helped to maintain the excellent and prestigious level of the works of art made at the behest of patrons or to be purchased by the community, but it has also made this sanctuary rich in valuable objects one of the favorite targets of anticlericals. In fact, the *protectio Beati Petri*, far from neutralizing attempts at depredation, has only accentuated them, as is demonstrated by a long series of pillages: the sack by the Ghibelline Muzio di Ser Francesco in the years 1319–21; the havoc wrought by the internal struggles between the noble families of Assisi; misappropriations by the communal public authorities (again at the end of the fourteenth century); confiscations by Napoleon's troops in the eighteenth century and at the beginning of the nineteenth, and again by the Italian state after unification.[35]

At the end of this brief historical account, it has to be said that in spite of the dramatic events and the dispersal of works of art and codices belonging to the Basilica and monastery, the collections on show in the museum of the treasury and the library are sufficient to temper our anger and regret over what has been lost.

[1] This is true not only for the museum of the treasury (which houses the oldest and most traditional objects), but also for the Frederick Francis Mason Perkins Collection (acquired more recently). It is equally true for the monastery library, whose existence is documented since 1265. A series of books on the Basilica and monastery as well their historical and artistic heritage, entitled "Il Miracolo di Assisi," has been published since 1969 by the Casa Editrice Francescana ofm. conv., Assisi.

[2] L. Alessandri, F. Pennacchi, *Inventari della sacristia del Sacro Convento di Assisi*, Quaracchi, 1920; L. Alessandri, *Inventario dell'antica biblioteca del S. Convento di San Francesco in Assisi*, Assisi, 1906.

[3] From the sixteenth century onward, the guidebooks written for pilgrims to the *corpus Beati Francisci* have systematically listed the precious reliquaries and their contents, as well as the pieces of liturgical gold work that now constitute the most admirable part of the Assisi treasure. See, for example: *Giardinello Ornato di varij fioretti. Raccolto da Fra Lodovico da Città di Castello* [after 1570], *detto il Filosofo, dell'Ordine Minore*, corrected reissue, Perugia, n.d.; G.A. Marcheselli, *Il Tesoro sacro e riverito che si conserva nella famosa basilica del Padre Serafico S. Francesco d'Assisi*, reissue, Assisi-Bassano, n.d.; V. Coronelli, *Sacro Pellegrinaggio alli celebri e devoti santuari di Loreto, Assisi ed altri che s'incontrano nel loro viaggio*, n.p. (but Venice), n.d.

(but 1700), pp. 33–45. Up until the beginning of the twentieth century, the liturgical treasure in Assisi was kept in the "secret sacristy," a room in the basement of the *campanile* that was entered from the "public sacristy" of the Lower Church.

[4] Cf. Various authors, *Fonti Francescane*, Assisi 1978 (1st reissue), p. 1271 and corresponding text in Matthew: 2, 11.

[5] Cf. M. Bihl (ed.), "E sermonibus Friderici de Vicecomitibus," in *Archivum Francescanum Historicum*, 1 (1908), 653.

[6] Cf. P. Magro, *La Basilica Sepolcrale di San Francesco in Assisi*, Assisi, 1991, pp. 89–95.

[7] G. Sbaralea (ed.), *Bullarium Franciscanum*, I, Rome, 1759, p. 40 (*Recolentes qualiter prima*) and p. 66 (*Speravimus hactenus*). See W. Schenkluhn, *La basilica di San Francesco in Assisi: Ecclesia specialis. La visione di Papa Gregorio IX di un rinnovamento della Chiesa*, Milan, 1994.

[8] Cf. Fonti Francescane, op. cit., pp. 1118–19.

[9] Cf. A.B. Langeli (ed.), *Le carte duecentesche del Sacro Convento di Assisi (Istrumenti, 1168–1300)*, from the series "Fonti e Studi Francescani–V," Padua, 1997, pp. 10–11.

[10] Cf. *Bullarium Franciscanum*, op. cit., p. 60.

[11] Cf. *Bullarium Franciscanum*, op. cit., p. 666.

[12] Cf. L. Alessandri, F. Pennacchi, *Bullarium Pontificium quod extat in archivio Sacri Conventus S. Francisci Assisiensis*, Quaracchi, 1920 et seq.

[13] Cf. P. Frutaz, "La Chiesa di san Francesco in Assisi, Basilica Patriarcale e Cappella Papale," in *Miscellanea Francescana*, 54 (1954), p. 399 et seq.; G. Abate, "La maestà del Romano Pontefice sulla Tomba di San Francesco," *Miscellanea Francescana*, 31 (1931), pp. 3–35.

[14] J. Lortz, *Un Santo Unico. Pensieri su Francesco d'Assisi*, Alba, 1958, p. 14.

[15] Cf. *Fonti Francescane*, op. cit., p. 560.

[16] L. da Pietralunga, *Descrizione della Basilica di San Francesco in Assisi*, introduction, notes and commentary by P. Scarpellini, Treviso, 1982, p. 51.

[17] L. Di Fonzo, "Sisto IV. Carriera scolastica e integrazioni biografiche (1414–1484)," in *Miscellanea Francescana*, 86 (1986) pp. 4356–445 ("For St. Francis and the sacred monastery of Assisi"); Various Authors, *Il Paliotto di Sisto IV ad Assisi. Indagini ed intervento conservativo*, series "Il miracolo di Assisi 9," Assisi, 1991; P. Magro, "Il Paliotto di Sisto IV ad Assisi," in *San Francesco*, LXXI/11 (1991), pp. 47–54.

[18] G. Palumbo, H. Blake, *Ceramiche medioevali assisiane. Un prezioso rinvenimento nel Sacro Convento di S. Francesco*, Assisi, 1972.

[19] C. Cenci, *Bibliotheca manuscripta ad sacrum conventum assisiensem*, series "Il miracolo di Assisi–4/I–II," Assisi, 1981. We know that a fair number of codices have been dispersed and are now in the Vatican Apostolic Library, the Augusta Library in Perugia and libraries in Grottaferrata, Poppi, St. Petersburg, Birmingham and even Perth (Australia). See vol. I, pp. 15–23 ("Increase and reduction in the number of codices").

[20] S. Nessi, "Il tesoro di S. Francesco in Assisi: formazione e dispersione," in Various Authors, *Il Tesoro della Basilica di San Francesco ad Assisi*, series " Il miracolo di Assisi 3," Assisi-Florence, 1980, pp. 13–23.

[21] A complete vision of the sanctuary at Assisi (architecture, iconography, stained-glass windows, liturgical objects) can be found in the monumental work sponsored by ENEL: Various Authors, *Basilica Patriarcale in Assisi. San Francesco. Testimonianza artistica, Messaggio evangelico*, Milan, 1991.

[22] A. Tomei, "Il disegno preparatorio di Jacopo Torriti per il volto del Creatore nella Basilica di Assisi," in *Bollettino d'Arte*, pp. 227–32; S. Romano, "Il disegno preparatorio per la Cattura di Cristo nella Basilica di Assisi," in *Bollettino d'Arte*, pp. 233–37.

[23] G. Marchini, *Corpus Vitrearum Medii Aevi. Italia I. L'Umbria*, Rome, 1973.

[24] S. Nessi, *La Basilica di San Francesco in Assisi e la sua documentazione storica*, series "Il miracolo di Assisi 5," Assisi, 1994 (2nd ed.), pp. 381–405 ("Illustrious patrons and devotees. The treasure of the basilica"). See too pp. 430–60 ("The chapels").

[25] S. Nessi, "Il Tesoro di San Francesco," op. cit., pp. 13–23.

[26] Ibid., p. 13.

[27] Various Authors, *La seta e la sua via*, Rome, 1995, p. 105.

[28] M. Assirelli, "Il movimento francescano e la Francia," in Various Authors, *Francesco d'Assisi. Documenti e Archivi. Codici e Biblioteche. Miniature*, Milan, 1982, pp. 310–18; S. Nessi, "Il Tesoro di San Francesco," op. cit., p. 16. The extremely generous patronage shown by St. Louis (1234–1271) to the Franciscans—in both Paris and Assisi—appears to justify the identification of his portrait carved in the stone frame of a "French storied window" (ca. 1270). Others have seen it as a representation of Frederick II, but there are few grounds to support such a hypothesis (E. Lunghi, "Presenza di Federico II nella Chiesa di San Francesco ad Assisi," in Various Authors, *Assisi al tempo di Federico II*, Assisi, 1995, pp. 213–42).

[29] M.G. Ciardi Dupré dal Poggetto, "Il primo papa francescano, Niccolò IV (1288–1292), e il suo influsso sulla miniatura umbra," in Various Authors, *San Francesco d'Assisi*, op. cit., pp. 358–65.

[30] D. Gaborit Chopin, "Reliquaire avec saint Francis et sainte Claire," in Various Authors, *L'art au temps des rois maudits, Philippe le Bel et ses fils*, Paris, 1998, pp. 193–95.

[31] V. Coronelli, *Sacro pellegrinaggio…*, op. cit., p. 37. See: G. Fratini, *Storia della Basilica e del Convento di S. Francesco in Assisi*, Prato, 1882, pp. 186–89; E. Dupré Theseider, "Il cardinale Albornoz in Umbria," in Various Authors, Storia e arte in Umbria nell'età comunale, II ("Atti del VI Convegno di Studi Umbri," Gubbio, May 26–30, 1968), Perugia, 1971, pp. 609–40.

[32] L. Marioli, "La collezione Federico Mason Perkins aperta nel Museo-Tesoro del Sacro Convento," in *San Francesco*, LXVI/10 (1986), pp. 29–35; F. Zeri, *La collezione Federico Mason Perkins*, series "Il miracolo di Assisi 8," Assisi, 1988, pp. 11–13.

[33] "Commemorazione del pellegrinaggio di Papa Giovanni XXIII in Assisi (1962-1992)," in *San Francesco*, LXXII/10 (1992), pp. 25–40.

[34] S. Nessi, "Il Tesoro di San Francesco," op. cit., p. 20 et seq.

[35] On the depredations suffered by the treasury following the Napoleonic campaigns and the unification of Italy, see S. Nessi, *La Basilica di San Francesco…*, op. cit., pp. 381–405 et seq.; for the library, see G. Zanotti, *Assisi. La Biblioteca del Sacro Convento*, Assisi, 1990, pp. 43–64 ("The Napoleonic Upheaval"), pp. 65–75 ("Establishment of the Municipal Library").

# FRANCIS OF ASSISI: HIS CULTURE, HIS CULT, AND HIS BASILICA

*Carl Brandon Strehlke*

*The Culture of Saint Francis*

We know of only one encounter between Saint Francis of Assisi and a work of art. In 1206 he wandered into the small church of San Damiano outside his hometown and kneeled in front of what his biographer Thomas of Celano called a painted cross (fig. 1). Tradition identifies it as a cross (fig. 2) now in the Basilica of Santa Chiara in Assisi. This imposing image of a triumphant Christ that challenges death with open eyes and rigid stance set Francis, then in his early twenties, on a new path.

Three years before Francis had returned home from enemy captivity in a war that had pitted Assisi, lead by its urban merchants, to which Francis's family belonged, against the town's exiled nobles whose property they had forcibly confiscated. Despite the class conflict Francis's great ambition was to become a knight like the foes he had fought. His father, Pietro Bernardone, a rich draper, indulged him, and had Francis fitted to join a makeshift army, which was planning to maraud in south Italy for a French nobleman. But the saint lasted only two days making it no farther than nearby Spoleto. Before he strayed into San Damiano, in another search for spiritual renewal, he had gone on a pilgrimage to Rome where he dressed up as a beggar in front of Saint Peter's. Now Francis believed that the cross in San Damiano commanded him to restore the church.

A building project required money to buy supplies and pay for labor. Intuitively guessing that his father would not be forthcoming, Francis borrowed a sum from a priest to purchase stones. But it did not prove enough so he took bolts of cloth from the family warehouse and left town to sell them.

Thomas of Celano relates that the bolts that the saint pinched were not ordinary cloth but expensive scarlet, a well shorn English wool which was so fine that it felt like silk. Scarlet was often dyed a bright red giving rise to that very meaning for the word. Not only was the wool expensive, but kermes, the basic material for the dye, had to be imported from the Middle East, making vermilion scarlets even more highly prized. Only the upper and professional classes wore them. For example, a picture of circa 1283 in Assisi shows the nobleman Favarone di Uffreduccio, father of Francis's first female follower, Saint Clare, dressed in scarlet robes lined in miniver (fig. 3). Martin de Canal in his chronicle of Venice, written in the mid-thirteenth century, described the officials of the glassmakers' guild

marching in a pageant honoring the new doge in scarlet. And later Boccaccio wrote of doctors coming to Florence from the university city of Bologna dressed in scarlets. The impression scarlets made might explain why it figures in the legend of another holy man of the period: Saint Galganus, a Tuscan gentleman who died the year of Francis's birth, is said to have given bolts of red wool away as alms.

Contemporaries would have also recognized the significance and hierarchy of textiles in religious art. In Alberto Sotio's crucifix of 1187 in Spoleto—a work Francis may well have known—the mourning Virgin wears a red mantle made of scarlet like that which Francis sold. The Christ depicted ascending to Heaven in the upper section wears a purple mantle. Purple was the color of royalty and Francis's family firm would not have dealt in textiles dyed that color although, in exaggeration, one biographer says the saint wore purple as a youth. The best purple silks were the monopoly of the Byzantine imperial workshops. Christ's sheer loincloth is a thin, gauze-like north Egyptian linen embroidered with colored silk. Much sought in Europe, the cloth, known as Alessandrian linen, was often used as a woman's veil, and appears as such in numerous paintings of the Virgin and Child.

Francis's surreptitious sale of the scarlet bolts created a riff with his father, who had him arrested. Francis cleverly avoided jail by declaring himself a penitent under church jurisdiction. Nevertheless Pietro Bernardone disowned him in a public ceremony in which Francis undressed and gave back his clothes and money. Recognizing Francis's gifts and yet desirous to control a wayward youth, the bishop took him in. A brief experience in a monastery as a dishwasher proved a disaster. Dishwashing ranked as one of the lowest professions (it appears as such in Thomas Aquinas's *Summa theologica*), and even Francis may not have been ready for the degradation.

Soon Francis was living in the impoverished, but socially recognized, position of a hermit doing good works like assisting in the town's leper colonies. This went on until one Sunday in 1208 or 1209, he was struck by a Gospel lesson in which Christ bids his disciples to leave all to follow him. Taking this as a personal bidding, Francis renounced all worldly goods and ornament, and made for himself a simple hooded tunic.

The rigid social structure of the medieval age meant

**Giotto (attributed to),** *Saint Francis Prays in San Damiano,* ca. 1290. Assisi, Basilica of San Francesco.

1

2

Anonymous Umbrian Artist, *Crucifix*, ca. 1175–80, tempera on panel. Assisi, Basilica of Santa Chiara.

that dress was an immediate give-away of status. Francis's earliest biographers cleverly play on this standard marking each step in his spiritual development by a change in attire. Even in his dandified youth Francis did not conform to convention. In *The Legend of the Three Companions*, a collection of stories gleaned from his closest followers eighteen years after his death, the young Saint Francis designs his own clothes, and flaunts social conventions by dressing above his station and by combining fancy and ordinary textiles. "He passed all limits in dress. He had the most sumptuous clothes made up even if they were not fitting to his social condition, and, in his search for originality he even sewed together in the same piece of clothing precious textiles with coarse ones." The same source recounts that while Francis was preparing to become a knight, he "got ready outfits of precious cloth, and even though he was less rich than his townsman (with whom he was leaving to become a knight), he was much more loose in spending."

When Francis renounced worldly goods, his obsession with clothes did not change, only the clothes did. Thomas of Celano writes: "He took his shoes off, he abandoned his cane, and he contented himself with a single tunic and he substituted the belt with a rope cord. From that instant he fashioned for himself a costume that reproduced the image of the cross…; and he made it very rough … and so poor and coarse that it would be impossible that anyone would envy it." Francis compared the brown costume to the plumage of his favorite bird, the lark, which "has the color of the earth: So the lark is a good example for why friars should not have elegant and beautifully tinted clothes, but clothes of modest price and of a color that is similar to the earth, which is the most humble element."

Despite the religious significance of the design, the new tunic with its hood made out of a single piece of rough cloth resembled that of the peasants who toiled Assisi's fields. This choice may have been a mark of solidarity. In 1210 a provision of an accord drawn up in Assisi to bring peace between the social orders confirmed the liberation of previously indentured agricultural workers. This had long been a sticking point: fearful of losing fieldworkers, this is what the nobles had most fought against in the war of 1202 which had seen Francis's capture.

Perhaps because of its resemblance to peasant attire, the dress of Francis and his first followers made a deep

3

Master of Saint Clare (Benvenuto Benvieni da Foligno ?), *Favarone di Uffreduccio Tries to Remove His Daughter Clare from the Nunnery*, ca. 1283, tempera on poplar panel. Assisi, Basilica of Santa Chiara.

impression. One observer declared that they were either one with God or real fools, because they lead a wretched life: they hardly eat, they walk barefoot, and they have vile clothes. Their look marked them as *quasi sylvestres homines*, either woodsmen or wild men. This scared people. On seeing them from afar girls were said to flee in fear that the friars' madness would bewitch them. Brethren who had been rich had trouble adjusting to this new life and dress. One effete and noble novitiate complained about the habit's hood, long length, and open sleeves. In comparison to the short tight male costumes of the age wearing a Franciscan habit must have felt like a tent.

Francis left precise instructions about the proper friar's dress. In the draft for the Rule written in 1221 he ordered that the humble clothes be mended only with sackcloth or burlap. In the Rule of 1223, which became the official Rule, he was a little more liberal allowing for a second habit and even shoes. But the concession bothered him. He felt many of the provisions of that rule were forced on him. In his final testament he reminisced that the first friars were content with a single habit that had been repaired inside and out, and, those who wished, also a belt and underpants. Francis hated friars wearing more than one or two layers of clothes. He himself did not let the cold bother him, and told Brother Leo that there was nothing more joyful than seeing icicles forming on the hem.

Other writings recall that if Francis judged a habit's cloth as unusually supple he would roughen it with a lining made from scratchy strands of rope. However, in the Rule of 1223 he also reminded his friars not to scorn men who wear soft and colored clothes, and who partake of delicate food and drink. Almost as if he was reminded of his own youthful days as a clotheshorse, *The Legend of the Three Companions* relates: "He insisted that the brothers not judge anyone, and not look with scorn on those who live in luxury and dress with exaggerated refinement and splendor." Truly this was a man with a soft spot for clothes and good dress.

Francis's own habit became an object of fetish devotion. Once when he passed through the town of Borgo San Sepolcro people tore off pieces as souvenirs. Similarly in Bologna in 1222 women and men went crazy trying to touch its fringe. The great archbishop of Pisa Federico Visconti remembered he had been lucky enough to have touched Francis. Because his clothes were often ripped to shreds, the saint had to

get new habits, a luxury that he frowned on in other friars.

Francis was buried without any relics having been taken except for some of his hair. This was not the usual procedure for a person who had died in the odor of sanctity. For example, when his greatest follower, the mesmerizing preacher Anthony of Padua, died in 1231, his jaw and tongue were removed and later encased in reliquaries. When Jordan of Giano went to Germany in the 1230s, Thomas of Celano gave him as relics bits of Francis's hair and tunics. Jordan was surprised how reverently the Germans received them—in part because he had not predicted that Francis would be an object of adulation and possibly because he thought the relics were meager fare. In the late 1200s and early 1300s travelling reliquaries with bits of Francis's tunics became popular (fig. 4). Produced by Franciscan friars themselves, the images on these reliquaries often repeat the compositions of frescoes in the Basilica of San Francesco in Assisi suggesting that their production was centered in Assisi.

Francis was not only adamant about clothes, he was violently repulsed by any material sign of well being. A famous story recounts how he repented for having slept on a feather pillow. He abhorred abundance and richness in furnishing, and he did not appreciate anything superfluous in tableware or crockery. One Easter dinner he refused to join his friars at a table that they had specially laid with white table cloths and glasses. He appeared instead at the door disguised as a beggar. Even nourishment presented problems for him. Remorseful at having eaten chicken, though racked by ill health and in need of substantial food, he asked a companion to lead him through town by a rope denouncing him for gluttony. Francis's behavior was often purposively theatrical. The beggar sitting in the hearth, the penitent lead like a criminal, and numerous other incidences like rolling in a pig sty and then appearing in front of the pope or preaching to the birds are obviously staged performances. He was aware of this, and himself said that he had to become crazed to become a man of God.

However, Francis's violent reactions against wealth and fine man-made things suggest an attraction for them. And indeed dreams of material splendor—marble thrones and mansions filled with shining armor—often occupied his sleeping hours. Disdainful of riches, Francis nevertheless had an exaggerated respect for

Italian artist working circa 1320, *Reliquary Diptych*. Baltimore, Walters Art Gallery.

4

Troyes written in the 1170s and 1180s (these tales in part sparked the "discovery" of King Arthur's remains at Glastonbury in 1191, further firing the imagination of Europeans everywhere). In a world in which the knight had become the subject of antiquarian interest as well as sainthood, knightly romances were considered a fit subject for church decoration. Not everyone appreciated this development: in the early twelfth century Bernard of Clairvaux had complained about sculptures of fighting knights and hunters winding their horns in monastic cloisters. In Italy notable examples are the chivalric tale depicted in the side portal of the Cathedral of Modena and the sculpture of Charlemagne's great knight Roland on the façade of the Cathedral of Verona. A remarkable story in *The Legend of Perugia*, an early account of Francis's life, illustrates how embedded these heroes were in his mind. To a friar's request for a breviary, the saint replied that Charlemagne, Roland, and Oliver and all the paladins and robust men who fought the infidels for Christ are greatly honored, but now there are those "who wanting to receive honor and human praise, it is enough to just hear about them." He meant it was just enough to hear about Christ, but in saying so he revealed a deep-seated taste for the knights of old. In principle Francis was against learning and did not want his friars to own books, but he showed himself to have been an assiduous reader of knightly romances.

As in his youth Francis had wanted to be a knight, as a friar he desired martyrdom. He had failed twice to reach North Africa and the Middle East where this was still possible for a Christian. Later a twinge of jealousy colored his pronouncement on hearing of the martyrdom in early 1220 of four friars, who had foolishly started preaching in the mosque of Marrakech, that no friar be singled out for honors. (The news of these deaths had motivated Saint Anthony to become a Franciscan, and try, like them, to seek martyrdom). In 1219, travelling with crusaders, Francis had finally made it as far as Dumyât (Damietta) at the mouth of the Nile delta. A fierce siege was then on, but Francis made contact with the enemy, preached to the Egyptian sultan al-Kamil, and even foolishly challenged the revered spiritual leader Fakhr al-Din-Farisi to a trial by fire. (Fakhr later was sent as an emissary to Frederick II in Sicily.) Jacques Vitry, bishop of Acre, the crusader stronghold in the Holy Land, dishearteningly noted that Francis did not convert a single Muslim,

good form. His youthful obsession with knighthood never left him. Courtesy, the trait that most distinguished knights, was for him a quality that friars should also cultivate. The early biographies mirror his chivalric idealism and read in part like knightly romances. Francis closely constructed his own conduct according to a courtly model: Like a knight devoted to his loved one, he called poverty his lady, he was a herald for Christ, and his friars were his companions of the Round Table and minstrels of the Lord. These analogies come from French and Provençal literature, which the saint greatly admired being an adequate speaker of French into which he often burst into song. When the young Francis played a beggar on the steps of Saint Peter's in Rome he babbled in French as if he were a pilgrim from abroad. In fact, his name, in Italian meaning Frenchman, was said to commemorate his birth while his father was away on business (he had been originally baptized Giovanni).

Like many of his upbringing, Francis was well versed in the romances and Arthurian tales of Chrétien de

French artisan working in Limoges possibly with a design by an Italian artist, *Reliquary of the Stigmata of Saint Francis of Assisi,* ca. 1230–40, enamel and gilt bronze. Paris, Musée du Louvre.

but only caused many in his own staff to become Franciscans.

Important elements in the Franciscan legend were visions and dreams. Saint Francis's greatest vision occurred on a September night of 1224 on Mount La Verna after a symbolic forty days of fasting and prayer. After his death followers testified that he had seen the crucified Christ in the form of a seraph and that his body was marked by the stigmata, or the wounds, that Christ suffered on the cross. While revelation of this miracle confirmed his sanctity for many, when Gregory IX de' Conti (r. 1227–1241), elected pope only a few months after Francis's death, canonized him, he omitted all mention of the stigmatization in his proclamation. And Gregory had long been Francis's good friend and supporter. His veneration knew no bounds: he was behind the first painted portrait of Francis, which is in the Benedictine monastery of Subiaco. Made before or just immediately after the canonization, it does not show the wounds. Over the next decade Francis's followers lobbied hard, and by the middle of the century the stigmatization became doctrine. Gregory also relented. As he wrote, a dream in which Francis showed him the wound in his side accounted for the about-face. Thomas of Celano had also used a dream as a way of illustrating why in 1209 Pope Innocent III de' Conti (r. 1198–1216) had placed Francis under his protection when the holy man showed up in the Lateran palace with a ragtag group of twelve followers. Co-opting a story taken from Dominican hagiography, Celano wrote that Innocent had a dream of Francis holding up the church. Like the Stigmatization, the subject of the two papal dreams became commonplace in depictions of Francis's life.

While dreams and visions were common enough literary devises in hagiography, Innocent III was not particularly susceptible to them. As pope he had helped Jean de Matha, a former classmate at the University of Paris, found the Trinitarian order dedicated to ransoming Christian slaves. Early sources relate that when Jean revealed his vision of Christ leading two shackled slaves—one white and one black, Innocent was not able to suppress a smile. However, even the pope could not overcome general credence; when he issued the founding charter, he went out of his way to take the vision seriously. It became the Trintarians' symbol, and appears as such in the mosaic of circa 1209 on the façade of their headquarters in Rome, San Tommaso *in formis.*

Francis's stigmatization had taken place on La Verna, a savage and wild mountain not far from Arezzo, which a local nobleman had donated as a spot for a hermitage. In art the place is usually depicted as isolated and inhabited by beasts and birds. A reliquary of the Stigmatization shows it dominated by trees (fig. 5). Indeed here on La Verna Francis's rapport with nature was as celebrated as his communion with the heavenly seraph. An early account says that on his arrival birds greeted him in great numbers. Appropriately, Thomas of Celano and Bonaventure of Bagnorea's official biographies both contain chapters on the saint's affinity with animals. They are respectively entitled: "Love of the saint for animate and inanimate creatures," and "The sentiment of piety. How creatures without reason seemed to love him." Celano also wrote episodes about Francis's friendship with a little bird, a falcon, bees, a pheasant, and a cicada. Other celebrated incidences relate how he calmed a fierce wolf and preached to the birds.

Similar stories are part and parcel of most medieval hagiography. They played on the complex feelings that people had about the animal kingdom. Francis's intuitive embrace of the animals belittled contemporary fears about them. Endowed with infinite symbolic meanings, animals were a recurrent subject of church decoration. For example, the façade of the Cathedral of Lucca, under construction in the early 1200s, contains all manner of animal imagery. And this was true of most other works of art then, be they the beasts decorating illuminated manuscripts or the lions and griffins incorporated into candleholders, pulpits, and church entrances. Animals were a reflection of the human world (medieval bestiaries often listed their human traits), and they mirrored the rigid categories of medieval society. In an account of one of Francis's sermons to birds he is described as preaching to doves, crows, and bull-finches, which contemporaries would have recognized to be the most common birds and the symbols of manual laborers.

Was Francis's sermon hiding a more dangerous reality? If Francis was not preaching to birds but to workers and farmers without permission, it was not only rabble rousing, but also in the early 1200s heretical because preaching was the preserve of the educated clergy. Local ecclesiastical authorities, jealous of this privilege,

5

*Christ Enthroned with the Sun and Moon and the Nursing Virgin*, early 1200s, marble. Assisi, Cathedral of San Rufino.

6

which was being built during the course of Francis's lifetime, has a relief of Christ surrounded by the sun and moon juxtaposed to a depiction of the nursing Virgin (fig. 6). The image seems to recall a passage in a letter written sometime before 1238 by Saint Clare of Assisi to the sister of the king of Bohemia, who had just founded a Franciscan convent in Prague. Speaking of Christ, Clare writes: "The sun and moon admire his beauty; his awards are valuable and of infinite greatness. Here I am referring to that Son of the Most High, to whom the Virgin gave birth, without losing her virginity. Hug his most sweet Mother, who gave birth to a Son that the heavens could not contain, yet she took him in the small cloister of her holy breast and carried him in her virginal womb." Although we do not know the precise date of the sculpture, the connection to Francis's *Canticle* and Clare's letter seems obvious, or, at very least, they all depend on common visual and theological traditions. It would seem to be in Assisi the one work of art that most reflects Francis's vision. Afterwards it was Francis himself who became a subject for art.

### Saint Francis's Life in Books and Pictures

Francis's cult was promulgated by the vast network of the order he created. Before his death it had already made an impact on Italian and European culture. In 1216 Bishop Jacques de Vitry had commented on the visible and reassuring presence of the Friars Minor midst the corruption of the papal court, then in Perugia, noting that they renounce all possessions, are totally detached from temporal things, go into the city by day, and retire to nights of contemplation in hermitages. He further remarked that they meet regularly. These assemblies, held all over continental Europe, served to govern the order and spread its mission, but also greatly enriched the friars' culture by putting distant groups in contact with each other.

A primary concern after Francis's canonization was an official life. Pope Gregory IX ordered Thomas of Celano, a learned friar who, however, had spent little time with the saint, to write it. Finished in February of the next year, this work is full of wonderful accounts of Francis's personality. So even though it closely follows the format of medieval saints' lives, the book has an immediacy that later biographies lack. As Francis's acquaintances aged, however, there was a sense that connection with him would be lost. Consequently, in 1244 Crescenzio Grizi, the Minister Gen-

were the very ones who tried to block the expansion of the friars. But most authors have not questioned if Francis actually talked to the birds—it suits his crazy behavior. Francis's acceptance of the animals as human-like would have been in keeping with much of the art of his day. For example, in Spoleto, very close to Bevagna, the little town where he had preached to the birds, the sculptures on the façade of the church of San Pietro show scenes of various animal legends as well as depictions of beasts of burden. Francis's sermon had an enduring impact: early Franciscan literature inspired Pier Paolo Pasolini's beautiful film *Hawks and Sparrows* which tells the story of a humble friar's attempt to get the birds to understand him.

In September 1225, toward the end of his life, Francis wrote a poem called the *Canticle of the Creatures* in which he celebrates all beings, and specifically the sun, moon, wind, fire, and earth, naming them sisters and brothers. He even includes death, which he dignifies as "our sister corporeal death." The canticle begins with two verses dedicated to Brother Sun and Sister Moon. The sun and moon as allegories of Christ and the Virgin were common Christian conceits. The lunette of the main portal of the Cathedral of San Rufino in Assisi, eral of the order, mandated at the General Chapter of Genoa that information be gathered from Francis's surviving disciples. This injunction engendered a number of new texts including *The Legend of the Three Companions* and *The Legend of Perugia*. These as well as other testimony served as a basis for Thomas of Celano's revised, or second life finished in 1247. It included many new episodes like that of the cross of San Damiano and the dream of Innocent III. It also did not mention by name Brother Elias, a principle character in the first biography, who had in the meantime been disgraced. The second life also differs from the first in the omission of references to Francis's frivolous youth and the almost total exclusion of miracles. The latter bothered some brethren, and, therefore, at the instruction of the next Minister General, Giovanni Parenti, Thomas of Celano composed the *Treatise on the Miracles of the Blessed Francis*. This was completed in 1253 and approved at the General Chapter of Metz in 1254.

These written lives provide a basis for judging the earliest images of the saint, which were just as important as the writings for promulgating the cult. In the absence of relics paintings served as manifestations of devotion. A picture (cat. no. 1/1) in the treasury of the Basilica of Assisi was reportedly painted on the very board on which Francis's corpse was washed. Recorded in the sixteenth century as over the entrance to the sacristy, originally it was likely in a more accessible area of the Basilica, and, therefore, part of its earliest public decoration. Its dating is still an open question, but it seems to me that it may be earlier than generally considered. It has been attributed to Giunta Pisano who in 1236 had painted a lost crucifix for the Basilica. The tabernacle became an important model: there is a near replica in the Pinacoteca Vaticana (cat. no. 1/2) and some of the scenes in an early panel once in San Francesco in Pisa (now in the Museo Nazionale di San Matteo), which has also been attributed to Giunta Pisano, clearly relate to it. The precise chronology of these paintings and the importance of the supposed model in Assisi need to be worked out. The association of the panel in Assisi with the ablution of Francis's corpse rendered it the status of a reliquary. This is also the case with a panel by the Master of Saint Francis in Santa Maria degli Angeli, which bears an inscription recording that it was painted on his deathbed.

In the first dated painting of Saint Francis (fig. 7),

Bonaventura Berlinghieri's retable in San Francesco in Pescia of 1235, there are not only miracles, but also depictions of more personal episodes in Francis's life: the Preaching to the Birds and the Stigmatization. These two scenes will become part of the official hagiography as laid out in the frescoes of Assisi. The number of other biographical scenes in two other panels painted in Tuscany, the great retable in the Bardi Chapel of Santa Croce in Florence and a retable in the Museo Civico of Pistoia from the Franciscan church of that city, prove that by the middle of the thirteenth century representations of Francis's life as opposed to his often posthumous miracles were becoming increasingly popular. The decision in the 1250s to publish a treatise on his miracles suggests that not everyone appreciated this trend and that prejudice for a traditional view that saintliness be manifest through miracles was strong. Interestingly none of the miracles represented in the early paintings will appear in the two biographical cycles in Assisi, which are both based on the official life of the saint written by Bonaventure of Bagnorea between 1260–63. While Bonaventure devoted a good half of his text to miracles (some of them not reported before), they took second place to his messianic vision of Francis.

Devotion to Saint Francis was not restricted to the order. In the bull of canonization Gregory IX mandated that the whole church celebrate his feast (fixed as October 4th). This greatly increased piety for the saint. At least three of the earliest paintings, while in Franciscan churches, were commissioned for private family chapels: the Mainardi for the panel in Pescia, the Tebaldi for the panel in Santa Croce in Florence, and the Cinquini for Giotto's panel in the Louvre originally in San Francesco in Pisa.

The very first image of Francis is the fresco in the Benedictine monastery of Subiaco, a place which Francis himself had visited. The fresco shows him without a halo, and, therefore, probably predates his canonization in 1228. It also contains a figure of a devotee, probably Lando, abbot of Subiaco from about 1227, but, more importantly, the fresco is in a chapel commissioned by Gregory IX. Another fresco in the same chapel seems to show Francis assisting Gregory at mass. According to an inscription, the chapel was finished in 1229, but the fresco with Francis probably dates between July and August of 1227

Bonaventura Berlinghieri,
*Saint Francis and Four Scenes
from His Legend*, 1235.
Pescia, San Francesco.

7

when Gregory was in Subiaco, and July 17, 1228, date of Francis's canonization.

Perhaps the most telling indication of the importance of images for the diffusion of Saint Francis's cult is a mid-thirteenth-century painting of the saint and four episodes of his legend in Orte, north of Rome. In the lower right is a scene showing a group gathered at an altar over which there is a bust-length portrait of the saint. The subject is apparently the miracle of a woman who saw the stigmata appear and disappear in a painting of the saint. Portraits promoted his cult but also came to work miracles themselves and served to convince the disbelieving. While these images were being made and venerated in all parts of central Italy, the Basilica in Assisi was being built. Soon its fresco cycles would be the standard for images of Saint Francis.

8

*Saint Francis's Basilica: Its Decoration and Problems of Attribution and Date*

Francis died on October 4, 1226, and two years later Gregory IX canonized him in a ceremony that took place in Assisi. The pope planned Assisi to become Italy's major pilgrimage site after Rome. Not only was he interested in promoting Francis's cult, he desired to assert the Holy See's presence in central Italy as the papacy had only in the past two decades managed to wrestle control of this territory from the Holy Roman Emperor. The day after the canonization Gregory laid the first stone of a basilica (fig. 8) on land that had been donated a few months previously by one Simone Puzarelli. The steep slope of the site on a promontory at the west end of town provided an ideal setting for the construction of two superimposed churches with separate entrances and a fortified convent. This unusual plan resembled the Benedictine complex of Subiaco—significantly, the place most closely associated with Saint Benedict of Nursia, the founder of European monasticism. Financing for the new Basilica, which Gregory wrote would be a special church (*Ecclesia Specialis*), came from various sources, but we also know from a document of 1232 that the citizens of Assisi were required to provide rations of grain to the construction site. Work proceeded at a rapid pace as on May 25, 1230 Francis's body was translated to a vault prepared under the high altar of the Lower Church. Shortly before the pope had named the Basilica the *caput et mater* (head and mother) of the Franciscan order.

The overseer on the site was Brother Elias, Francis's close companion and himself from Assisi. It was he who had arranged for the original grant of land. His election as Minister General of the order in 1232 moved the project along even more quickly. Elias's vast authority comes through in a document dated 1238 in which the monks of the nearby Benedictine abbey of Santa Croce at Sassovivo petition Gregory IX to force the friar to send back the engineer Giovanni of Penne. Elias obviously felt no hesitation about hiring talented workers from other sites. Later he was even accused of exacting money from Franciscan convents for the building in Assisi. Bells cast in 1239 significantly bear his name as well as those of the pope and the Emperor Frederick II. The date and names are telling: In 1238 Elias had been sent by the pope as an ambassador to Frederick II, but his mediation failed, and in March 1239 Gregory IX excommunicated the emperor calling him the beast of the Apocalypse. Elias's own governance was challenged at a heated meeting presided over by the pope on May 15th in Rome. It ended in his suspension from the leadership. Shortly after he joined Frederick II in Tuscany, and Gregory IX excommunicated him.

The Basilica must have been well along before Elias was deposed as he was shown as a suppliant at the foot of Giunta Pisano's lost cross of 1236. In the seventeenth century the cross was on the rood screen of the

Upper Church. Its very existence suggests that the building was ready for decoration even though only a year before on the anniversary of Francis's death Gregory IX had to celebrate an outdoor mass presumably because the Basilica was not fit for large crowds. However, there is a record of one other important mass being held in the Lower Church by Cardinal Rinaldo (later Alexander IV) during which a miracle occurred: A stone hit and mortally wounded a woman who at the end of the mass miraculously revived. The story of the falling stone, still preserved as a relic, suggests that the church was under construction. The façade of the Upper Church was certainly completed before Gregory's death in August 1241 as the two sculptures

of eagles on it refer to his coat-of-arms. Soon after, in 1246, the town of Assisi donated land in front of the Basilica's two entrances to create squares.

During the construction the design of the Basilica changed. The most significant modification was the extension of the nave of the Upper Church by one bay. But also the architectural style changed from Romanesque to Gothic. The new style appears in the first bay of the nave and the narthex of the Lower Church. The Upper Church (fig. 9) is in a completely Gothic style that resembles in part contemporary French models. It has been compared to the Cathedral of Angers finished about 1240 although the analogy is really only generic. Two-storied churches were not

**View of the interior of the Upper Church of the Basilica of San Francesco, Assisi.**

9

common, but precedents can be found in French royal and ecclesiastical chapels. And, as Wolfgang Schenkluhn has shown, the Cathedral of San Nicola Pellegrino in Trani, built between 1175–86 with modifications made starting in 1222, provides a good Italian example. There in the Lower Church, as at Assisi, the body of the saint is preserved.

The Basilica in Assisi was intentionally designed to project an image of papal authority in central Italy. The plan, with particularly prominent transepts, recalls Saint Peter's in Rome, and some of the architectural features of the Upper Church seem to derive from what is known of the destroyed papal audience chamber on the second floor of the Lateran Palace. The original arrangement of the saint's tomb in the Lower Church was based on the *confessio* of Saint Peter's and the Chapel of the Holy Sepulcher in Jerusalem. In addition, the double doors at the entrance of the Lower Church copy the entrance to the Basilica of the Holy Sepulcher. Most pilgrims visiting the site would have understood the architectural symbolism, which emphatically associated Francis with Christ and the Apostles, and the monument itself with Rome and the papacy.

The Basilica was not consecrated until 1253, because as it was nearing completion, the pope, Innocent IV Fieschi (r. 1243–1254), had been forced outside of Italy as a result of the conflict with Frederick II. After a seven-year absence, he returned residing at first in Perugia. In April 1253 he moved to Assisi. On May 25th he consecrated the Basilica, and in July he issued a bull approving the use of donations to complete and decorate it. Thirteen years later Pope Clement IV de Foulques (r. 1265–1268) extended this privilege for three years. By 1271 the construction and early decoration seems to have come to an end as a record exists of a donation of five poplars for making a door, which were probably for the entrance to the Lower Church. The two papal bulls probably coincide with the execution of the early stained glass and frescoes. In the 1250s German masters fashioned glass for the windows in the apse of the Upper Church depicting Old and New Testament scenes. This part of the church was the papal preserve (a throne for the pope is located at the end of the apse), and, therefore, Innocent IV was probably behind the decision to hire the foreign artisans. His long sojourn in Lyon from 1244–50 accounts for his taste for figured glass, which was typical of northern European churches. Money that came in as a result of his bull would have underwritten the huge expense. Work may have begun before the church's consecration. It was certainly finished before 1260 when the General Chapter of Narbonne promulgated an edict against excessive decoration in Franciscan churches and specifically against colored glass. The text makes an exception for church apses most probably reflecting the situation at Assisi and the completion of the windows there. The decree, however, restricts the subject matter to the Crucifixion, the Virgin, the Baptist, Francis and Anthony.

The Constitutions of Narbonne also frowned on painting, but, at Assisi, under papal control, the rule was ignored. The first surviving frescoes are in the narthex and nave of the Lower Church (fig. 10) through which all pilgrims passed to worship at the tomb of Saint Francis in the crossing. Only a few bits of the narthex frescoes survive. The frescoes in the nave were damaged by later construction. They show on one side episodes from the life of Saint Francis and on the other from the life of Christ. The scheme, which emphasizes the parallelism of Christ and Francis's lives, derives from Bonaventure's official biography of the saint. The decision to write a new life was reached at the meeting in Narbonne. The erudite Bonaventure, Minister General since 1257, wished to respond to attacks on the Franciscans that were coming out of Parisian academic circles. And he was also concerned about standardizing the office that other orders were using for the feast of the saint. (Interestingly in 1257 he had provided copies of Celano's first life to the Cistercians as an example.) Bonaventure retreated to Mount La Verna, place of Saint Francis's stigmatization, to gather inspiration for his new work. Known as *The Major Legend*, it was finished in Paris. There copies were prepared for the 1263 General Chapter, which was held in Pisa. Three years later at the General Chapter of Paris it was decreed that all earlier accounts of Francis's life be destroyed. The few copies of the early biographies that survived were only rediscovered—in some cases in Cistercian libraries—in the eighteenth and nineteenth centuries. Iconographic reasons suggest that the frescoes in the nave were begun before the mass destruction, because in the scene of the Stigmatization the seraph is shown without a cruciform halo (fig. 11) whereas in Bonaventure's text the seraph is specifically identified

View of the interior of the
Lower Church of the Basilica
of San Francesco, Assisi.

10

11

as Christ. The frescoes could still have been in progress in 1266 when Clement IV extended privileges about donations for the completion of the Basilica. The artist is an anonymous painter known as the Master of Saint Francis. His other major work was for the church of San Francesco al Prato in Perugia for which, sometime after 1262, he provided an altarpiece (cat. no. 6) over the tomb of Francis's companion Giles, and a large crucifix, now in the Galleria Nazionale di Perugia, dated 1272. The Perugian Franciscans likely hired the painter on the basis of his previous work in Assisi. All the master's documented work was for Franciscan establishments, and he had even been given the honor of painting a portrait of Saint Francis on a board on which it was said the saint had died. It is not known where the painter was from although he is most often called Umbrian. The classicizing architectural decoration of the frescoes in Assisi as well as in the panels with saints that come from the Perugia al-

tarpiece show a knowledge of contemporary Roman painting, and the exaggerated sagging pose of Christ in the 1272 crucifix seems to show the influence of Cimabue's crucifix in San Domenico in Arezzo. Both the crucifixes by Cimabue and the Master of San Francesco display a mannered stylization of the crucified body of Christ that is not evident in known works by Giunta Pisano, who painted the lost crucifix of 1236. Interestingly enough the large cross in the Basilica of Santa Chiara in Assisi that can be dated in the early 1280s is similar in style to the Perugia crucifix showing how in the late 1260s and early 1270s what was happening in the Basilica of San Francesco had become the dominant model for painting elsewhere in the region. Such can be seen in the work of the so-called Master of Montelabate, who worked in the 1280s in the Benedictine abbey of Montelabate (near Perugia), in a style that mediates between the Master of Saint Francis and Cimabue.

Master of Saint Francis,
*Apparitions from the Old
and New Testament*, 1270s,
glass. North transept,
Upper Church, Basilica
of San Francesco, Assisi.

A great deal of the stained glass in the transept and nave of the Upper Church has been attributed to the Master of Saint Francis. Whether that artist's hand can actually be seen in the design of these windows, which underwent radical fifteenth- and nineteenth-century restorations, is not easily determined, but their monumental aspect does indeed suggest a painter. The scale of the scenes in these windows differs considerably from the German windows in the apse and the other windows in the Upper Church which are by French or English masters working in the 1260s. The Transalpine masters worked in a smaller, more contained format, which was not as conducive to the architecture of the building and the plan for large-scale frescoes. While they may have taught the local master how to work in glass, the award of the commission to a skilled Italian fresco painter reflects a new preference for hiring professional painters for decorative art projects. This practice continued most notably in the Lower Church where there are windows by Simone Martini and other identifiable painters such as the Master of Figline. Given the destruction of most of the Master of Saint Francis's frescoes in the Lower Church, the windows in the Upper Church represent some of the most inventive compositions produced in Italy in the mid-thirteenth century. For example, the window (fig. 12) in the north transept showing the apparitions of Christ and Old Testament stories prefiguring those apparitions are of a monumentality and elegance that is found in no other central Italian painting of the period. They show a keen interest in the representation of pictorial space and the grouping of figures that will be the primary concerns of artists working in the latter part of the century and most particularly in the frescoes of the nave of the Upper Church. The windows of the Upper Church were to contemporaries probably the most impressive part of the whole decor: in 1291, during a visit to Assisi, the mystic Angela of Foligno had a vision of Francis in the bosom of Christ, which was clearly inspired by the iconography of one of the windows (fig. 13).

The great Florentine artist Cimabue and his workshop frescoed most of the apse and transept of the Upper Church (fig. 14). The program is vast: the frescoes show stories of the Virgin, the Apostles Peter and Paul, the Archangels, and the Apocalypse. The four Evangelists are in the vault at the crossing, and two monumental crucifixions fill the two walls of the transept's

12

Master of St. Francis,
*Saint Francis in the Bosom
of Christ*, 1270s, glass.
South side of the nave,
Upper Church, Basilica
of San Francesco, Assisi.

east ends. The scenes of Christ in Glory and the Transfiguration in the upper part of the north transept and the Apostles in the gallery separating the upper and lower levels are not by Cimabue. In iconography and style these frescoes, except for six of the Apostles, are English. Whether the artist was indeed from England or an Italian imitating a northern manner is a matter of some debate. An Italian, probably Roman, master, possibly Jacopo Torriti himself, painted the six other Apostles in the gallery, and the Roman masters, in collaboration with Cimabue's workshop, also executed the extensive architectural decoration on the ribbing of the vaults and elsewhere. This continues into the nave of the church and unifies all the narrative scenes in a common illusionist architectural setting. This element suggests that the frescoes of the Upper Church were all part of one campaign of decoration that dates to a circumscribed period of time (not decades as some authors have argued).

The architectural decoration connects the project at Assisi with Roman painting as first executed during the pontificate of Nicholas III Orsini (r. 1277–1280), and most particularly the few classicizing decorative fresco fragments that survive from his private quarters in the Vatican and the frescoes of the upper part of the Sancta Sanctorum, the oratory in the Lateran that this pope had completely refurbished. In addition, Cimabue's frescoes of the Apostles Peter and Paul reflect the scheme, if not also the compositions, of the lost frescoed decoration in the atrium of Old Saint Peter's in Rome. While Bonaventure had stressed Francis's similarity to the Apostles and emphasized Franciscan devotion to Mary, who, in Cimabue's frescoes, is shown as the head of the Apostles, Peter and Paul are quintessentially Roman and papal saints.

An indication of the date is found in the fresco of the Evangelist Mark (fig. 15) in the vault of the crossing (recently destroyed by the earthquake). The fresco includes a view of Rome with the Senate on the Capitoline Hill on which the arms of the Orsini family appear. The arms probably refer to Nicholas III, who in 1278 was also elected a Roman senator. That same year another member of the family, Cardinal Matteo Rosso Orsini, was nominated protector of the order holding the office to 1285. However, the arms can only be considered a *terminus post quem*.

The decoration proceeded in direct contrast with the Minister General Bonagrazia of Persiceto. He was of

13

Cimabue, *Crucifixion*,
ca. 1277–80, fresco.
Southeast transept,
Upper Church, Basilica
of San Francesco, Assisi.

14

the influential Spiritualist party that did not want to compromise Francis's original vision of simplicity and utter poverty (Francis is said to have only asked that Franciscan oratories be well swept). Bonagrazia came firmly out against sumptuous church decoration by forcing reconfirmation of the Constitutions of Narbonne at the General Chapter of 1279. This meeting took place in Assisi suggesting that the ongoing work in the Basilica bothered Bonagrazia. Nicholas III reacted immediately refuting the Franciscans' stance in a bull that implicitly underscored his personal commitment to the Basilica's decoration. It is not clear, however, whether he was the one to commission the frescoes. Luciano Bellosi has most recently argued with significant stylistic reasons that the frescoed decoration of the Upper Church began three pontificates later, under the Franciscan Nicholas IV.

Despite the papal overtones of Cimabue's frescoes, the iconography celebrates specifically Franciscan themes and, in particular, the apocalyptic and prophetic aspects of Franciscan thought associated with the Spiritualists. Bonaventure in his biography of the saint had also picked up on this visionary strain. While most Franciscans believed in the messianic nature of Francis's mission, emphasizing that was sure to placate the Spiritualists who were increasingly uncomfortable with the direction of the order. Bonaventure had made Francis out to be the Alter Christus (the other Christ) and the Angel who opens the Sixth Seal of the Apocalypse. While the latter is never represented as a subject of Franciscan art, angels and apocalyptic imagery dominate the frescoes in the transept, and the very tone of this part of the cycle can be easily interpreted as a concession to Spiritualist concerns.

The frescoes, already in bad condition in Vasari's time,

Cimabue, *The Evangelist Mark,*
after 1278, fresco. Crossing,
Upper Church, Basilica
of San Francesco, Assisi.

have lost almost all of their color, and are, therefore, very difficult to evaluate from a stylistic point of view. However, the dates of several paintings that can be associated either stylistically or iconographically with them confirm a dating in the late 1280s. Vigoroso of Siena's polyptych from the church of Santa Giustina in Perugia (now in the Galleria Nazionale) shows a remarkable assimilation of Cimabue's style that must have come from direct contact with Assisi. A recent restoration has shown this painting to be dated 1291. Duccio's design for glass of the oculus of the apse of Siena cathedral, executed 1287–89, picks up on motifs present in the frescoes of the Virgin. Cimabue also painted a *Maestà with Saint Francis of Assisi* in the

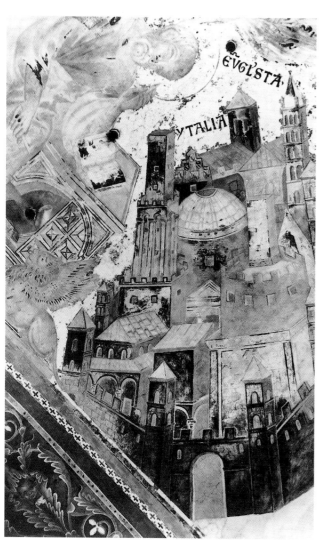

15

north transept of the Lower Church. The throne of that painting bears many similarities to the throne in Duccio's *Rucellai Madonna,* contracted in 1285, suggesting yet another point of contact between the great Sienese and Florentine masters.

The frescoes in the nave contain several programs. In the upper part are two rows of Old and New Testament stories. In the lower part is the famous legend of Saint Francis. On the inner façade is the Ascension of Christ and the Pentecost and above the door roundels of the Virgin and Child and the Apostles Peter and Paul. There are also two painted vaults: one has bust length images of Christ, the Virgin, the Baptist, and Saint Francis, and the other the Doctors of the Church. The scheme of showing parallel cycles of the Old and New Testaments derives from the decoration of the basilicas of Rome and most specifically Saint Peter's.

The frescoes present many problems of dating and attribution. Most of the Old and New Testament frescoes and the vault (fig. 16) with the busts are by a Roman master who is usually identified as Jacopo Torriti. Torriti's best-known work was for the Franciscan Pope Nicholas IV Masci (r. 1288–1292). The pope commissioned from him mosaics for the apses of the Basilicas of San Giovanni Laterano and Santa Maria Maggiore (the latter finished after the pope's death). In both, Nicholas IV had images of Saint Francis included. As the first pope from the order, he took care to promote Francis to near apostolic status in Rome's most sacred religious sites. The two mosaics include Torriti's prominent signature (and the one in the Lateran a possible self-portrait). These signatures are unprecedented in the decoration of any Roman basilica and indicate the extent of Torriti's fame.

In Assisi, the Old and New Testament stories were executed starting from the transept in the west to the front door in the east. Torriti and his workshop interrupted their work in the first bay, probably because Torriti was called to Rome sometime before the death of Nicholas IV to work in Santa Maria Maggiore. In Assisi another master artist took over. He undoubtedly worked with members of Torriti's large enterprise. This new artist executed the last Old and New Testament stories of the first bay, the façade frescoes, and the legend of Saint Francis. His identification (and sometimes the separation of the hands between the Saint Francis's legend and the other frescoes) is one of the central problems of early Italian art.

Jacopo Torriti, *Bust of Christ*,
ca. 1285–87, fresco.
Vault of the nave,
Upper Church, Basilica
of San Francesco, Assisi.

16

Giotto (attributed to),
*Isaac Refuses to Bless Esau,*
ca. 1288, fresco.
Nave, Upper Church, Basilica
of San Francesco, Assisi.

17

The earliest literary source identifying the artist of the Franciscan legend as Giotto is Vasari writing in 1568. He stated that the Assisi frescoes were executed during the generalship of Giovanni Minio of Murrovalle (1296–1304). Earlier notices about Giotto's work in Assisi by Ghiberti and Vasari in the 1550 edition of the Lives of the Artists do not specify the Saint Francis stories. Vasari visited Assisi in 1563 and 1566, and based his revised attribution on local sources. Vasari's escort there was the painter Dono Doni who also later provided the art historical information for friar Ludovico of Pietralunga's valuable manuscript description of the Basilica. A much earlier source for the attribution to Giotto is the Ferrarese chronicler Riccobaldo who in 1313 wrote that Giotto had worked in Assisi, Rimini, and Padua. Riccobaldo, however, could be referring to the frescoes in the transept and Magdalene Chapel of the Lower Church, which were executed by Giotto and his workshop in the first decade of the fourteenth cen-

tury. In this century German and Anglo-American art historians have denied Giotto's authorship of the legend because of what are perceived as the big differences with the frescoes in the Scrovegni Chapel in Padua which date between 1303 and 1306.

The American art historian Millard Meiss signaled two frescoes (fig. 17) showing the story of the patriarch Isaac and his sons Jacob and Esau as key works in the problem of the attribution. The innovative conception of space and the modeling of the figures with an attuned sense of the fall of light and shade distinguish them from the other biblical scenes. While Meiss's observations are true—the Isaac frescoes are extraordinary, the same kind of modeling and compositional devices can be found in the Franciscan legend. Could this "Isaac Master" be Giotto and was he the artist who continued to direct the work in the nave?

Recent findings by Bruno Zanardi about the production of the Saint Francis legend show that while one master may have overseen the project, a huge team worked on the frescoes. Zanardi determined this by a careful mapping out of the *giornate*, or working days, used to create the cycle. His work supplants data previously published by Meiss and the restorer Leonetto Tintori. There are at least five hundred and forty-six *giornate*. Scaffolding was erected so that teams of artists could be working on the left and right sides of a single composition (or even a bay consisting of three scenes) at the same time. Furthermore, a large number of set compositions, or templates, known in Italian as *patroni*, that could be adapted for different figures, were used. Therefore, whoever the main master be, he was in charge of a vast enterprise that was working quickly to finish the project.

A sticking point with regard to any serious consideration of the attribution of the Franciscan legend is its date. In recent years Luciano Bellosi has made persuasive arguments for dating the frescoes to the papacy of Nicholas IV. His thesis can be outlined as follows. On assuming the papacy, Nicholas IV issued a series of bulls in favor of the Basilica, and made significant donations to it. Saint Francis is shown beardless in accordance with the new iconography promoted by the pope. The saint first appears as such in Torriti's mosaic in the apse of Santa Maria Maggiore, finished in 1296, but commissioned by Nicholas IV before 1292. The costumes and the hair of the figures in Assisi reflect styles that pre-date Giotto's frescoes in Padua.

Giotto (attributed to), *Innocent III's Dream of Saint Francis Holding Up the Church*, ca. 1288–92, fresco. Nave, Upper Church, Basilica of San Francesco, Assisi.

Giotto (attributed to), *Gregory IX's Dream of Saint Francis Showing Him the Wound in His Side*, ca. 1288–92, fresco. Nave, Upper Church, Basilica of San Francesco, Assisi.

18

19

They were already common around 1283, the probable date of the tabernacle with scenes from the life of Saint Clare in Santa Chiara in Assisi (fig. 3). The figure style and architectural compositions of the frescoes are reflected in the frescoes of the Sala dei Notari of the Palazzo dei Priori of Perugia, decorated circa 1296 and 1297, and in Filippo Rusuti's mosaics on the façade of Santa Maria Maggiore, commissioned by the Colonna cardinals and finished before 1297, the year the Colonna were disgraced by Pope Bonaventure VIII Caetani (r. 1294–1303).

In the important fresco of *Innocent III's Dream of Saint Francis Holding Up the Church* (fig. 18), the saint is shown supporting the portico of the Lateran Basilica, which Nicholas IV had restored. Furthermore,

Francis holds it with his right arm. This detail is new. In earlier representations including the frescoes in the Lower Church of Assisi by the Master of Saint Francis, the saint sustains the church on his back following the phrase in Bonaventure's *Major Legend*, "*proprio dorso submissio.*" Interestingly, in the inscription of Torriti's mosaic in the apse of the Lateran Basilica (1291), commissioned by Nicholas IV himself, a connection is made between Innocent III's dream and Nicholas's restoration of the Lateran. Francis is said, as in the fresco in Assisi, to have held up the church "*humerum supponens*" meaning by his arm. The connections between Nicholas's papacy and the iconography of the Saint Francis cycle seem clear enough to warrant dating the frescoes during his reign. Nicholas was so at-

Follower of Giotto, *Cardinals Gian Gaetano and Napoleone Orsini being presented by Saints Francis of Assisi and Nicholas of Bari to Christ*, before 1306, fresco. St. Nicholas's Chapel, Lower Church, Basilica of San Francesco, Assisi.

20

tached to Assisi that he even had the papal throne in Assisi serve as the model for the new papal throne in the renovated Lateran.

The papal iconography is particularly apparent in the reordering of the episode of *Gregory IX's Dream of Saint Francis Showing Him the Wound in His Side* (fig. 19). In Bonaventure's life it is recounted that Gregory had this dream before the canonization. In the cycle this scene is shown after the canonization not only to correct Bonaventure's historical sequence, but, more particularly, to emphasize the authority of the pope in pronouncing on such miraculous matters.

The change in dating of the Saint Francis cycle means the attribution to Giotto can be seriously entertained. The most significant piece of evidence is provided by a painting signed by Giotto himself. It is the tabernacle in the Louvre showing Saint Francis receiving the stigmata and a predella with three other scenes from the Franciscan legend. All four compositions derive directly from the Assisi cycle. The only difference is that in the scene of the dream of Innocent III the apostle Peter also appears. Giotto's tabernacle comes from the church of San Francesco in Pisa, and while the patron probably asked that the scenes repeat the compositions in the mother church in Assisi, Giotto is

not likely to have copied them so slavishly if they were not his own inventions. Secondly, the Pisan patron may have hired Giotto because he painted the frescoes in the first place. The Louvre panel is not dated. Renovations to the Pisan church were begun around 1261 and finished around 1286, and in the year 1300 the façade of the church was being covered with marble. Between 1286 and 1300, the construction was completed and the building was ready for decoration. The coat-of-arms on the painting is that of the Cinquini (also Cinquino or Cinquina) family, an important mercantile family of the Kinsica section of Pisa. Often the arms on the painting have been erroneously identified as those of the Ughi, a Florentine family in exile in Pisa. The two families' arms, each consisting of a shield of *vaio*, or fur patterns, are near identical, but it is the Pisan family that had two chapels in the transept. In one of these chapels there was once the early thirteenth-century painting of Saint Francis and stories from his life attributed to Giunta Pisano. It is not clear what member of the Cinquini family commissioned the Giotto, but the poet and merchant Natuccio Cinquini is a possibility. In the year 1296 he held an important office in the Kinsica district and in 1297, late in life, he married a woman of the prominent Buonconte family. He seems to have died in Pisa between 1299 and 1301.

While work was proceeding on the decoration of the Upper Church it became clear that the Lower Church needed to be expanded. The nave could not accommodate all the pilgrims and several important personages wished to be buried there. Several new chapels were built at the end of the thirteenth century and the beginning of the fourteenth century, ruining the Master of Saint Francis's frescoes in the nave. The specific dates of their construction are not documented. Observations of the masonry only show that the Magdalene chapel on the north side of the nave was built before the Saint Nicholas chapel at the end of the north transept. The chapels along the north nave created a second nave which pilgrims could use as an alternative route to reach the tomb of Saint Francis in the crossing.

The first chapel to be decorated was the one dedicated to Saint Nicholas. The chapel contains the tomb of Gian Gaetano Orsini who died in Perugia during the long conclave of 1292–94. Irene Hueck has argued that the cardinal's tomb must postdate the tomb prepared

Pietro Lorenzetti, *Virgin and Child with Saints John the Baptist and Francis*, ca. 1320, fresco. Chapel, Lower Church, Basilica of San Francesco, Assisi.

21

in the Vatican for Boniface VIII and consecrated in May 1296 because it obviously depends on it. The chapel contains frescoes of the legend of Saint Nicholas of Bari and of other saints as well as a dedication fresco over the door showing Cardinals Gian Gaetano and Napoleone Orsini being presented by Saints Francis and Nicholas to Christ (fig. 20). A public act was drawn up in the chapel in March 1306 implying that the decoration was completed before that date. Furthermore, Giuliano of Rimini in his altarpiece now in the Isabella Stewart Gardner Museum, dated 1307, and the Master of Cesi in his eponymous altarpiece in Cesi, dated 1308, copied figures from the chapel's frescoes. A number of trecento drawings showing figures and scenes from the chapel also attest to the frescoes' popularity.

The dedication fresco originally had three other figures of cardinal deacons on each side. These were revealed in the cleaning of 1974. Hueck argued that they were cardinals at the Perugian conclave, which in 1294 finally elected Celestine V Angeleri (r. 1294; d. 1296). The fresco would have commemorated its conclusion. As there are five cardinal deacons in the picture and only four existed in 1294, Hueck dated it to after 1295 when another Orsini cardinal, Francesco Napoleone, was created. The fresco was probably changed to show only two donors after 1297 when the Colonna cardinals were deposed (they were among the original cardinals shown), and a war was declared against them by Boniface VIII. But by then most of the other cardinals were dead, and Napoleone Orsini, the late Gian Gaetano's brother and papal legate in Umbria until 1301, was paying for the decoration of the chapel.

Napoleone Orsini was also the patron of the Saint

Giotto, *Raising of Lazarus*,
ca. 1307–08, fresco.
St. John the Baptist Chapel,
Lower Church, Basilica
of San Francesco, Assisi.

Giotto and His Workshop,
*The Holy Family on the way
to Jerusalem*, ca. 1309, fresco.
North transept, Lower Church,
Basilica of San Francesco,
Assisi.

22

23

John Chapel in the south transept opposite the Saint Nicholas Chapel. He seems to have established it in 1300 after his conquest of Gubbio on Saint John the Baptist's day of that year. He planned it as his mortuary chapel, but the decoration was not begun until many years later. Giuseppe Marchini connected a document dating 1318, in which the Venetian government gave permission to glass workers from Murano to work in Assisi, to the central window of this chapel. The window showing the meeting of John the Baptist and Christ and the Annunciation to Zacharias is stylistically close to contemporary Venetian painting. Presumably the glass would have been executed before any paintings. The chapel has only one fresco (fig. 21). By Pietro Lorenzetti, it is below the window, and shows the Virgin and Child and Saints John the Baptist and Francis in a fictive arcade of columns. A similar fresco appears in the Nicholas Chapel following a precedent made by Cimabue in the transept where there is a beautiful, but little-known image, set as in an arcade, of the Virgin and Child, the two Maries, and Saint Joseph working as a carpenter. The date of Lorenzetti's fresco is not certain, and although it is usually placed in the mid-teens, the prominence of the Virgin's veil may be associated with a relic that Napoleone Orsini donated to the church on March 10, 1320.

Sometime after 1297 the friars decided to remove the rood screen separating the nave from the crossing. This facilitated the movement of pilgrims and allowed them direct access to the tomb. It also made it easier to come and go from the Magdalene Chapel, because its entrance into the nave abutted the rood screen. The friars lent Teobaldo Pontano, the Franciscan bishop of Assisi, money to decorate that chapel, and they also let him re-employ the Cosmatesque marbles of the screen as a *dado*. The frescoes (fig. 22) are mature works of Giotto that date shortly after the Scrovegni Chapel in Padua, which was finished by March 1306. A notary's document drawn up on January 4, 1309 in which Giotto is recorded as having been recently present in Assisi provides a date for the execution of these frescoes as well as of those in the north transept, which are also by Giotto and his workshop. They represent the infancy of Christ (fig. 23), the Crucifixion, and two miracles of Saint Francis. The correspondences of the infancy cycle with scenes of similar subjects in Padua is close, implying the use of set compositions

Tuscan artist, *Drawings after
frescoes by Giotto, the Master
of Saint Nicholas, and Simone
Martini in the Lower Church
of Assisi*, ca. 1320, vellum,
22.3 × 21.8 cm. Cambridge,
Fogg Art Museum, 1932.65 recto.

24

that the workshop could execute given Giotto's perhaps sporadic presence at the site. Some of these compositional models might explain why a number of trecento drawings of the Assisi scenes exist (fig. 24). The patron of the transept frescoes was most likely the Franciscan friar without a halo seen between Saints Francis and Anthony at the bottom of the cross in the large Crucifixion scene. It has been suggested that he was Michele of Cesena, elected Minister General in 1316. If so, the frescoes would have to have been completed before 1322 when he broke with the pope on the question of Franciscan ownership of property. However, a date before Michele became General is in my opinion more possible because of Giotto's presence in Assisi in 1309. The friar may be Gonsalvo of Valboà, the Spanish Minister General, who was head of the order from 1304 when Giovanni Minio of Murrovalle was nominated a cardinal by Boniface VIII. Gonsalvo died in April 1313 and was followed by Alessandro Bonino, who died on October 5, 1314. It took two years before the next Minister General, Michele of Cesena, was chosen. Vasari's statement about Giotto working during the time of Giovanni Minio of Murrovalle may refer to the Lower Church frescoes. Minio was appointed cardinal protector of the order in 1307.

A distinct member of Giotto's workshop continued the decoration in the vaults of the crossing where there are four large allegories of the Franciscan virtues of poverty (fig. 25), chastity, and obedience, and Saint Francis in glory. The iconography is new. Both obedience, in terms of the Franciscan vow to obey the pope, and poverty, in terms of the saint's original vision of an order that did not own anything, were much discussed during the second decade of the fourteenth century. The debate had caused a rift in the order, and the two opposing parties became identified as the Spirituals and Conventuals. Between 1309–12 official discussions were held to see if the two positions could be reconciled, and even the pope, Clement V de Got (r. 1305–1314), presided over some of the meetings. The Spiritualists had important supporters among the rulers of Naples and Sicily as well as members of the Curia including Napoleone Orsini who had long been involved with the Basilica of San Francesco. In fact, the pope called Orsini's chaplain, Ubertino of Casale, to defend the Spiritualist view. He was the author of the highly influential *Arbor vitae crucifixae Jesu*

*Christi* (1305), which can be seen in part as a source for the iconography of the frescoes.

The subject matter would suggest a conscious conciliatory effort to address openly questions of interest to both parties. The frescoes would have to date before a definitive break occurred in 1322 after Pope John XXII issued a series of bulls against the Spiritualist position on apostolic poverty. At the General Chapter held that year in Perugia the pope's decision was repudiated, and Michele of Cesena broke with him. Partly because of the dissent of the Spiritualists, allegorical Franciscan art disappears. The frescoes would have to have been executed before these tragic events, and probably even before Michele of Cesena became Minister General in 1316. His election took place in Naples and he was widely seen as an ally of King Robert of Naples, who was particularly sympathetic to the Spiritualists. The frescoes are Giottesque and Florentine. Significantly, during Michele's term Florentine artists lost their hold on work in the Basilica.

The original fresco in the apse of the Lower Church, which logically would have been painted at the same time as the allegories, is destroyed. It depicted saints in glory around the crucifixion. Ludovico of Pietralunga described it as incomplete (in parts only the heads were painted). The only indication of a date comes from Ludovico's account: He mentions the presence of a friar bishop who has to have been Saint Louis of Toulouse, canonized in April 1317. Ghiberti attributed the fresco to Giotto's Florentine follower Stefano, whereas local sources gave it to Puccio Capanna, an artist from Assisi documented in the 1340s. If the Stefano attribution is correct, or if at least it was a Florentine, the decoration continued smoothly from the north transept through the crossing. If it were by the later painter, it would mean that completion of this part of the Lower Church was more piecemeal than generally thought.

The frescoes of the south transept depicting the Passion (fig. 26) represent a distinct change as the artist is not a Florentine but the great Sienese painter Pietro Lorenzetti. The date is a matter of some discussion particularly because some writers have asserted that there was no work done in the church during the Ghibelline take-over of Assisi. In September 1319 the local Ghibelline leader Muzio di Francesco, with the aid of cohorts from Arezzo, seized Assisi, and in March 1320, to bolster their finances, they requisitioned the

Follower of Giotto (Stefano
Fiorentino ?), *Allegory of
Poverty*, ca. 1309–12, fresco.
Crossing, Lower Church,
Basilica of San Francesco,
Assisi.

25

Pietro Lorenzetti,
*Lamentation*, early 1320s,
fresco. South transept,
Lower Church, Basilica
of San Francesco, Assisi.

26

Basilica's treasury where a good section of the papal coffers had been deposited as well as several cardinals' personal property. Napoleone Orsini was so disgusted that even though he had been a rallying point for the Ghibelline cause in Tuscany, he decided not to be buried in Assisi. However, he and others secretly negotiated with the Assisi rebels to buy back some of their own property, and, coincidentally on the very day the treasury was seized, Orsini had signed over the relic of the Virgin's veil. Between 1320–23 Lorenzetti was working on an altarpiece for the *pieve* (baptismal church) of Arezzo commissioned by Bishop Guido Tarlati, the militant Ghibelline ruler of that city and a strong supporter of Muzio di Francesco. Therefore during the Ghibelline dominance in Assisi, Lorenzetti could easily have had open access to the Basilica. It is likely that Lorenzetti worked in Assisi in conjunction with his projects for Tarlati in Arezzo, which did not only include the altarpiece, but also, according to Vasari, frescoes in the apse of the *pieve.*

The dating of certain paintings of Lorenzetti's early career merits reexamination in light of the probable date of the Assisi frescoes. Lorenzetti spent much of the thirteen-teens outside of his native Siena. One of his earliest works for an important non-Sienese patron is the *Virgin and Child* from the *pieve* of Cortona. I would propose for it a date in conjunction with Henry VII's grant of special privileges to that city in 1312. Because of the panel's location in Cortona's principal church, like Duccio's *Maestà* in the Cathedral of Siena, the Lorenzetti acted as a potent civic symbol of a newly franchised city. A work that closely relates to the Assisi frescoes is Lorenzetti's crucifix from San Marco in Cortona. The Christ is similar to the one in the fresco of the Crucifixion. The Cortona crucifix can be dated before 1319 on the basis of Segna di Bonaventura's close copy of it in a cross in Arezzo.

The patrons of Pietro Lorenzetti's frescoes in Assisi are not known although their portrait and coat-of-arms were painted below the large Crucifixion. The two coats-of-arms are the same. Only the portrait of the man on the right-hand side survives but it is likely that the portrait on the left-hand side was also of a man. Usually when a married couple is depicted, the female portrait appears on the right, which in heraldry is the distaff side. The arrangement in the Lorenzetti might mean that the donors were father and son. The arms are very similar to the arms on the tomb of one Master Giuliano di Master Simone in the Basilica's cemetery. This tomb is dated July 1307, but Giuliano's son could have overseen the decoration. The devotional fresco of Saint Vittorino, the much-venerated bishop of Assisi, in the border below the Crucifix may indicate that the donor was local. In this same area Lorenzetti frescoed five lost busts of companions of Saint Francis who were buried in the Basilica. His fresco of five other companions below Cimabue's *Maestà* in the north transept still survives.

The last great trecento chapel in the church is on the south side of the nave. It was founded by Cardinal Gentile Partino of Montefiore who was a Franciscan and had been created a cardinal priest in 1298 by Boniface VIII, with the title San Martino *in montibus.* In a document of May 30, 1312 six hundred gold florins were set aside for a chapel in San Francesco. The cardinal died on October 12th of the same year. The chapel contains a series of magnificent frescoes (fig. 27) by Simone Martini, and the windows were also designed by him. The date of his work can be gauged by the depiction of Saint Louis of Toulouse, the brother of King Robert of Naples, who was canonized on April 7, 1317. As this was in the entrance arch

Simone Martini, *Saint Martin of Tours Renounces Arms*, ca. 1315–16, fresco. St. Martin Chapel, Lower Church, Basilica of San Francesco, Assisi.

and, therefore, one of the last parts of the chapels to be completed, Simone Martini could have begun the chapel before the event, which, in any case, had been in the works for some time. Simone also frescoed images of five saints in the north transept including one of the newly canonized saint. Simone's great altarpiece in Naples made in honor of Louis's canonization is similar in style to the Assisi frescoes, but might actually postdate them. Work on the Assisi frescoes would have begun after Simone's fresco of the *Maestà* in the city hall of Siena. He signed that fresco in 1315, but made extensive renovations to it for which he was paid in December 1321, and those changes reflect the style of the work in Assisi.

The chantry in the nave of the Lower Church is dedicated to Saint Stanislaw, an eleventh-century Polish martyr bishop, who was canonized in August 1253 during Pope Innocent IV's sojourn in Assisi. Coats-of-arms indicate that the patrons were the local Soldani family. The chapel may date to when one Giovanni Soldani became custodian of the convent in 1337. The native painter Puccio Capanna, who in Vasari is celebrated as one of Giotto's closest followers, executed the frescoes depicting two stories from the saint's legend, the Crucifixion, and the Coronation of the Virgin. The last scene was left incomplete. This same artist, whose only documented activity dates to 1341/2 and 1347, also executed the large Crucifix in the Chapter House of the convent.

Another follower of Giotto frescoed the *Maestà* in the sacristy. He is the Master of Figline named after a tabernacle in the main church of Figline, a town near Florence. The same artist frescoed a chapel in the Franciscan Basilica of Santa Croce in Florence. He also designed glass for both Santa Croce and the Lower Church of Assisi. He has sometimes been identified with the Giovanni di Bonino, an artist from Assisi, who executed glass for the Cathedral of Orvieto in 1334, and who worked in Perugia the following year. The trecento pictorial decoration of Francis's Basilica comes full circle in the chapel of Saint Catherine of Alexandria in the Lower Church. The frescoes depicting the life of that saint were painted by Andrea of Bologna in the 1360s for the Spanish cardinal and military leader Egidio Albornoz. Like Napoleone Orsini in the early 1300s, he had brought the rebel cities of Umbria back under the yolk of the papacy. The cardinal probably had called a Bolognese artist because of

27

his connections to that university city where he had founded a college for Spanish students.

By the mid 1320s Assisi was no longer the great stage for the newest and best in Italian painting, but before that, despite competing claims from Rome and Florence, we might truly say that here the great age of Italian art was ushered in. Like the Franciscan Chapter Meetings, which brought diverse groups together in one locale, the Basilica was a gathering point for the greatest Italian artists of the age. The experiments that they conducted in the Basilica of the humble friar laid the groundwork for the development of Italian Renaissance art.

*Bibliographical Note*
The bibliography on Saint Francis and the Basilica of San Francesco in Assisi is enormous. All the quotations from the lives of Saint Francis come from *St. Francis of Assisi: Writings and Early Biographies. English Omnibus of the Sources for the Life of St. Francis*, M.A. Habig (ed.), Chicago, 1972. The critical edition in the original Latin is *Legendae S. Francisci Assisiensis saeculis xiii et xiv conscriptae*, with introductions by M. Bihl, in *Analecta franciscana*, X (1926–41). See also *Fontes franciscani*, E. Menestò and S. Brufani (eds.), Assisi, 1995. The critical English version of Saint Clare's writings and legend is *Clare of Assisi: Early Documents*, edited by R.J. Armstrong with a preface by V. Namoyo, New York, ca. 1988.
On medieval scarlets see J.H. Munro, "The Medieval Scarlet and the Economics of Sartorial Splendour," in *Cloth and Clothing in Medieval Europe: Essays in Memory of Professor E. M. Carus-Wilson*, London, 1983, pp. 13–70 and on Saint Galganus's legend *Leggenda di santo Galgano confessore: Testo volgare inedito del XIV secolo*, F. Cardini (ed.), Siena, ca. 1982. Jordan of Giano's account of his trip to Germany with relics of Saint Francis is in *Chronica Fratris Jordani*, H. Boehmer (ed.), *Collection d'études et de documents*, VI, Paris, 1908. For Angela of Foligno's own description of her visits to the Basilica in the 1290s see Angela of Foligno, *Complete Works*, translated with an introduction by P. Lachance and a preface by R. Guarnieri, New York, 1993. For the connection of Giotto's Louvre tabernacle with the Ughi family see J. Gardner, "The Louvre Stigmatization and the Problem of the Narrative Altarpiece," *Zeitschrift für Kunstgeschichte*, 45 (1982), pp. 220–21. On the Cinquini altars see F. Paliaga and S. Renzoni, *Le chiese di Pisa: Guida alla conoscenza del patrimonio artistico*, Pisa, 1991, pp. 39–40. On San Francesco in Pisa see O. Banti, *La chiesa di S. Francesco come luogo di aggregazione civile, cuturale, e religiosa della società pisana nel medioevo e nell'età moderna*, Pisa, 1984. On the Cinquini see M. Pagano, "Cinquino, Natuccio," *Dizionario biografico degli italiani XXV* (Rome, 1981), pp. 647–49.
A useful critical review of the literature on the Basilica and its decoration is found in Pietro Scarpellini's annotated edition of Ludovico di Pietralunga's *Descrizione della Basilica di S. Francesco e di altri santuari di Assisi*, Treviso, 1982. This book summarizes early sources and the important nineteenth and twentieth-century bibliography. For the latest information about the architecture and its sources see W. Schenkluhn, *San Francesco in Assisi: Ecclesia Specialis, Die Vision Papst Gregors IX, von einer Erneurung der Kirche*. Darmstadt, 1991, which has also been published in Italian (*San Francesco in Assisi: Ecclesia Specialis. Fonti e ricerche*, 5, Milan, 1991).
The following list, while not pretending to be complete, contains many other useful references.
F. Bologna, "Vetrate del Maestro di Figline," *Bollettino d'arte*, XLI (1956), pp. 193–96.
G. Marchini, *Le vetrate italiane*, Milan, 1956.
J. White, "The Date of the Legend of St. Francis at Assisi," *The Burlington Magazine*, XCVIII (1956), pp. 344–50.
M. Meiss, *Giotto and Assisi*, New York, 1960.
M. Meiss, "Reflections on Assisi: A Tabernacle and the Cesi Master," in *Scritti di storia dell'arte in onore di Mario Salmi*, Rome, 1962, pp. 74–111.
L. Tintori and M. Meiss, *The Painting of the Life of St. Francis in Assisi*, with *Notes on the Arena Chapel*, New York, 1962.
E. Battisti, *Cimabue*, Milan, 1963.
A. Smart, "Ghiberti's 'quasi tutta la parte di sotto' and Vasari's Attribution to Giotto at Assisi," *Renaissance and Modern Studies*, VIII (1963), pp. 5–24.
G. Zaccaria, "Diario storico della basilica e sacro convento di S. Francesco in Assisi (1220–1927)," *Miscellanea francescana*, 63 (1963), pp. 75–120, 290–361, 495–536; and 64 (1964), pp. 165–210, 433–73.
F. Bologna, *Cimabue*, Milan, 1965.
F. Bologna, *Gli affreschi di Simone Martini ad Assisi*, Milan, 1965.
G. Previtali, *Gli affreschi di Giotto ad Assisi*, Milan, 1965.
G. Volpe, *Pietro Lorenzetti ad Assisi*, Milan, 1965.
A. Monferini, "L'Apocalisse di Cimabue," *Commentari*, XVIII (1966), pp. 25–55.

G. Previtali, *Giotto e la sua bottega*, Milan, 1967 (revised editions 1974 and 1993).
F. Bologna, "Povertà e umiltà. Il San Ludovico di Simone Martini," *Studi storici*, X (1969), pp. 231–59.
A. Smart, *The Assisi Problem and the Art of Giotto*, Oxford, 1971.
*Giotto e i giotteschi in Assisi*, with an introduction by G. Palumbo, *Il miracolo di Assisi*, 1, Rome, 1969.
*Giotto e il suo tempo. Acts of the Congresso Internazionale per il VII centenario della nascita di Giotto* (1967), Rome, 1971.
S. da Campagnola, *L'angelo del sesto sigillo e l'"alter Christus": Genesi e sviluppo di due temi francescani nei secoli XIII–XIV*, Rome, 1971.
G. Marchini, *Corpus vitrearum medii Aevii: Italia. Volume 1: Umbria*, Rome, 1973.
V. Martinelli, "Un documento per Giotto ad Assisi," *Storia dell'arte*, 19 (1973), pp. 193–208.
G. Ruf, *S. Francesco e S. Bonaventura: Un'interpretazione storico-salvifica degli affreschi della navata nella chiesa superiore di San Francesco in Assisi alla luce della teologia di S. Bonaventura*, Assisi, 1974.
H.B.J. Maginnis, "Assisi Revisited. Notes on Recent Observations," *The Burlington Magazine*, CXVII (1975), pp. 511–17.
A. Tantillo Mignosi, "Osservazioni sul transetto della Basilica Inferiore di Assisi," *Bollettino d'arte*, LX (1975), pp. 129–42.
H.B.J. Maginnis, "The Passion Cycle in the Lower Church of San Francesco, Assisi," *Zeitschrift für Kunstgeschichte*, 39, (1976), pp. 193–208.
R. Simon, "Towards a Relative Chronology of the Frescoes in the Lower Church of San Francesco at Assisi," *The Burlington Magazine*, CXVIII (1976), pp. 361–66.
L. Bellosi, "Moda e cronologia. A) La decorazione della Basilica Inferiore di Assisi," *Prospettiva*, 10 (1977), pp. 21–31.
H. Belting, *Die Oberkirche von San Francesco in Assisi*, Berlin, 1977.
*Assisi al tempo di San Francesco, Atti del V Convegno Internazionale* (1977), Società Internazionale di Studi Francescani, Assisi, 1978.
Stanislao da Campagnola, *Le origini francescane come problema storiografico*, Perugia, 1978.
I. Hueck, "Le vetrate di Assisi nelle copie del Ramboux e notizie sul restauro di Giovanni Bertini," *Bollettino d'arte*, LXIV (1979), pp. 75–90.
*Il Maestro di Figline: Un pittore del trecento*, exhibition catalogue, L. Bellosi (ed.), Florence, 1980.
*Il Tesoro della Basilica di San Francesco ad Assisi*, Florence, 1980.
L. Bellosi, "La barba di San Francesco," *Prospettiva*, 22 (1980), pp. 11–34.
E. Borsook, *The Mural Painters of Tuscany*, Oxford, 1980.
M. Boskovits, "Gli affreschi della Sala dei Notari a Perugia e la pittura in Umbria alla fine del XIII secolo," *Bollettino d'arte*, LXVI (1981), pp. 1–42.
I. Hueck, "Cimabue und das Bildprogramm der Oberkirche von San Francesco in Assisi," *Mitteilungen des Kunsthistorischen Institutes in Florenz*, XXV (1981), pp. 279–324.
I. Hueck, "La Basilica francescana di Assisi nell'Ottocento; alcuni documenti su restauri progettati ed interventi eseguiti," *Bollettino d'arte*, LXVI (1981), pp. 143–52.
G. Ruf, *Das Grab des hl. Franziskus: Die Fresken der Unterkirche von Assisi*, Freiburg, 1981.
Stanislao da Campagnola, *Francesco d'Assisi negli scritti e nelle biografie dei secoli XIII–XIV*, Assisi, 1981.
J. Canon, "Dating the Frescoes by the Maestro di San Francesco at Assisi," *The Burlington Magazine*, CXXIV (1982), pp. 65–69.
*Francesco d'Assisi: storia e arte*, Milan, 1982.
S. Nessi, *La basilica di Assisi e la sua documentazione storica*, Assisi, 1982.
Acts of the conference *Roma anno 1300* (May 19–24, 1980), Rome, 1983, with important contributions on Assisi questions by Luciano Bellosi, Giorgio Bonsanti, Irene Hueck, and Valentino Pace.
D. Blume, *Wandmalerei als Ordenspropaganda: Bildprogramme im Chorbereich franziskanischer Konvente Italiens bis 14. Jahrhunderts*, Worms, 1983.
M. Boskovits, "Celebrazioni dell'VIII centenario della nascita di San

Francesco: Studi recenti sulla Basilica di Assisi," *Arte cristiana*, LXXI (1983), pp. 203–14.

I. Hueck, "Der Lettner der Unterkirche von San Francesco in Assisi," *Mitteilungen des Kunsthistorischen Institutes in Florenz*, XXVIII (1984), pp. 173–202.

I. Hueck, "Ein Dokument zur Magdalenenkapelle der Franziskirche von Assisi," in *Scritti di storia dell'arte in onore di Roberto Salvini*, Florence, 1984, pp. 191–96.

L. Bellosi, *La pecora di Giotto*, Turin, 1985.

A.S. Hoch, "A New Document for Simone Martini's Chapel of St. Martin at Assisi," *Gesta*, 24 (1985), pp. 141–46.

J. Poeschke, *Die Kirche von San Francesco in Assisi und ihre Wandmalerein*, Munich, 1985.

S. Romano, "Pittura ad Assisi, 1260–1280: Lo stato degli studi," *Arte medievale*, 2 (1985), pp. 109–21.

J. Stubblebine, *Assisi and the Rise of Vernacular art*, New York, 1985.

A.S. Hoch, "The Identity of a Saint in the Chapel of St. Martin at Assisi," *Arte cristiana*, LXXIV (1986), pp. 103–5.

I. Hueck, "Die Kapellen der Basilika San Francesco in Assisi: die Auftraggeber und die Franziskaner," in *Patronage and Public in the Trecento*, Florence, 1986, pp. 81–104.

A.S. Hoch, "St. Martin of Tours: His Transformation into a Chivalric Hero and the Franciscan Ideal," *Zeitschrift für Kunstgeschichte*, L (1987), 471–82.

C.B. Strehlke, "A Celibate Marriage and Franciscan Poverty Reflected in a Neapolitan Trecento Diptych," *The J. Paul Getty Museum Journal*, 15 (1987), pp. 79–96.

R. Goffen, *Spirituality in Conflict: Saint Francis and Giotto's Bardi Chapel*, University Park, Pennsylvania, 1988.

A. Martindale, *Simone Martini*, Oxford, 1988.

C. Volpe, *Pietro Lorenzetti*, edited and with an essay by M. Lucco, Milan, 1989.

A. Tomei, *Jacobus Torriti pictor. Una vicenda figurativa del tardo Duecento romano*, Rome, 1990.

I. Hueck, "Ein umbrisches Reliquiar in Kunstgewerbemuseum Schloss Köpenick," *Forschungen und Berichte. Staatliche Museen zu Berlin*, 31 (1991), pp. 183–88.

A.S. Hoch, "The Dedication of the St. Elizabeth Altar at Assisi," *The Burlington Magazine*, CXXXIII (1991), pp. 36–37.

A. Tartuferi, *Giunta Pisano*, Soncino, Italy, ca. 1991.

K. Krüger, *Der frühe Bildkult des Franziskus in Italien: Gesalt- und Funktionswandel des Tafelbildes im 13. und 14. Jahrhundert*, Berlin, ca. 1992.

I. Carlettini, "L'Apocalisse di Cimabue e la meditazione escatologica di S. Bonaventura," *Arte medievale*, VII:1 (1993), pp. 105–28.

C. Frugoni, *Francesco e l'invenzione delle stimmate*, Turin, 1993.

F. Martin, "Die Apsisverglasung der Oberkirche von S. Francesco in Assisi: Ihre Entstehung und Stellung innerhalb der Oberkirchenausstattung," *Manuskripte zur Kunstwissenschaft in der Wernerschen Verlagsgesellschaft*, 37, Worms, 1993.

M.V. Schwarz, "Zerstört und Wiederhergestellt. Die Ausmalung der Unterkirche von S. Francesco in Assisi," *Mitteilungen des Kunsthistorischen Institutes in Florenz*, XXXVII (1993), pp. 1–28.

*Galleria Nazionale dell'Umbria, Dipinti, sculture e ceramiche: Studi e restauri*, C.B. Valsassina and V. Garibaldi (eds.), Florence, 1994.

*Il gotico europeo in Italia*, V. Pace and M. Bagnoli (eds.), Milan, 1994, with contributions on Assisi by Martina Bagnoli and Frank Martin.

D. Gordon, "The Mass Production of Franciscan Piety: Another Look at Some Umbrian Verres Eglomisés," *Apollo*, CXL, 394 (1994), pp. 33–42.

E. Lunghi, *Il crocefisso di Giunta Pisano e l'icona del Maestro di San Francesco alla Porziuncola*, Assisi, 1995.

E. Lunghi, *The Basilica of St. Francis at Assisi: The Frescoes by Giotto, his Precursors, and Followers*, translated by C. Evans, London, 1996.

B. Zanardi, *Il cantiere di Giotto: Le storie di San Francesco ad Assisi*, with an introduction by F. Zeri and an essay by C. Frugoni, Milan, 1996.

F. Martin, *Die Glasmalereien von San Francesco in Assisi*, Regensburg, 1997.

C. Frugoni, *Francis of Assisi: A Life. New York*, 1998 (original edition Turin, 1995).

L. Bellosi with G. Ragionieri, *Cimabue*, Milan, 1998.

# PAINTINGS

## Master of the Treasury

Italo-Byzantine (?), active second third
thirteenth century

**1/1**
*Saint Francis and Four Posthumous
Miracles*
Tempera on panel, 111.5 × 154.5 cm,
overall; 95 × 137.5 cm, picture surface
Assisi, Museo-Tesoro della Basilica
di San Francesco

1/1

**Unknown Master**
Umbrian, active second third
thirteenth century

**1/2**
*Saint Francis and Four Posthumous
Miracles*
Tempera on panel, 67 × 86.5 cm
Vatican City, Pinacoteca Vaticana

1/2

These two panels are among the most significant and controversial Italian paintings of the entire thirteenth century. Both portray Saint Francis, standing full-length holding an open book and a cross, surrounded by four of his posthumous miracles. Saint Francis's book in the Vatican panel is blank while that in Assisi is inscribed with the passage from the gospel of Saint Matthew (19:21) to which the Saint's biographers say he opened by chance one day and thereafter dedicated his life to a mission of poverty: SI VIS PERFECTU/S ESSE VADE ET VE/NDE OMNIA QUE HAB/ES ET DA PAU-PER/IBUS [If you would be perfect, go, sell what you possess and give to the poor].

In both panels the saint is surrounded by the same four miracles enacted after his death. The first of these, at the upper left, is the miracle of the deformed girl, whose neck "had been monstrously bent and her head had grown down to her shoulders" (Tommaso da Celano, *Legenda Prima*, book III, chapter 2). On the day of Francis's interment in the chapel of San Giorgio, she placed her head upon the tomb and was cured. Below this scene is the miraculous healing of the cripple Bartolomeo da Narni. "The most holy Francis showed himself one night in a dream to this man, commanding him to go to a certain bath, where he, moved by great compassion for him, wished to free him from his illness… The man then began to drag himself to the place as best he could with the aid of a cane… As he approached the bath, he missed the way, for it was night; and again he heard the voice saying to him that he was not walking along the right way, and it directed him to the bath. And when he had come to the place and had entered the bath, he felt one hand placed upon his foot and another on his leg, gently stretching it out. Immediately he was cured" (Tommaso da Celano, *loc. cit.*). At the upper right of both panels is a possessed woman exorcised of the devil. Concluding the cycle at the lower right is the healing of a cripple, thought to be Niccolò da Foligno.

The Assisi *Saint Francis and Four Posthumous Miracles* was first described in the Basilica of San Francesco by Ludovico da Pietralunga around 1570, at which time it was hanging above the entrance to the sacristy in the Lower Church. Fra Ludovico stated that it was then, and presumably had been by long earlier tradition, much venerated not only as a supposed portrait of the saint, but also for having been painted on a board said to have been used to wash Francis's body at his death. The original location of the Vatican panel is unknown: it is unrecorded prior to its appearance in the Biblioteca Apostolica Vaticana in the last century, though it was at that time presumed to have come from Assisi as well (Fratini, 1882, p. 41). The close correspondence between the two panels has engendered endless debate over whether one is a copy of the other (not in the modern sense of a close stylistic replica but rather in faithfully reproducing the narrative content); if so, which may claim precedence; if not, whether both are copies of an earlier prototype which does not survive; how early or late they might have been painted; whether they are by different painters or the product of a single artist or workshop; and whether either (or both) could have been painted by Giunta Pisano, who was commissioned by Fra Elia in 1236 to paint the great Crucifix (lost) for the newly built Basilica of San Francesco.

Most of these discussions are based on iconographic rather than stylistic arguments, and no documentary evidence has yet been discovered to throw any further light on the issues. Those scholars (see especially Scarpellini, 1980; Frugoni, 1993) who have considered the panels at any length do so in the context of a small corpus of thirteenth-century images portraying Saint Francis and his miracles, the majority of which are similar to these in content if not in form. It is probable that "portraits" of Saint Francis existed from the time of his death in 1226, certainly they must have been known by the date of his canonization in 1228. However, of all the sur-

viving thirteenth-century images of the saint, only one, in San Francesco, Pescia, is dated—1235—and signed by its artist, Bonaventura Berlinghieri. Though it cannot be demonstrated, this is commonly presumed to be the earliest known likeness of the saint. Like the Assisi and Vatican panels, it shows a standing figure of Francis holding a book (the Assisi and Vatican panels are alone in this group in showing him with a cross as well), flanked by smaller representations of some of his miracles, in this case six in number but again four of them posthumous. Unlike the Assisi and Vatican panels, it is painted in a vertical format with a pedimental top, a shape followed by all the other Tuscan representations of the saint from the thirteenth century (Museo di San Matteo, Pisa; Bardi Chapel, Santa Croce, Florence; Museo Civico, Pistoia; etc., see Kruger, 1992). The horizontal, rectangular format of the Assisi and Vatican panels is recognizably more archaic, and so these two paintings, though generally dated as much as two decades after the Pescia altarpiece, are widely considered to reflect a much earlier prototype, one that must have been influential in developing the cult of Saint Francis by popularizing the stories of miraculous cures affected at his tomb (the most thorough analysis of the probable sequence of development of the images supporting this cult is to be found in Frugoni, 1993; see also Scarpellini, 1982b, pp. 94–99).

A date for the Assisi Saint Francis significantly later than Bonaventura Berlinghieri's painting in Pescia is repeated throughout most of the vast literature on the subject and is based on two assumptions. The first of these is that visual imagery necessarily postdates the publication of textual sources with which it conforms. In this case it has long been recognized that while the first two miracles portrayed on the Assisi and Vatican panels unequivocally depend on Tommaso da Celano's first life of Saint Francis (1228), as possibly does the fourth miracle, the third has been identified with the story of a pos-

sessed girl of Norcia appearing only in his *De Miraculis* of 1245–50 (Bughetti, 1926). A story of the exorcism of a possessed woman is featured in the *Legenda Prima*, however, and a scene of exorcism appears on Bonaventura Berlinghieri's panel of 1235. It is therefore possible either that the painted scene in the Assisi panel is not meant to refer specifically to the miracle of the girl of Norcia as described in the *De Miraculis* or that the story was in common currency before its publication. In either event, iconography alone cannot be adduced as a conclusive means for dating the panel.

It was also noted by Thode (1885), and repeated by nearly all writers since, that the artist of the Assisi Saint Francis panel very carefully reproduced the high altar of the Lower Church at Assisi in his rendering of the last two of Francis's miracles, and that this altar was not consecrated until 1253. Kleinschmidt (1926) pointed out, however, though his observation has been largely if not entirely ignored in the subsequent literature, that this date cannot be accepted as a *terminus post quem* for execution of the painting since it was actually the date of the formal consecration of the two churches by Pope Innocent IV and consequently of the two high altars as well. Both altars, and especially that in the Lower Church, which was already a conspicuously important pilgrimage shrine, must have existed for some time prior to this. Venturi (1907) did not believe this structure represented the high altar of the Lower Church but rather Saint Francis's original tomb in the chapel of San Giorgio. If for either reason it is not necessary to date the Assisi panel as late as 1253, it is also not necessary to assume that it reflects an earlier, lost prototype. It is at least possible that it is itself the prototype, painted sometime in the second quarter of the century, from which later panels such as that in the Vatican depend, a possibility perhaps more in keeping with its status as a venerated relic as well as icon.

The question of dating the Assisi and Vatican panels has primarily interested authors concerned with establishing the

position these images may have occupied in the history of the Franciscan legend. It is also an important though not determining factor in another, equally contested issue, that of their authorship. Beginning with Sebastiano Ranghiasci as early as 1820, the Assisi panel has consistently been associated with the only artist known by name to have worked in Assisi during the quarter century following Francis's death, Giunta Pisano. Giunta, one of the few artists active anywhere in Italy in the early thirteenth century who is known today by name, is documented between 1236, when he painted a large Crucifix for San Francesco that included a portrait of Fra Elia as donor (lost), and 1254 (see Tartuferi, 1991). Three large crucifixes signed by him survive—in Assisi (Santa Maria degli Angeli), Pisa (Museo di San Matteo), and Bologna (San Domenico) —and these reveal him to have been a pioneer in the introduction to Italian painting of a naturalizing style based partly on Byzantine sources, as well as a master whose talents fully justify his modern reknown, the founder of a school of followers in each of the three centers where he is known to have been active: Assisi, Bologna, and especially his native Pisa. The strongly Byzantinizing style of the Assisi Saint Francis, coupled with its universally admired quality—it is indisputably one of the most sophisticated and accomplished Italian panels surviving from the decades preceding Cimabue's own revolutionary interpretations of Byzantine sources— have led a number of authors to assign it to Giunta Pisano himself (Sirén, 1922; Tartuferi, 1991; and most outspokenly Boskovits, 1973b, 1993), if probably as a late work representing a second period of activity at Assisi after 1250.

It is difficult to compare either the "portrait" of Saint Francis or the small narratives of his miracles on the Assisi panel with the monumental, iconic figures on Giunta's three signed crosses, and most writers have preferred to see the former as the work of a follower of Giunta sometimes labelled, for convenience, the Master of the Treasury

(Scarpellini, 1980a; Caleca, 1986; Todini, 1989; Toscano, 1990; Kruger, 1992; Frugoni, 1993; Ragionieri, 1993; Lunghi, 1995). Among these scholars, opinion is divided as to whether the Assisi and Vatican panels might be by the same hand. Although Scarpellini (1980), for example, rejected Boskovits' attribution of the two paintings to Giunta, he agreed that they were probably the work of a single artist or workshop, and he was followed in this opinion by Todini (1989). Tartuferi (1991), on the other hand, accepted Boskovits' attribution of the Assisi panel to Giunta, but preferred to see the Vatican panel as the work of a different, derivative artist whom he characterized only as a Pisan follower of Giunta. Whether the Vatican panel, if accepted as by a follower of Giunta, might be Pisan or Umbrian has also been a point of contention, as has its precise relation to the Assisi panel. Most authors recognize its reductive detail and broader, more brightly colored handling as of marginally less distinguished quality than the Assisi panel. Some interpret this as a sign of its being a copy of the Assisi panel, though many believe it is only a slightly later replica of a third painting (lost) that the Assisi panel itself copies. Boskovits (1973b, 1993) alone believes that the Vatican panel may possibly have preceded the Assisi version.

None of Giunta Pisano's three signed crosses contain narrative scenes that permit comparison to those on either the Assisi or Vatican panels. Indeed, the only such scenes on any panel attributable with some confidence to Giunta, the Saint Francis panel in the Museo di San Matteo, Pisa, are fundamentally different in their exposition of drama and characterization of emotion, as well as in such basic technical devices as figure style and organization of space. Comparisons of the two figures of Saint Francis in Assisi and the Vatican to that in Pisa or to any of the painted crosses by Giunta is also unconvincing, and it must be concluded that adducing Giunta's name for either of these two paintings is based solely on inference from his historical importance. The painter of the Assisi Saint Francis aspires to many of the same naturalistic effects that Giunta introduced to Italian painting, but he achieves his ends in an essentially different idiom, one far more directly related to Byzantine sources than Giunta's paraphrases of Byzantine motifs and techniques.

It is impossible to overemphasize the Byzantine aspects of the Assisi Saint Francis, both in the manner in which the saint's features and hands are rendered and more significantly in the composition of the small narratives flanking his effigy. The division of each composition into symmetrically disposed halves around a vacant center, the remarkably precocious projection of space, the abundance of architectural detail, the elegantly attenuated proportions of the figures, and the prismatic patterns of their drapery folds more than anything else recall the most sophisticated products of Constantinopolitan icon painting of the twelfth and early thirteenth centuries. All these qualities are unprecedented in Italian painting and, with the exception of their only partially successful imitations in the Vatican panel, do not subsequently reappear in Italian art before the last two decades of the thirteenth century, in the paintings of Cimabue and Duccio. Neither Giunta Pisano nor any of his followers mastered or even demonstrated an interest in such complex spatial devices as the view from below up into the vaulting of a ciborium in the miracle of the deformed girl on the Assisi panel, or the complicated structure of the entrance alcove on the building behind the possessed woman in the miracle of exorcism. Architectural backgrounds for Italian artists of the thirteenth century have a symbolic rather than scenographic significance, and are invariably constructed of a simple screen of emblematic structures aligned parallel to the picture plane.

The possibility, first raised by Adolfo Venturi in 1907, must be considered whether the Assisi panel might have been painted not by an Italian but by a Byzantine artist working in Assisi. That such might have been the case is historically plausible, given Francis's own missionary connections with the East and after his death the continuous involvement in Constantinople and Jerusalem of the Franciscan order. In this context, it is perhaps interesting to recall a little-noticed remark in a seventeenth-century Franciscan chronicle (L. Wadding, *Annales Minorum*, I, p. 212, cited in Thode, 1885, p. 75), referring to early portraits of Francis painted by a Greek artist, Melormus, one of the most famous masters of that time ("...gli antichi ritratti che sono stati dipinti... dal pittore greco Melormus, uno dei maestri più famosi di quel tempo"). No other reference to such an artist is known, so it is impossible to confirm his existence or to suggest that he may have been the artist of the Assisi *Saint Francis and Four Posthumous Miracles*. It is even possible that "Greek" was in this case not meant literally but simply as a designation of the antiquated style of the painting ("maniera greca" was a descriptive formula applied indiscriminately to dugento and trecento pictures from Vasari's time onwards). On the other hand, it is also possible that the tradition was founded on a fact that can no longer be documented but that should not for that reason be discarded altogether.

Although the artist of the Vatican Saint Francis permitted himself some freedom in rearranging the compositions of the narratives from the Assisi panel, he took great pains to reproduce a number of details from their architectural backgrounds, clearly without fully understanding their spatial significance. In every instance his results may be described as a compromise between a Byzantine innovation and an Italian tradition. There is no apparent reason to consider this artist Pisan (as suggested by Tartuferi) or even Tuscan generally. His evident familiarity with the Assisi panel implies that he was active there for at least part of his career (no other paintings have yet been convincingly attributed to his hand), and the broad, decorative borders separating the scenes at the top from those on the bottom are more reminiscent of Umbrian manuscript illumination than of any other source. It is not even clear that he can be considered a direct follower of Giunta Pisano—similarities between the two artists may be the result of their common interest in Byzantine sources. For the present it seems prudent to designate him simply as an unknown Umbrian master, and to consider the Vatican panel as painted probably around the middle of the thirteenth century. [LBK-PP]

*Bibliography*: Ranghiasci, 1820, p. 13; Fratini, 1882, p. 41; Thode, 1885, pp. 75–76; Venturi, 1907, pp. 84–87; Sirén, 1922, pp. 164–72; Bughetti, 1926, pp. 693–700; Kleinschmidt, 1926, pp. 306–10; Boskovits, 1973, pp. 349–50; Volbach, 1979, pp. 22–23; Scarpellini, 1980a, pp. 34–38 (with previous bibliography); Scarpellini, 1982a, pp. 79–80, 345–47; Scarpellini, 1982b, pp. 98, 119–20; Caleca, 1986, II, p. 583; Todini, 1989, p. 132; Toscano, 1990, p. 623; Tartuferi, 1991, pp. 16–17, 70; Kruger, 1992, pp. 206–9; Boskovits, 1993, p. 103 n. 197; Frugoni, 1993, pp. 281, 311 n. 86, 324, 327, 335–45, 349–50 n. 21, 351 n. 34, 352 n. 44, 353 n. 46, 355 n. 63, 356 n. 72, 415–16 n. 14; Ragionieri, 1993, p. 530, Lunghi, 1995, pp. 77–78 n. 156.

## Master of the Blue Crucifixes
Umbrian or Emilian, active second
third thirteenth century

**2**

*Double-sided Crucifix*
Tempera on panel, 109.5 × 77 cm
Assisi, Museo-Tesoro della Basilica
di San Francesco

This double-sided Crucifix (the recto is nearly effaced, while the paint surface on the verso is extremely well-preserved, outside of small local losses) is perhaps the most distinguished member of a small group of painted crosses that may be associated with the early spread of Franciscan devotions to the image of the Crucified Christ. It is in all likelihood identical with a Crucifix described in one of the earliest preserved inventories of the sacristy of San Francesco at Assisi in 1430, and was therefore probably painted for the Basilica originally, as was another double-sided Crucifix by the same hand now in the Wallraf-Richartz-Museum, Cologne (found by Johann-Anton Ramboux in a refuse heap beneath a tower in the Sacro Convento and purchased by him from the Capitolo in either 1820 or 1835–36: Scarpellini, 1980). The cross in Cologne is smaller (82 × 51 cm) than the Assisi cross and omits the mourning figures of the Virgin and Saint John the Evangelist from the apron, but is otherwise nearly identical to it in design and in its exceptionally high quality of execution.

The earliest writers to refer to the Assisi cross considered it the work either of Giunta Pisano himself (Guardabassi, 1872; Venturi, 1907) or of Giunta's closest and most talented follower in Umbria, the Master of Saint Francis (Thode, 1890). Giunta is documented as having painted a monumental crucifix for the Basilica of San Francesco in 1236. Although this work does not survive, a reflection of its probable appearance may be gleaned from another crucifix signed by Giunta in the church of Santa Maria degli Angeli at Assisi. This cross, as well as two other crosses signed by Giunta—in San Domenico, Bologna, and the Museo di San Matteo, Pisa—portrays Christ with His eyes closed in death, His body pulling downwards and swaying in an exaggerated curve to the left. This form of painted crucifix, emphasizing the pain and suffering of Christ's sacrifice, was a Byzantine innovation introduced to Italy in the early thirteenth century and embraced with particular enthusiasm by the Franciscans. Earlier Italian painted crosses showed Christ alive, His eyes open, His body erect in an emblematic triumph over death. Although Giunta's cross is not the earliest known example of this new form, it is one of the most powerful in its expressive, almost realistic portrayal of Christ's suffering.

In part the early attributions to Giunta of the Treasury cross reflect a recognition of its conspicuously high quality. Osvald Sirén (1922) first made an effort to isolate its author as a personality distinct not only from Giunta Pisano, but also from the Master of Saint Francis, a less delicate and serene, more expressive and calligraphic artist. Sirén noted that the painter of the Treasury cross must have worked in Emilia as well as Umbria since two other paintings attributable to him were to be found in the church of San Francesco in Bologna. Although these are no longer generally accepted as being by the same hand, others have since come to light—notably a painted Cross in the Pinacoteca in Faenza—that suggest Sirén's intuition was accurate. Sirén dubbed his artist the Master of the Franciscan Crucifixes, a slightly confusing appelative that was changed by Garrison (1949) to the Master of the Blue Crucifixes: "His cross in Assisi shows a remarkable chromatic experiment, all the drapery and most of the decorative parts being in tones of very beautiful blue."

In characterizing his Blue Crucifix Master as the most sensitive follower of Giunta working in Northern Umbria (i.e. around Perugia and Assisi), Garrison intended to break up the group of paintings that had been assembled by Sirén and enlarged by Evelyn Sandberg-Vavalà (1929) into unrelated, sometimes individual works by a number of minor masters. Subsequent writers (Bologna, 1962; Scarpellini, 1980; Lunghi, 1986; Todini, 1986, 1989; Tartuferi, 1991) have instead observed only two main tendencies within this group: one that is entirely dependent on Giunta Pisano's cross in San Domenico, Bologna, that is recognizably Emilian in character, and that is in any event noticeable primarily in paintings still in Emilia, and another that is as reminiscent of Umbrian painting as it is of the San Domenico cross. This latter, more numerous group—now indicated by the name Master of the Blue Crucifixes—is recognized to include works probably painted in Emilia-Romagna as well as Assisi and therefore to constitute an important bridge between those two centers of artistic production.

Like the Master of Saint Francis, it is generally claimed that the Master of the Blue Crucifixes was profoundly influenced by Giunta Pisano and may have worked for some period as his assistant. However, where the Saint Francis Master exclusively reflects the style of Giunta in the Santa Maria degli Angeli cross, the Blue Crucifix Master has more in common with the refinement and elegance of Giunta's later cross in Bologna (contrary to the opinion of most writers, Tartuferi [1991] and Boskovits [1993] believe the Bologna cross to be Giunta's earliest work, possibly painted before 1230; this seems unlikely). It is at least possible, however, that rather than being a late follower of Giunta active in the third quarter of the thirteenth century, the Master of the Blue Crucifixes may have been a younger contemporary of Giunta aware of his work at Assisi but developing out of an autonomous Umbrian tradition. The two artists share an interest in certain Byzantine conventions of form, but their painting techniques and decorative interests have little in common. The Treasury cross, though sometimes dated around 1275, may possibly have been painted as early as 1240–50.

Where Giunta Pisano is known today through the survival of three monumental painted crosses, and the Master of Saint Francis is associated with monumental decorative campaigns in the Basilica of San Francesco at Assisi (ca. 1260) and San Francesco al Prato, Perugia (ca. 1270), the Master of the Blue Crucifixes instead appears to have specialized in small-scale panel paintings for private as well as ecclesiastical patrons. Two of his processional crosses were painted for San Francesco, but if he received commissions for monumental work there as well, it does not survive. The lyrical and engaging pictorial idiom he perfected is fully appropriate to the intimate scale and devotional rather than didactic purposes of his paintings. In this arena he is unrivalled among dugento painters prior to the advent of Duccio at the end of the century. [LBK-PP]

*Bibliography*: Guardabassi, 1872, p. 19; Thode, 1890, p. 16; Venturi, 1907, p. 18; Sirén, 1922, pp. 222–23, 339; Sandberg-Vavalà, 1929, pp. 845–48; Garrison, 1949, pp. 13, 184; Scarpellini, 1980, pp. 38–41 (with previous bibliography); Lunghi, 1986, II, p. 596; Todini, 1986, II, p. 376; Todini, 1989, I, p. 125; Tartuferi, 1991, pp. 82–83.

## Master of the Blue Crucifixes
Umbrian or Emilian, active second
third thirteenth century

**3/1**

*The Mourning Virgin*
Tempera on panel, 81 × 31.5 cm
Washington, D.C., National Gallery
of Art (no. 808)

**3/2**

*The Mourning Saint John the Evangelist*
Tempera on panel, 80.5 × 31.5 cm
Washington, D.C., National Gallery
of Art (no. 809)

These two figures originally occupied extensions, or terminals, at either end of the transverse arms of a painted crucifix, following a convention adopted in Italy in the early thirteenth century. Twelfth century crosses, in which the figure of the Crucified was shown alive in triumph over death, frequently included ancillary figures such as these or complete narrative scenes of the Passion painted on the apron of the cross alongside the body of Christ. With the adoption in the thirteenth century of the Byzantine formula of Christ portrayed with His eyes closed in suffering, attendant figures were frequently (though not invariably, see the preceding entry) moved to isolated compartments at the ends of the arms, sometimes, as here, shown full-length in attitudes of mourning, sometimes, as in the three signed crosses by Giunta Pisano, shown half-length as icons. That the present figures were indeed cut from the arms rather than the apron of a cross (as was suggested by Garrison) is indicated by the horizontal wood grain of the panels. The Washington *Virgin* and *Saint John the Evangelist*, then in the collection of Philip Lehman, New York, were included by Sirén (1922) in his initial reconstruction of the oeuvre of the painter he called the Master of the Franciscan Crucifixes. Although this designation was retained by Van Marle (1923), Sandberg-Vavalà (1929), and Shapley (1979), it has been discarded by all other writers both as confusing and as referring to a non-homogeneous group of paintings. Sandberg-Vavalà associated the Washington panels with a painted cross at Santa Maria in Borgo, Bologna, that she

added to Sirén's original group. She was followed by Garrison (1949), the first to dispute the coherence of the Master of the Franciscan Crucifixes, who assigned the Washington panels to a Bolognese artist he called the Borgo Crucifix Master. Gertrude Coor-Achenbach (cited in Shapley, 1979) endorsed this attribution, claiming that the Washington panels were actually the missing terminals excised from the Borgo Crucifix.

More recent authors (e.g. Lunghi, 1986; Todini, 1989) have recognized that the Washington panels have little in common with the purely Emilian style of the Santa Maria in Borgo crucifix outside of their mutual dependence on the example of Giunta Pisano. Among the pictures first discussed as a group by Sandberg-Vavalà, they relate far more closely to the terminals of a painted crucifix in the Pinacoteca at Faenza or again to the mourning figures painted on the apron of the double-sided cross in the Museo-Tesoro della Basilica di San Francesco at Assisi. Both of these are now recognized as key works by the Master of the Blue Crucifixes, and there can be little doubt that the Washington panels were painted by him as well. Both figures may be considered middle terms—in the arrangement and decoration of their draperies and rendering of their facial features and in the drawing of Saint John's hair—in the artist's development between the terminals of the Faenza cross and the consumate elegance of the apron figures on the Treasury cross in Assisi, but which of these was painted before the other and which decades of the thirteenth century their conception and execution might span are still matters of debate. [LBK-PP]

*Bibliography*: Sirén , 1922, pp. 221–22, 339; Van Marle, 1923, p. 402; Sandberg-Vavalà, 1929, pp. 845, 855; Garrison, 1949, p. 221; Shapley, 1979, I, pp. 311–13 (with previous bibliography); Lunghi, 1986, II, p. 596; Todini, 1989, I, p. 125; Tartuferi, 1991, p. 94.

## Master of the Blue Crucifixes
Umbrian or Emilian, active second
third thirteenth century

**4**

*Double-sided Processional Cross*
Tempera on panel, 38 × 23 cm
Northampton (Mass.), Smith College
Museum of Art
(no. 24:18-1)

Of significantly more modest dimensions than either of the two processional crosses painted by the Master of the
Blue Crucifixes for the Basilica of San
Francesco (Assisi, Museo-Tesoro della
Basilica; Cologne, Wallraf-Richartz-
Museum), the Northampton cross is at
least their equal in refinement and delicacy of execution. Its exceptional quality led Roberto Longhi (1948) to attribute it directly to Giunta Pisano as a
late work, though all other authors have
considered it among the group of Emilian and North Umbrian paintings assembled by Sirén (1922) and Sandberg-
Vavalà (1929) under the rubric Master
of the Franciscan Crosses. Garrison
(1949), who believed this group of
paintings to be entirely heterogeneous
beyond their common debt to Giunta's
example, nonetheless classified the
Northampton cross among their number ("Bolognese [?] or less probably
North Umbrian [?] Giuntesque"). Zeri-
Natale (1984) thought it "quasi certa-
mente di origine Umbra" (almost certainly of Umbrian origin), while
Wagstaff (1965) and Tartuferi (1991)
thought the cross might be by a Tuscan
painter. It is ignored by Todini (1989),
and in fact is overlooked in much of the
literature concerned with debating the
Emilian or Umbrian origins of this important group of works.
It was Enzo Carli (1958) who stressed
the resemblance of the Northampton
cross to several of the key works of
Sandberg-Vavalà's "Franciscan Cross
Master" that are now recognized as by
the Master of the Blue Crucifixes: the
Faenza crucifix, the terminal figures in
the National Gallery of Art, Washing-
tón, and a small panel of the *Crucifixion*
in the Museum of Fine Arts, Boston
(Coor-Achenbach, 1949; Kanter, 1994a,
pp. 113–15). Bologna (1964), Scarpellini (1980), and Todini (1986, 1989) have

defended the attribution of these paintings to the Master of the Blue Crucifixes
and their arguments may be extended to
the Northampton cross as well. On both
sides of this cross, which are nearly identical, the figure of Christ is painted with
the same fluid line and confident white
highlighting as in the Treasury cross in
Assisi. His facial features are rendered
with the same elegantly stylized pathos;
the gentle curve of His body is the same,
as is the delineation of the musculature
in His arms, torso, and legs and the animated folds of drapery in His perizoma.
The predominantly red palette of the
Northampton cross is unusual, but the
purity and intensity of its color is altogether typical of this Master.
The shape of the Northampton cross is
also unusual. It was related by Sandberg-
Vavalà to earlier metalwork examples
and to a small painted cross in the Cini
Foundation, Venice, sometimes attributed to Giunta Pisano but more recently
to a Tuscan painter known as the Master
of Santa Maria Primerana (Tartuferi,
1991, p. 98) or the "Master of the Crucifix no. 434 in the Uffizi" (Boskovits,
1993, p. 438). This shape, and the relatively small size of the Northampton
cross, must have been determined by its
use not as a temporary altar fixture to be
carried periodically in procession but as
a permanent attachment to a staff, probably borne by a bishop. This class of object may have been somewhat more
common originally than the rare surviving examples indicate, but it is likely that
they were not numerous until the fourteenth century, when they began to assume more decorative and freely inventive shapes, such as those of the crosses
from Yale (Master of the Gubbio Cross)
and Cleveland (Expressionist Master of
Santa Chiara) included in the present
exhibition. [LBK-PP]

*Bibliography*: Sandberg-Vavalà, 1929,
pp. 99–100, 858–61, 872 n. 42; Longhi,
1948, pp. 32–33; Garrison, 1949, p. 179;
Carli, 1958, p. 36; Wagstaff, 1965, p. 30;
Zeri-Natale, 1984, pp. 3–4; Tartuferi,
1991, p. 18; Boskovits, 1993, pp. 438,
801.

## Master of the Blue Crucifixes
Umbrian or Emilian, active second
third thirteenth century

**5**

*Virgin and Child*
Tempera on panel, 24.5 × 17.5 cm
Private Collection

Despite its small size, this little-known panel must be counted among the masterpieces of thirteenth-century painting in Italy. It was first published by Filippo Todini (1986, 1989), who recognized it both as the work of the Master of the Blue Crucifixes and as having formed one valve of a diptych with a panel representing the Crucifixion now in the Museum of Fine Arts, Boston (Kanter, 1994a). The Boston *Crucifixion* is extensively scarred and abraded. Its original quality can be intuited through its damages but a true idea of the former richness of its color and handling can only be gauged by comparison to this *Virgin and Child*, which is preserved in a remarkably pure state. The freely brushed white highlights and deep violet shadows of the Virgin's mantle, the loose, rapidly-painted folds of the Child's orange cloak or of the hem of the Virgin's cowl and shawl, the delicately modelled features of both faces and all four hands, and the deceptively naturalistic treatment of the mordant gilt striations (an inherently abstract medium appropriate to more hieratic, iconic representations) in the Christ Child's robes all denote an artist of superb technical capacity and visual imagination.

That this *Virgin and Child* once formed a diptych with the Boston *Crucifixion* is not open to doubt. The panels are approximately the same size, are constructed in the same fashion, and bear remnants of original hinges at the same heights on their right and left edges, respectively. The holes drilled in the top center of both panels may have been added later to accommodate hanging straps: they are not typical of early diptychs and they have not created radiating crackle patterns in the gold ground that might have been expected if they pre-existed the panels' gessoing and gilding. It is also unlikely that the painted leaf-and-dart pattern decorating the frame mouldings and partially covering the red inscription on the background at either

side of the Madonna is original, as that motif became popular in Italian frames only in the sixteenth century and is largely unknown prior to the fifteenth century.

The lettering of the background inscription (Mother of God) in Greek (typical of Italian paintings of the Virgin and Child of the thirteenth century), together with the presence of prominent gold striations highlighting the Christ Child's draperies suggest the possibility that a Byzantine icon may have inspired the Master of the Blue Crucifixes' invention of this composition. The touching gesture of the Child resting the sole of His right foot on the Virgin's wrist and nestling His cheek against hers is distantly derived from the Byzantine *Donskaya* type, but is here rendered with an emotional tenderness and immediacy that is purely Italian.

Portable diptychs for private, personal devotion such as this are exceedingly rare prior to the mid-fourteenth-century. Only three complete examples from the thirteenth century are known, and of these this pair of panels by the Master of the Blue Crucifixes may be the earliest. Another pair, comprised of a *Madonna and Child* formerly in the National Gallery in London and a *Crucifixion* in the Szépmüvészeti Múzeum, Budapest (Davies and Gordon, 1988, pp. 98–99) is frequently attributed to a Tuscan artist but might plausibly be considered Umbrian (the London panel was, perhaps not coincidentally, purchased in Assisi). The other pair, both panels of which are in the Art Institute of Chicago (Lloyd, 1993, pp. 131–35) is of more problematic attribution but has recently been proposed as the product of an Italian artist working in the Latin Kingdom of Jerusalem, possibly at Acre around 1275. Contacts between Crusader artists in the East and painters in Umbria have long been noted, but the direction in which influences flowed between them is still a matter of debate. [LBK-PP]

*Bibliography*: Todini, 1986, II, p. 376; Todini, 1989, I, p. 125; Kanter, 1994a, pp. 113–15.

**Master of the Blue Crucifixes,**
*The Crucifixion.*
**Boston, Museum of Fine Arts,**
**Gift of Edward Jackson Holmes**
**(28.886). By permission.**

## Master of Saint Francis
Umbrian, active third quarter thirteenth century

**6/1** *The Prophet Isaiah*
Tempera on panel, 53.6 × 25.6 cm
Assisi, Museo-Tesoro della Basilica
di San Francesco

**6/2** *The Apostles Saints Bartholomew
and Simon*
Tempera on panel, 47.6 × 22.8 cm
New York, The Metropolitan Museum
of Art, Robert Lehman Collection, 1975
(1975.1.104)

**6/3** *The Apostle Saint John the
Evangelist*
Tempera on panel, 49.5 × 24 cm
Washington, D.C., National Gallery
of Art (no. 811)

**6/4** *The Apostle Saint James Minor*
Tempera on panel, 50 × 24 cm
Washington, D.C., National Gallery
of Art (no. 810)

**6/5** *The Apostle Saint Peter*
Tempera on panel, 48 × 23 cm
Private Collection

**6/6** *The Apostle Saint Andrew*
Tempera on panel, 48.3 × 22.7 cm
Perugia, Galleria Nazionale
dell'Umbria (inv. no. 23)

**6/7** *Saint Francis*
Tempera on panel, 48 × 21.7 cm
Perugia, Galleria Nazionale
dell'Umbria (inv. no. 24)

**6/8** *Saint Anthony of Padua*
Tempera on panel, 54 × 24 cm
Perugia, Galleria Nazionale
dell'Umbria (inv. no. 21)

**6/9** *The Deposition*
Tempera on panel, 54 × 48.5 cm
Perugia, Galleria Nazionale
dell'Umbria (inv. no. 22)

**6/10** *The Lamentation*
Tempera on panel, 54 × 48 cm
Perugia, Galleria Nazionale
dell'Umbria (inv. no. 22)

6/1

These ten panels together formed part of one of the greatest Italian altarpieces of the thirteenth century. The five panels now in the Galleria Nazionale dell'Umbria at Perugia, representing the Deposition, Lamentation, Saint Anthony of Padua, Saint Francis, and Saint Andrew (this saint is always referred to as Matthew in earlier literature; a recent cleaning undertaken at the Galleria Nazionale [see Romano, 1994, p. 58] uncovered an inscription on the arch above the figure reading "SANCTUS [F]UIT IN PATRAS," thus indicating Andrew, the Apostle martyred in the Peloponnese) were first grouped by Henry Thode (1885) with the frescoes of the life of Saint Francis decorating the nave of the Lower Church of San Francesco at Assisi as the work of a gifted and spirited follower of Giunta Pisano, who rejected the restrictive Byzantine conventions of that painter to create an effectively new narrative style. Thode named this painter the Master of Saint Francis after the venerated "portrait" of Saint Francis by the same hand in the church of Santa Maria degli Angeli at Assisi, and characterized him as the greatest master in Italy before Cimabue. This assessment has been accepted by generations of scholars since, with additional attributions expanding the outlines of the painter's career and establishing him as the head of a productive and influential workshop.

Among the earliest additions to the oeuvre of the Master of Saint Francis were five panels that could be linked to those in Perugia by their common format and related subjects, forming what at first were believed to be two independent altarpieces. The Isaiah in the treasury of the Basilica of San Francesco at Assisi was first noted by Raimond van Marle in 1919, and was joined by Garrison (1949) with the two Passion scenes and the Saint Anthony of Padua in Perugia, with which it shares the same columns and trilobe framing arches, as the surviving fragments of an exceptionally large altarpiece that possibly once stood on the high altar of the Lower Church of San

Francesco. Garrison reconstructed a second altar comprising the Perugia Saint Francis and Saint Andrew and four other panels, all representing Apostles, that had come to light in the years since Thode's initial study. The Saint Peter, Saint John the Evangelist, Saint James Minor, and Saints Bartholomew and Simon had all once belonged to the Camposanto Teutonico in Rome and were sold to the Lehman and Stoclet collections sometime between 1921 and 1928 by Anton de Waal, rector of the Arciconfraternità della Pietà del Camposanto Teutonico (Pope-Hennessy and Kanter, 1987, p. 80).

These two supposedly independent altarpieces were first recognized as the front and back face of a single altarpiece by Jürgen Schultze (1961; 1963), who accepted Garrison's suggestion that it may have functioned as the high altarpiece of the Lower Church of San Francesco in Assisi, basing the hypothesis on the presence of the Isaiah in the treasury of the Basilica. Scarpellini (1980) doubted this identification since the Isaiah is not recorded at the Basilica prior to 1919 and none of the other panels are mentioned in any of the numerous early inventories of the Basilica, and since the high altar of the Lower Church probably did not have an altarpiece: the priest said mass from behind it, facing the congregation of pilgrims in the nave, not before it. He suggested, furthermore, that as the two Passion scenes in Perugia were described as early as 1793 in the sacristy of San Francesco al Prato in Perugia by W.Y. Ottley, that church was a more likely provenance for the entire altarpiece than was San Francesco in Assisi.

This proposal was defended with further circumstantial arguments of provenance by Dillian Gordon (1982), who added the highly plausible argument that the altarpiece may have been painted to stand on an altar table above the sarcophagus of the Beato Egidio, one of the companions of Saint Francis, in San Francesco al Prato. The relics of the Beato Egidio (d. 1261 or 1262) were interred in a classical sar-

6/3

6/4

cophagus (now in the Oratory of Saint Bernardino in Perugia) the carved decoration of which closely mirrors the painted and carved decoration of the altarpiece fragments, and which approximates in length the probable total width of the altarpiece. Gordon proposed an absolute *terminus post quem* for the altarpiece of 1266, since the depiction of the stigmata in the Perugia Saint Francis are of two colors, brown on the hands and feet and red on the saint's ribs, following a passage in Saint Bonaventure's *Legenda Maior* which was declared canonical in that year. She further suggested 1272, the date inscribed on a monumental painted cross by the Master of Saint Francis (now in the Galleria Nazionale dell'Umbria) that formerly hung above the high altar of San Francesco al Prato, as a likely *terminus a quo*, assuming that the altarpiece and the cross were parts of a single comprehensive decorative campaign.

Gordon also established, through close physical examination of the wood grain on the backs of the panels, the exact reconstruction of the altarpiece of which they formed part. According to her findings, the surviving panels from the front face of the altarpiece, the Isaiah, Deposition, Lamentation, and Saint Anthony of Padua, in that order from left to right, comprised the entire right half of the structure. A larger center panel probably representing the Crucifixion (missing) would have stood immediately to the left of the Isaiah, with four corresponding panels showing in all likelihood another prophet, a saint (probably Francis), and two further scenes from the Passion missing from the left half of the structure. The six panels remaining from the rear of the altarpiece comprised the entire left half of that side, arranged in order from left to right: Saint Francis, Saints Bartholomew and Simon, Saint James Minor, Saint John the Evangelist, Saint Andrew, and Saint Peter. Of these six, the Saint Francis, Saints Bartholomew and Simon, and Saint Andrew could be shown to have been cut from the same piece of wood (in other words to have stood directly back-to-back) with the Saint Anthony of Padua, Lamentation, and Deposition, respectively, so it is clear that no further panels are missing at either end from this half of the altarpiece. The contention of Sergio Fusetti and Paolo Virilli (1994, pp. 60–62) that the front face was longer by one additional figure at either end must be dismissed, though they are correct in observing that the Isaiah and Saint Anthony of Padua did not originally have columns on their left and right edges, respectively. These panels apparently abutted the center panel or the outer frame only with a floating corbel supporting their framing arches and without an intermediate column as in the innermost panels.

The resultant altarpiece, when complete with the now missing panels and with its (undoubtedly) substantial carved frame and decorative insets of colored and gilded glass, must have been of a majesty, complexity, and beauty unparalleled in thirteenth century panel painting. An impression of its impact, however diminished by its fragmentary state, is still evident today in the fresh, glowing colors of the surviving panels, the calligraphic freedom of their draughtsmanship, and the exuberant decorative patterns of their painted architecture. Its importance can scarcely be underestimated if one considers the impact it must have made *in situ* (if Dillian Gordon's hypothesis is correct), beneath the magnificent painted cross by the Master of Saint Francis, one of the largest and most beautiful surviving from the thirteenth century, and above a richly carved sarcophagus containing the much-venerated relics of one of Saint Francis's original companions. Presumably painted after, perhaps by as much as a decade (see Cannon, 1982), the frescoes filling the nave of the Lower Church of San Francesco at Assisi, one of the most visited pilgrimage sites on the Italian peninsula, it clearly established the Master of Saint Francis as the foremost painter of his time in central Italy. [LBK-PP]

6/5

*Bibliography*: Thode, 1885, p. 77; Van Marle, 1919, pp. 9–21; Garrison, 1949, pp. 161–63, 170–71; Schultze, 1961, pp. 59–66; Schultze, 1963, pp. 141–45; Scarpellini, 1980b, pp. 42–46 (with previous bibliography); Gordon, 1982, pp. 70–77; Christiansen, 1982, pp. 14–17; Todini, 1986, II, p. 376; Lunghi, 1986, II, p. 624; Pope-Hennessy and Kanter, 1987, pp. 78–80, 286–87; Todini, 1989, pp. 184–85; Frugoni, 1993, p. 299; Ragionieri, 1993, p. 530; Romano, 1994, pp. 58–60; Fusetti and Virilli, 1994, pp. 61–62; Lunghi, 1995, p. 79.

6/6

6/7

## Jacopo Torriti (attributed)
Roman, active last quarter
thirteenth century

**7**

*The Creator*
Preparatory drawing (red chalk
on plaster), 75 × 57 cm
Assisi, Museo-Tesoro della Basilica
di San Francesco

The fresco of the Creation of the World, on the upper section of the right-hand wall of the Upper Church of Assisi, marks the beginning of the cycle depicting episodes from the Old Testament. It starts at the bay adjacent to the transept, while the opposite wall is decorated with scenes from the New Testament.

Each of the two cycles is made up of sixteen scenes arranged on two levels, on each side of the single-light windows in the walls of the nave.

Over the course of an extensive program of conservation work carried out in the 1950s by the Istituto Centrale del Restauro, the preparatory drawings for fairly large areas of the frescoes were discovered, including those of the Creation of the World, Creation of Eve, Sacrifice of Isaac, Nativity, and Arrest of Christ. Totally different from the *sinopia*—traced in red chalk directly on the bare surface of the *arriccio*, over which a layer of plaster (or *intonaco*) is then laid—the preparatory drawing represents the intermediate and crucial phase of the creative process when, after the conception and the rough sketch of the fresco (the *sinopia*), the artist moves on to the preliminary execution of the painting.

It is at this moment that the artist's style, his technical skill or the peculiarity of his manner are revealed with the immediacy of the simple line, before application of the color. Thus the preparatory drawing is the stage where the painter expresses himself with greatest freedom, as he is less conditioned by an iconographic tradition or by established methods of execution.

The restoration of the fresco of the Creation of the World brought to light the preparatory drawing for the Creator's face, a work carried out by a talented painter with a classical training. In addition, his technique of composition is extremely refined and displays great inventiveness.

The critical debate over the identification of the artists who worked in the Upper Church is far from resolved, but among the painters who took part in the first phase of decoration of the nave, one personality emerges with particular force. This was Jacopo Torriti, a great painter and mosaicist who signed the two most important apsidal decorations in Rome at the end of the thirteenth century, at San Giovanni in Laterano (1291) and Santa Maria Maggiore (1296).

Both works were commissioned by the first Franciscan pontiff, Girolamo Masci, elected pope under the name of Nicholas IV (1288–1292). From 1274 to 1279, he had also been minister general of the Order and had certainly supervised the work on the Upper Church. In 1288, Nicholas IV issued a bull authorizing the provincial minister and guardian of the monastery at Assisi to utilize, "de discretorum fratrum ejusdem ecclesie Sancti Francisci consilio," the alms received from pilgrims to "facere conservari, reparari, ædificari, emendari, ampliari aptari et ornari Ecclesias Sancti Francisci de Assisio Sanctae Mariae de Portiuncola" (*The Registers of Nicholas IV*, vol. I, p. 13 n. 74).

The papal bull was intended to get the decoration of the Upper Church under way again, and it was apparently in 1288 that the Roman painters to whom the scenes in the first two and a half bays starting from the transept are attributed commenced work. And their "leader" must have been Torriti, since his touch characterizes almost the entire decoration of the nave, even if the majority of the frescoes were painted by his followers (Tomei, 1990a). The master's hand is most clearly recognizable in the vault of the Deësis in the second bay out from the transept and in the Creation of the World. On the vault of the Deësis Christ, the Virgin, Saint John the Baptist, and Saint Francis are depicted in the round shields held by angels. The critics are unanimous in thinking that this fresco is entirely by Torriti, as is demonstrated by the evident resemblance between the images and the figures of Christ and the Virgin in the apsidal mosaic of Santa Maria Maggiore (Scarpellini, 1982b; Tomei, 1990a).

To return to the fresco of the Creation of the World and therefore to the preparatory drawing for the face of the Eternal Father, Torriti's name has been put forward several times (and with justification), first by Zimmermann (1889) and then by numerous other authors (Toesca, 1927; Matthiae, [1965–66]; Boskovits, 1981; Bellosi, 1985). Other experts are inclined to attribute it to Filippo Rusuti on the basis of a comparison with the figure of Christ in Majesty in the mosaic on the façade of Santa Maria Maggiore, executed and signed by this artist probably sometime before 1297 (Strzygowski, 1888; Bologna, 1969a; Belting, 1977; Gandolfo, 1988). While there are undeniable—though generic—similarities between the fresco in Assisi and Rusuti's mosaic, analysis of the preparatory drawing makes it possible to establish a clear connection with the Christ in the apsidal mosaic of Santa Maria Maggiore. The two images have a number of extremely significant details in common, such as the shape of the eyes, nose and mouth, as well as the rendering of the hair. In addition, one notes an identical sense of modeling, with the same masterly handling of the structure of the facial planes and a powerfully naturalistic plasticity. Thus these two works differ markedly from Rusuti's mosaic, characterized by a certain fixity of expression and some obviously conventional elements. On the other hand, the face of the Eternal Father and that of Christ on the vault of the Deësis—a work unanimously attributed to Torriti—are almost identical. In fact it seems to be a somewhat less powerful version of the type used in the fresco at Assisi and, to an even greater extent, of the model produced by Torriti in the apse of Santa Maria Maggiore. So one can therefore conclude that the same cartoon was probably used and translated into mosaic by distinctly different stylistic means. Yet it must be pointed out that, in comparison with the freedom of expression and fineness of execution displayed by the preparatory drawing of the Eternal Father, the painted figure in the fresco in the nave at Assisi seems less spontaneous and more heavily conditioned by the weight of an ancient iconographic tradition, perhaps the one inaugurated by the Old Testament frescoes painted in the fifth century in the Basilica of San Paolo fuori le Mura in Rome.

In the definitive version—that is after the color had been applied—the Father's face has in effect undergone what could be called a process of "iconization," i.e. of assimilation to the ancient and prestigious models that have influenced the realization of this fresco. Moreover, the thick outlines of the work produce an archaic effect and emphasize the formal structure of the image.

On the other hand the fresco retains the refined chiaroscuro of the preparatory drawing, which skillfully defines the planes of the face and reveals the technique of a mature painter, alive to the symbolic and monumental values of the figurative culture of late antiquity and early Christian culture.

The drawing of the Eternal should therefore be attributed to Torriti who, during the few years he spent in Rome and Assisi, was the only artist to have adopted the classical pictorial lexicon in such a precise fashion. This is clearly demonstrated, in the fresco of the Creation of the World, by the lively naturalism of the animals depicted in the lower part of the scene and above all by the two personifications of light and of darkness, which are absolutely identical to the small presiding geniuses that people the river scene in the mosaic executed by Torriti in Santa Maria Maggiore.

Finally, on the level of style and composition, the distinguishing features of the Eternal Father can also be found in the preparatory drawing for the face of Christ in the scene of the Arrest (Istituto Centrale del Restauro, Rome), a work by another artist working in Torriti's entourage (see Tomei, 1997).

The preparatory drawings also permit

us to reconstruct the activity of Torriti and his disciples in the nave. In point of fact, these artists can be distinguished not only by specific stylistic features, but also by their technical skills. They used an original and clearly-defined method of execution that was plainly the mark of their workshop, a method that can also be discerned in that part of the nave—and not elsewhere—where Torriti worked, from the fresco of the Creation of the World to that of the Arrest. [AT]

*Bibliography*: Thode, 1885; Strzygowski, 1888, p. 156; Zimmermann, 1889, pp. 256 et seq.; Toesca, 1927; Soldati, 1928; Nicholson, 1930; Zocca, 1936; Lochoff, 1937; Toesca, 1948; Gnudi, 1958; Carità and Mora, 1959; Bologna, 1960; Bologna, 1962; Matthiae [1965–66], II, p. 217 et seq.; Bertelli, 1969; Bologna, 1969a; Venturoli, 1969; Volpe, 1969; Belting, 1977; Mora, Mora and Philippot, 1977; Scarpellini, 1980a and 1980b; Boskovits, 1981; Scarpellini, 1982b; Brandi, 1983; Bellosi, 1985, pp. 121 et seq.; Todini, 1986; Tomei, 1989; Tomei, 1990a; Tomei, 1996; Boskovits, 1997; Tomei, 1997.

## Master of the Gubbio Cross
Umbrian (?), active ca. 1285–ca. 1320

**8**

*Double-sided Processional Cross*
Tempera on panel, 51.8 × 37.5 cm,
recto
Yale University Art Gallery
Bequest of Maitland Fuller Griggs
(1943.238)

This beautifully-preserved processional cross is painted with nearly identical images of the crucified Christ on both faces. Full-length standing figures of the mourning Virgin and Saint John the Evangelist fill the large, elegantly shaped trilobe terminals at either end of the transverse arm of the cross, while a mourning angel is painted above the cross in the upper terminal, facing towards the Virgin at the left on the obverse and towards Saint John at the right on the reverse. At the foot of the cross on its front face a diminutive figure of Saint Francis kneels in devotion, while Saint Clare occupies the same position on the back face. The outermost lobes at the top and sides and two lobes at the bottom at the level of the painted suppedaneum are decorated with delicately painted quatrefoil discs, and the entire gold ground is enlivened with an engraved pattern of ivy tendrils of a remarkable complexity and sophistication of design.

The Yale cross was first associated by Garrison (1949) with another double-sided processional cross of nearly the same size (56 × 38 cm) in the Galleria Nazionale dell'Umbria at Perugia as the work of an artist appropriately if somewhat expansively dubbed the "Processional Cross Master." The Perugia cross is very closely related to the Yale panel in figure style and expressive content though it is more archaic in form, including figures from the Passion on the apron of the cross and placing Christ's feet spread in different directions on the subpedaneum. This last motif recalls the solution introduced by Giunta Pisano to the problem of portraying Christ's agony on the Cross while remaining faithful to the decorative principles of Byzantine painting. The Yale cross instead adopts the more naturalis-

tic placement of Christ's feet developed with such powerful authority by Giotto in his early crucifixes at Santa Maria Novella and at Rimini. The shape of the Yale cross, furthermore, has little to do with that of earlier painted examples on either a large or a small scale, and may be derived from goldsmith's work or crystal carving. The unusual engraving of its gold ground may also be derived from such a source, or it may reflect the exuberant decoration that fills the background of illuminated initials in Perugian manuscripts of the early decades of the fourteenth century. Such differences from the otherwise conventional format of the Perugia cross suggest that though apparently painted by the same artist, the Yale cross probably dates several decades later, reflecting on an intimate scale the revolution in pictorial thinking being enacted on the walls of the Upper Church in Assisi in the last decade of the thirteenth century.

While it is clear that the Yale cross is the product of exposure to the team of artists working on the walls of the Upper Church of San Francesco, no consensus of opinion has been offered for the stylistic origins of the Perugia cross. Its relationship to the style of Cimabue on the one hand and the Roman masters working around Jacopo Torriti and Pietro Cavallini on the other has generated a confusing array of arguments (Santi, 1969; Parenti, 1994) over the artist's possible origins in Tuscany, Rome, or the one place most subject to the influence of both those centers, Assisi. Volpe (cited in Boskovits, 1973b) introduced another factor to the equation by recognizing a large painted Crucifix in the Pinacoteca at Gubbio as a work of the same hand, rechristening him the Master of the Gubbio Cross. Boskovits (1973b; followed by Lunghi, 1982, p. 210) associated the mixture of Tuscan and Roman influences in the Perugia, Gubbio, and Yale crosses with the polyglot culture of the "cantiere d'Assisi" and in particular with the same particular blend of styles in the work of the so-called Master of the Capture of Christ active among the frescoists of the

Upper Church of San Francesco. It is possible that the Master of the Gubbio Cross may have trained in Assisi with the Master of the Capture of Christ sometime in the 1280s, while debated additions to his oeuvre (Donnini, 1975; Fratini, 1986; Todini, 1989), a number of which are also to be found in Gubbio, suggest that he may subsequently have transferred his activity there. Proposals that he might be identifiable with one of the three principal manuscript illuminators active in northern Umbria in the early years of the fourteenth century, the so-called Primo Miniatore Perugino (Conti, 1981), or with the artist Palmerino di Guido documented as active in Gubbio in 1321 (Manuali, 1982), are to be rejected, but emphasize the affinities of a painting such as the Yale cross with Umbrian art of the early fourteenth rather than late thirteenth century. [LBK-PP]

*Bibliography*: Garrison, 1949, pp. 25, 178; Santi, 1969, p. 36; Seymour, 1970, pp. 99–101; Boskovits, 1973b, pp. 11–12; Donnini, 1975, pp. 8–9; Manuali, 1982, pp. 8–11; Fratini, 1986, II, p. 605; Todini, 1989, I, p. 123; Parenti, 1994, p. 89.

**Master of the Gubbio Cross**
Umbrian (?), active ca. 1285–ca. 1320

**8**
*Double-sided Processional Cross*
Tempera on panel, 51.8 × 37.5 cm,
verso
Yale University Art Gallery
Bequest of Maitland Fuller Griggs,
(1943.238)

## Expressionist Master
## of Santa Chiara
Umbrian, active ca. 1290–ca. 1330

**9**

*Double-sided Processional Cross*
Tempera on panel, 61.3 × 44.2 cm
Cleveland, Museum of Art
Purchase from the J. H. Wade Fund
(43.280)

Like the double-sided processional cross from the Yale University Art Gallery also included in this exhibition, the Cleveland cross was painted for a Clarissan patron, an image of Saint Clare filling the lower quadrilobe terminal on the front face (the Cleveland and Yale crosses are two of the earliest to include a half-length saint other than John the Evangelist in one of its terminals). The upper terminal on that side is filled with a mourning angel in steep and dramatic foreshortening, while the lateral terminals are occupied by the traditional figures of the mourning Virgin and Saint John the Evangelist. On the reverse of the cross Saint Francis replaces Saint Clare in the lower terminal. The mourning angel in the upper terminal is shown in profile flying up and away from the Crucified Christ below him, as though he were actually designed to fill a space below the right arm of the cross and inappropriately transposed to this position. The lateral terminals are again occupied by the Virgin and Saint John the Evangelist, the former shown in an unusual pose with her hands joined at her waist, perhaps following the model of Giotto's early painted crucifix in Santa Maria Novella, Florence.

This beautifully carved and painted cross was acquired for the Cleveland Museum of Art as a fifteenth-century Florentine work (Francis, 1945). Federico Zeri (1956, cited in Wixom, 1974) called it Venetian, fourteenth century, while Richard Offner (1956) instead considered it Umbrian. Boskovits (1968) refined Offner's attribution, assigning it for the first time to an artist identified only a short while earlier by Longhi (1963) as the Expressionist Master of Santa Chiara. This artist, author of an important triptych in the church of Santa Chiara in Assisi and of a dip-

tych in the Louvre, took his unusual name from the exaggeratedly dramatic quality of his frescoes of the life of the Virgin and the burial of Saint Clare in the right transept of the church of Santa Chiara. Later authors (Boskovits, 1968; Scarpellini, 1969) added to the list of his works additional frescoes in the vaults of Santa Chiara, several panels and frescoes in Gubbio, and a number of other independent panels, making him one of the primary figures in the development of early fourteenth-century painting in Umbria.

Among the attributions added to the nucleus of works originally assigned to the Expressionist Master of Santa Chiara were four large painted crosses that had formerly been grouped together under the rubric Master of the Montefalco Cross. This artist had been identified as Giotto's earliest Umbrian collaborator, in part responsible for the later scenes from the life of Saint Francis in the Upper Church of San Francesco at Assisi (Previtali, 1967). With the amalgamation of these paintings into the oeuvre of the Expressionist Master of Santa Chiara, the latter was recognized as the principal exponent of Giotto's style in northern Umbria from the later 1290s (the probable date of the frescoes in Santa Chiara) through the first three decades of the fourteenth century. Several authors, notably Boskovits (1968), have contended that the Expressionist Master's hand is also visible assisting Giotto in the execution of the frescoes in the chapels of Saint Nicholas and the Magdalene in the Lower Church of San Francesco, during the great Florentine master's second campaign of work in Assisi. From this contention, coupled with the presence of a number of his works in Gubbio, has arisen a proposal to identify the Expressionist Master of Santa Chiara with the Eugubine painter Palmerino di Guido (active 1301–ca. 1340), mentioned in a document of 1309 as an assistant or associate of Giotto in Assisi (Neri Lusanna, 1977; Todini, 1980; Lunghi, 1986). This identification is plausible but not demon-

strable, and it has not met with universal acceptance (Angelini, 1988).

Among the works widely accepted as by the Expressionist Master of Santa Chiara, the Cleveland cross most closely resembles some from the group once assembled around the Montefalco cross, notably a painted crucifix in Spello, and the transept frescoes in Santa Chiara itself. The strongly Giottesque figure canon of these paintings, almost statuesque in their tactility, is animated by an over-excited sensibility verging on the melodramatic. Despite their small scale, the same

nervous pathos, less typical of Italian than of Northern European art, is apparent in all the figures of the Cleveland cross, which is likely to date towards the beginning of the Expressionist Master's career, probably in the first decade of the fourteenth century. [LBK-PP]

*Bibliography*: Francis, 1945, pp. 3–5; Offner, 1956, pp. 166–67 n. 1; Boskovits, 1968, pp. 126–27; Wixom, 1974, pp. 138–39 (with previous bibliography); Lunghi, 1986, p. 632; Todini, 1989, I, p. 138; Chong, 1993, p. 147.

# Master of the Sterbini Diptych
Veneto-Byzantine, probably second
quarter fourteenth century

**10**

*Virgin and Child*
Tempera on panel, 33.2 × 26.7 cm
Assisi, Museo-Tesoro della Basilica
di San Francesco,
Perkins Collection

A small group of early-fourteenth-century panels, all representing the Virgin and Child, have been associated with this Madonna from the Perkins collection as the work of a single master or workshop probably active in Venice, or elsewhere along the Adriatic coast of Italy, strongly influenced by the Greek or Cretan traditions of icon painting. The group takes its name from a diptych formerly in the Sterbini collection and now in the Museo di Palazzo Venezia, Rome, representing in the left wing the Virgin and Child with Saint Joseph and Saints Lawrence, Philip, and John the Baptist, and in the right wing the Crucifixion, the Stigmatization of Saint Francis, and Saint Louis of Toulouse (Santangelo, 1948, p. 5, figs. 1–2). Another picture, in the Museo Regionale in Messina, is a triptych showing the Virgin and Child with Saints Bartholomew and Agatha (Zeri, 1992b, no. 18). The other Madonnas in the group—formerly with Salvatore Romano, Florence; formerly collection of Lord Clark of Saltwood (Garrison, 1949, nos. 65, 92); and the Perkins Madonna—may have been parts of diptychs as well, but if so their companion panels are not known to survive.

The salient characteristics, first recognized by Richard Offner (as quoted in Zeri, 1988, p. 82) linking these five paintings are primarily iconographic. In all of them, the figure of the Virgin reproduces faithfully some common prototype. Not only are her facial features identical in all of them, but the folds of her drapery are identically disposed and the fingers of both her hands are spread in the same fashion. The Christ Child is the same physical type in all five paintings as well, although the Perkins panel differs from the others in showing Him turned towards His mother with a gesture of blessing and holding a scroll in His left hand. In the Sterbini, Romano, Lord Clark, and Messina panels He turns away from His mother to toy with a bird on a string, raising His left leg in a lively and playful pose. In this respect, the Perkins panel is closer to the Byzantine iconic models that inspired the entire group, while the others introduce an admixture of Italian elements sometimes attributed to Sienese Ducciesque or Lorenzettesque influence (Shorr, 1954, p. 103; Zeri, 1992b, pp. 11, 55).

It is not clear to what extent the similarities among these five panels necessarily imply their common authorship, or whether they ought instead be considered products of a Veneto-Byzantine tradition of icon painting, in which the personality of the artist is submerged in his attempts to recreate faithfully the presence of a much-venerated image. The panel formerly in Lord Clark's collection, for example, is strongly Byzantinizing in style as well as content, as is the diptych from the Sterbini collection, and both could easily have been efforts of the Greek artistic community working in Italy. The Perkins panel and that formerly in the collection of Salvatore Romano look decidedly more like Venetian or Paduan paintings of the second quarter of the fourteenth century, and might as easily have been produced by an Italian as a Greek craftsman. As such, the designation "Master of the Sterbini Diptych" is a label of convenience intended to isolate the similarities among a group of paintings but not to assign them to a single artistic personality in any conventional sense. Dates for the five panels in the Sterbini group may vary over a period of several decades, but none of them present internal evidence that could assist in establishing a relative chronology. The Sterbini diptych itself must post-date 1317, the year in which Saint Louis of Toulouse (who is portrayed in the right wing) was canonized. A date ca. 1330–40 was proposed for the Perkins panel by Zeri (1988), a suggestion that is not contradicted by comparison to other works produced in Venice or in Venetian territories at that time. [LBK-PP]

*Bibliography*: Zeri, 1988, pp. 82–83.

89

## Master of San Martino alla Palma
Florentine, active first third fourteenth century

**11**

Portable tabernacle:
*Virgin and Child Enthroned
with Saints Peter and John the Baptist
and Two Angels; The Nativity;
The Crucifixion*
Tempera on panel, 55 × 30 cm,
central panel; 48.5 × 14.6 cm, wings
Assisi, Museo-Tesoro della Basilica
di San Francesco, Perkins Collection

This tabernacle triptych, which is preserved with its original frame mouldings and iron hinges intact, is an early and extremely simple example of a type of private devotional object that would become increasingly popular and increasingly elaborate in structure and decoration throughout the fourteenth century. It represents a conventional image of the Madonna and Child enthroned in its center panel, with diminutive figures of Saints Peter and John the Baptist, undoubtedly patrons of the tabernacle's original owner, and angels in adoration. In the left wing is a slightly unconventional portrayal of the Nativity, showing the Virgin gently laying the Christ Child in the manger while Saint Joseph offers a prayer of thanksgiving, apparently following a description in the pseudo-Bonaventure's *Meditationes in Vitam Christi.* Two other early fourteenth-century paintings illustrating the same text appear to have been intended for Franciscan patrons, and it has been suggested that the Perkins tabernacle may have been as well (Offner, 1947). The right wing is filled with a more traditional image of the Crucifixion, with the Virgin and Saint John the Evangelist standing at the foot of the Cross. Mourning or Adoring angels are skillfully arranged to fill the triangular gables of each wing.

The earliest writers to discuss the Perkins tabernacle mentioned little more than its relationship to Giotto and some of his followers, especially Bernardo Daddi. Richard Offner (1933) was the first to clarify this observation by attributing it to a painter he at first named the Amico di Daddi and later

the Master of San Martino alla Palma, after an altarpiece in the parish church there. For Offner, the Master of San Martino alla Palma was the oldest and in many respects the most gifted and distinctive of Bernardo Daddi's immediate followers, while Bernardo Daddi was in turn the greatest Florentine painter of the early fourteenth century after Giotto. He furthermore considered the Perkins tabernacle to be the earliest known work by the Master of San Martino alla Palma, an opinion shared by Federico Zeri (1988). Both scholars dated the painting around 1325–30, a period then thought to represent the beginning of Daddi's career as well and thus the earliest likely moment for reflections of his style to appear in another painter's work.

Few scholars have subsequently questioned Richard Offner's attributions to the Master of San Martino alla Palma, but serious questions have been raised concerning the dates of his activity, his chronology, and his relation to Bernardo Daddi, who is himself now recognized to have been active well before 1325. Miklos Boskovits (1984), for example, proposed that the Master of San Martino alla Palma was trained among an earlier generation of artists, including the Master of Saint Cecilia, Lippo di Benivieni, and the Master of the Saint George Codex, with whom he is especially closely related and who may possibly have been his original mentor. In this view, the earliest works by the Master of San Martino alla Palma, probably dating around 1310, are more archaic than those of Bernardo Daddi's numerous followers, and only his late works display any real influence of Daddi's style. Among these late works Boskovits includes the Perkins tabernacle, accepting the date proposed for it by Offner of ca. 1325–30 but considering this the close rather than the beginning of the Master of San Martino alla Palma's career.

So little documentation and so few firmly dated works survive from the early trecento that it is difficult to accept either of these divergent theories

without certain reservations. It does seem, however, that the majority of the Master of San Martino alla Palma's extraordinarily animated and expressive paintings—he was truly one of the most talented painters in Florence in the first decades of the fourteenth century—date earlier than Offner supposed, if perhaps not by as much as twenty years, as Boskovits contends. But it is unlikely that Offner was wrong in dating the Perkins tabernacle ca. 1325–30. It is difficult to envision any earlier date for the composition of the Nativity scene in the left wing, while the architecture of the Virgin's throne is more typical of paintings from the 1330s than of any earlier time. It is also important to note that beneath the simple projecting pediment at the top of the central panel is a raised trefoil frame moulding, unique in the Master of San Martino alla Palma's oeuvre and virtually unknown in Florentine painting before the late 1320s. The attribution and date of the Perkins tabernacle are, therefore, less matters of debate than are opinions regarding its significance. If it is considered the Master's earliest work, he must be recognized as a talented but essentially derivative artist. If it is assumed to be a mature, even a later effort by the painter, as seems more likely, then he can be recognized as an innovative if still elusive protagonist in the development of late Gothic and Renaissance style in Florence. [LBK-PP]

*Bibliography*: Offner, 1933, p. 83 n. 53; Offner, 1947, pp. 4, 5 n. 1, 6, 8, 12–13; Boskovits, 1984, pp. 67–68; Zeri, 1988, pp. 18–19.

# Pietro Lorenzetti
Sienese, documented 1306 (?)–after 1344

**12**

*Virgin and Child*
Tempera on panel, 70.5 × 44.5 cm
Assisi, Museo-Tesoro della Basilica
di San Francesco, Perkins Collection

Pietro Lorenzetti was one of the principal masters of Siena in the early fourteenth century, occupying a position of
undisputed prominence among artists
of the generation following the death of
Duccio around 1318. His monumental
and highly expressive figure style and
narrative sensibilities, which have much
in common with the powerful sculptur-
al idiom of Giovanni Pisano, were influential well beyond the confines of the
Sienese commune. His earliest important altarpieces were painted for Cortona and Arezzo, the latter dated 1320,
and he was entrusted sometime in the
second decade of the century with the
fresco decoration in the south transept
(and elsewhere) of the Lower Church of
San Francesco at Assisi. He was, with his
fellow Sienese Simone Martini, the first
artist to break the Florentine monopoly
on commissions in Assisi, and among
the last of the truly great innovators of
the fourteenth century to exercise his
talents in the Basilica.

The Perkins *Virgin and Child* is a beautiful example of Pietro's work from the
height of his maturity, painted a decade
or more after he had completed his frescoes in Assisi. The expressive colloquy
established by the figures, with the
Christ Child peering intently, perhaps
questioningly into His mother's face
while she instead engages the viewer
(once the supplicant) with a benign but
unwavering stare, is typical of the immediacy and emotive impact of his
paintings following the Carmine altarpiece of 1328. The deep shadows flicker-
ing across the faces of the mother and
Child and their full, rounded proportions, nearly filling the space available
within the frame mouldings and forcing
the visible remnants of gold ground to
the extreme margins of the panel, represent a marked development beyond the
stately, measured, and more linear approach to composition that prevailed in

Siena in the preceding decades and that
continued in the work of Simone Martini and his followers. Pietro Lorenzetti's own (presumably numerous) disciples were adept at imitating his figural
vocabulary and decorative motifs, but
none could approximate his penetrating
understanding of human character, or
the ease with which he rendered it in
two dimensions.

Relatively few scholars of Pietro Lorenzetti's work have discussed the Perkins
Madonna at any length, and it has not
received the critical attention that its
exceptional quality merits. In large
part this is due to the compromised
state in which it was known for many
generations, having only recently been
returned to its original shape (it had
been enlarged to a complete rectangle
by the addition of new pieces of wood
fit into the upper corners) and freed of
extensive and coarse, probably eigh-
teenth- or early-nineteenth-century
repaints. But for a long, narrow strip of
damage following a split in the panel
that rises through the Virgin's right
hand to a height just below the Christ
Child's right hand, the painting now
reads as the masterpiece it is. Its newly
revealed shape, furthermore, has led to
a proposal (Laclotte, 1976; Zeri, 1988)
for identifying a companion panel in
the figure of *Saint Clare* now in the
Kress Collection at the University of
Georgia at Athens. This panel, which is
severely damaged, is cut to the same
shape and has a similar set of punch
marks decorating the figure's halo.
This shape, however, is not unusual in
Pietro Lorenzetti's oeuvre and is
shared with at least two other Madonna's, one formerly in the Serristori collection, Florence (Volpe, 1989, no.
A10), and one from San Giovanni Battista at Campriano now stored at the
Pinacoteca Nazionale, Siena (Torriti,
1990, fig. 76). Nor are the patterns
Pietro used to fill haloes as reliable as
evidence of association as they might
be for some other painters. In fact, the
Athens Saint Clare is portrayed in
somewhat greater than half-length and
in a panel slightly too tall and narrow

to have fit comfortably alongside the
Perkins Madonna in a single altarpiece.
In these respects it more closely resembles the ex-Serristori Madonna, with
which it agrees stylistically as well, and
which is a much more likely candidate
for the center panel of the structure that
also originally housed the Athens panel.
The particular form of the repaints that
once covered the Perkins Madonna is
typical of paintings preserved in the
early nineteenth century out of context
as independent devotional panels, and it
is possible that no other panels from its
original altarpiece (there can be no
doubt that it once functioned as the
center panel of an altarpiece) survive. It
should be noted, however, that the engaged mouldings that run around three
sides of the panel are unusual in form,
yet they recur in the three surviving
panels from an altarpiece by Pietro
Lorenzetti dated 1332, painted for Santa
Cecilia at Crevole and now preserved in
the Pinacoteca Nazionale, Siena (Torriti, 1990, fig. 76). Furthermore, the damaged upper corners of the Perkins
Madonna show traces of once having
borne gable mouldings (now cut away)
identical to those in the Crevole fragments. Only the decoration of the
haloes in those panels, which are inscribed with the names of the saints,
differs from that in the Perkins Madonna, and it is unclear whether they
should be considered possibly fragments of a single complex or simply
parts of two different altarpieces that
followed the same, somewhat unusual
carpentry design. It is worth noting that
the Campriano Madonna attributed to
Pietro Lorenzetti came from a church in
the immediate vicinity of Crevole and
has a shape similar to the Perkins
Madonna and the Crevole Saints, possibly indicating a number of local vari-
ants on this particular altarpiece form.
The Campriano Madonna is unlikely to
have stood with the Crevole Saints in a
single altarpiece. It is punched, as they
are not, along the borders of its gold
ground as well as in the haloes, and it
seems to be a considerably later work.
[LBK-PP]

*Bibliography*: Laclotte, 1976, p. 18 n. 7;
Zeri, 1988, pp. 48–49; Volpe, 1989, p.
202, no. A4 (with previous bibliography); Skaug, 1994, I, p. 226, II, chart 7.5.

# Pietro Lorenzetti
Sienese, documented 1306 (?)–after 1344

**13**

*Saint Margaret* (?) *or Cecilia* (?)
Tempera on panel, 67.2 × 46 cm
Assisi, Museo-Tesoro della Basilica
di San Francesco, Perkins Collection

Our understanding of the precise outlines of Pietro Lorenzetti's career is still
somewhat vague, in part due to the limited number of dated or firmly documented paintings by him, and in part
due to his pervasive influence over contemporaries and followers in Siena.
There remains very little agreement
over the extent to which assistants or
even imitators may have been responsible for a number of paintings commonly attributed to him, with schools of
thought ranging from the severely restrictive to the openly expansive. A case
in point is represented by this panel
of a Virgin Saint from the Perkins
collection. It has long been recognized
as having formed part of an altarpiece
with a Virgin and Child in the Loeser
collection at the Palazzo Vecchio,
Florence, a Saint Catherine of Alexandria at the Metropolitan Museum of
Art, New York, a Bishop Saint from the
De Noailles collection, Paris, an Apostle
in the collection of Amedeo Lia at La
Spezia, and two triangular pinnacles in
the National Gallery at Prague showing
a youthful Martyr Saint and a Hermit
Saint (Zeri, 1988, figs. 1–6). All of these
panels have, either separately or as a
group, wandered in and out of attribu-
tional controversies centered on the
existence of a so-called Dijon Master
(after a small devotional triptych in the
museum there), or as he has recently
been renamed, the Loeser Master (Maginnis, 1980), active in Pietro Lorenzetti's
entourage. For some scholars, the existence of such a personality is undeniable, even if an accurate list of works as-
signable to him is still open to debate.
For at least one scholar (Frinta, 1976) he
can with some confidence be identified
with an actual historic personality, Mino Parcis da Siena, documented as an
assistant or collaborator of Pietro
Lorenzetti in 1321 and plausibly the father of an important painter of the next
generation: Jacopo di Mino del Pellicciaio. For still other scholars the existence of a Dijon or Loeser Master is a
myth and all the works assigned to him
instead comprise the late style of Pietro
Lorenzetti himself, painted after the
Birth of the Virgin altarpiece of 1342
from Siena Cathedral (Volpe, 1989, pp.
44–45; Chelazzi Dini, 1997, p. 132). This
last point of view is largely based on the
extremely high quality of most of the
paintings in the "Loeser Master" group:
for at least one adherent of this theory,
the Perkins Saint "è da annotare fra i
capolavori di Pietro [is to be numbered
among the masterpieces of Pietro
Lorenzetti]" (Volpe, 1989, p. 188).
Judging these paintings only on the basis of their quality it is difficult to see
them as anything but the work of Pietro
Lorenzetti. The lively humanity of the
Virgin and Child in the Loeser panel
and the convincing plasticity of textures
and volumes in their draperies, the
pathos of the Amedeo Lia Apostle, and
the intimate details of the Perkins
Saint—such as the saint's shy tug at her
shawl, the trailing ends of hair braids
casually resting on her shoulders, and
the beautifully visualized (if much damaged) wreath of flowers in her hair—be-
speak the intervention of a great and inventive artist and conform to our expec-
tations of Pietro Lorenzetti himself. The
difficulty lies in reconciling problems of
chronology. If these paintings, and the
others attributed to the "Loeser Master,"
are by Pietro, it is the consensus of opinion that they must date to the last
decade of his career, specifically after
1342 (Pietro is believed to have died in
the plague of 1348), as they do not conform in style to the sequence of his dated paintings earlier than that. The
Loeser altarpiece itself, however, is constructed in an archaic format, with
round-arched picture fields, silver decorated spandrels (no longer preserved on
the Perkins panel), and triangular pinnacles: structural and decorative features popular in the 1320s. It employs a
Byzantinizing device of gold striations
highlighting drapery folds (again not
visible in the Perkins Saint) that had
largely disappeared from Sienese painting after 1320, and it employs a set of
punch tools atypical of Pietro Lorenzetti's paintings but which have been
identified (Frinta, 1976) in the work of
Jacopo di Mino del Pellicciaio, therefore
already absent from Pietro's shop, as
early as 1342. From this it has been concluded (Skaug, 1994) that the Loeser
polyptych must have been painted earlier than 1342, and consequently that it is
unlikely to be by Pietro Lorenzetti.
These conflicting observations, even
those apparently more objective or "scientific" than others, are all capable of alternative interpretations, and the issue
is therefore difficult to resolve with only
the evidence presently available.
For most of its known history, the
Perkins Saint has been referred to as
Margaret, an identification summarily
dismissed by Zeri (1988) in favor of an
identification as Saint Cecilia. Both
saints are sometimes shown holding a
small cross and wearing a crown of
flowers, and the figure in this case bears
no other attributes that could aid in distinguishing between possible alterna-
tives. It should be noted that another
image of Saint Cecilia by Pietro Lorenzetti, among the three surviving panels
from the Crevole altarpiece of 1332,
bears no resemblance to the present
painting. [LBK-PP]

*Bibliography*: Zeri, 1988, pp. 50–53;
Volpe, 1989, pp. 56, 186–92 (with previous bibliography); Skaug, 1994, I, pp.
230–31, II, chart 7.6; Baetjer, 1995, p. 45.

## Master of the Perkins Saint Paul

Tuscan (Lucchese ?), third quarter
fourteenth century

**14**

*Saint Paul*
Tempera on panel, 57.4 × 32.8 cm
Assisi, Museo-Tesoro della Basilica
di San Francesco, Perkins Collection

The majestic figure of Saint Paul is clad in a pale rose-colored mantle lined with yellow. He holds the sword of his martyrdom in his right hand, and in his left a volume of his epistles bound in red leather. The painting has suffered losses both from flaking and abrasion, and its panel support is fragmentary, but more than enough survives to appreciate both its original shape and its imposing quality. Federico Zeri (1988, p. 70) suggested that the saint was originally portrayed full-length, but the raised beard of gesso along the edges of the gold ground seems to indicate instead that he was always shown half-length, framed on either side with a double order of columns the base of which rested on the present bottom edge of the panel, with small capitals about half-way up, at the level of the saint's elbows. This is an unusual framing solution which may ultimately aid in tracing the painting's still mysterious origins.

Three other fragmentary figures of saints identified by Zeri must have accompanied the Perkins Saint Paul as lateral panels of a polyptych. At the far left of the structure stood an unidentified Bishop Saint formerly in the Ireland-Smith collection, London (sold Sotheby's, London, February 7, 1972, lot 42), followed by the Perkins Saint Paul immediately to the left of the missing central panel, which presumably represented the Madonna and Child. To the right of the center panel and turned decisively towards it was a Saint Peter now in Wawel Castle, Cracow, flanked by a Saint James in the collection of Piero Corsini, New York. Zeri added to this group a fragmentary triangular panel representing Christ the Redeemer (Museo di Palazzo Venezia, Rome), which probably stood in a pinnacle surmounting the center panel. Flanking it, in pinnacles above the lateral panels, may have stood two panels showing the Virgin Annunciate and the Annunciatory Angel (present whereabouts unknown) also identified by Zeri, and Saints Bartholomew and John the Baptist in the Allen Memorial Art Museum (Oberlin College, Oberlin, Ohio), first published by Andrea De Marchi (1998a, pp. 405, 407).

The author of these remarkable panels, first called the "Master of the Perkins Saint Paul" by Richard Offner, has generally been thought to have been Sienese, but was sometimes said to have been a contemporary of Sassetta in the early fifteenth century (see Palumbo, 1973, p. 57). Federico Zeri (1987, pp. 20–23), however, proposed a date for them just before the middle of the fourteenth century, and correctly observed that while they are undoubtedly Tuscan, they cannot be associated with any artist from the principal centers of Siena, Florence, or Pisa. Not only is their figure style and palette singularly unusual, but the punch tools used to decorate their gold grounds reappear in none of those centers (see Skaug, 1994). Zeri suggested, as a tentative hypothesis, that the Master of the Perkins Saint Paul might have been Lucchese, not on the basis of convincing comparison to surviving Lucchese paintings so much as by eliminating other possibilities.

Zeri's proposal was accepted by Andrea De Marchi, who refined his observations and agreed with him in noting the influence of the young Antonio Veneziano on the Master's figure style, as well as its influence in turn on the earliest works of Angelo Puccinelli in Lucca. Assuming these stylistic parameters as a point of departure, a date for the Perkins Saint Paul and its companion panels around 1360–65 would seem reasonable. The earlier dating (ca. 1340) proposed by Zeri is precocious, placing the altarpiece too close in time to the examples by Bernardo Daddi on which it is distantly dependent. [LBK-PP]

*Bibliography*: Palumbo, 1973, p. 57; Zeri, 1987, pp. 20–23; Zeri, 1988, pp. 70–73; De Marchi, 1998a, p. 405.

## Master of the Perkins Saint Paul
Tuscan (Lucchese ?), third quarter
fourteenth century

**15**

*Madonna and Child Enthroned with*
*Saints Catherine of Alexandria and Paul*
Tempera on panel, 50.5 × 25.5 cm
Assisi, Museo-Tesoro della Basilica
di San Francesco, Perkins Collection

This beautiful and beautifully preserved panel—only the Virgin's mantle has suffered some flaking losses and the usual darkening of pigments—originally formed the left wing of a portable devotional diptych. Remnants of hinges are still visible on the right edge of its engaged frame, where it would have been joined to a panel of similar shape and size probably representing the Crucifixion, though no panel of that subject by this artist is known to survive. Saint Paul, standing before the Virgin's throne on the right, may be identified, as in the previous painting, by the sword of his martyrdom and the volume of epistles that he carries in his hands. Opposite him, Saint Catherine of Alexandria wears the crown and ermine-lined cloak of a princess, and is accompanied by the instrument of her attempted martyrdom, a large spiked wheel. The reverse of the panel, painted black, bears an as yet unidentified coat of arms: or, a bend gules, with two crows or ravens.
Mason Perkins, Richard Offner, Federico Zeri (1988, p. 74), and Andrea De Marchi (1998a) all recognized that the artist

of this panel was the Master of the Perkins Saint Paul, also responsible for the preceding entry in this catalogue. For Zeri, the softer modeling and delicate palette of this little panel suggested a date perhaps as much as twenty years later than the Saint Paul and therefore around 1360. Just as it may be necessary to date the Saint Paul later than Zeri supposed, however, so the date of this painting might safely be pushed back closer to or shortly after 1370. The elaborate Gothic design of the Virgin's throne, with its finely rendered crockets, spires, and finials and the elegant cosmatesque inlay on its back and on the risers of its seat and step, looks forward even as far as some of the designs of Lorenzo Monaco in the last decade of the fourteenth century, while the subtle rendering of light cast uniformly from the left and glancing off the forward projections of the throne is as sophisticated as in any painting of this scale from the trecento. Although the name, origin, and chronology of the Master of the Perkins Saint Paul remain a tantalizing mystery, there can be little doubt that the quality of his surviving paintings entitles him to consideration among the major artists of the mid-fourteenth century in Tuscany. [LBK-PP]

*Bibliography*: Zeri, 1987, p. 23; Zeri, 1988, p. 74; De Marchi, 1998a, p. 405.

## Lorenzo Monaco
Florentine, active ca. 1387–1423/24

**16**

*Madonna of Humility*
Tempera on panel, 84 × 58.7 cm
Assisi, Museo-Tesoro della Basilica
di San Francesco,
Perkins Collection

Perhaps the most beautiful and best preserved painting in the Perkins bequest to the Sacro Convento, Lorenzo Monaco's *Madonna of Humility* presents a number of problems of dating and interpretation. Nearly every scholar to have considered the painting has recognized in it the hand of the great Camaldolese master of the International Gothic style, although Sirén (1905) and Van Marle (1927) believed it to be at best a product of his workshop while Giglioli (1906) inexplicably attributed it to Cennino Cennini. More recently, Marvin Eisenberg (1989, pp. 176–77) discussed it in the context of a group of paintings that at the time he believed not to be by Lorenzo Monaco but subsequently acknowledged as probably the artist's earliest works. The simplest but most eloquent case for attributing the panel directly to Lorenzo Monaco was put by Federico Zeri (1988, p. 30): "Lo stile di questo splendido dipinto (eseguito per committenti privati) è quello di Lorenzo Monaco… Lo stato, eccezionalmente felice, del dipinto, consente di rilevarne l'assai alta qualita, che esclude l'intervento della bottega alludendo alla totale autografia." For Zeri, the Perkins *Madonna of Humility* was to be dated to the first years of the fifteenth century, close to the great altarpiece of 1404 in Empoli or the nearly contemporary Madonna and Child in the Pinacoteca Nazionale at Bologna. Kanter (1994b, pp. 303–4) reiterated Zeri's appreciation of the painting's quality but associated it instead (as had Eisenberg) with works of the preceding decade, dating it around 1395.

The difficulty of assessing Lorenzo Monaco's work prior to the 1404 Empoli altarpiece is largely due to confusion surrounding his career as a manuscript illuminator. Three of the great choirbooks he illuminated for Santa Maria degli Angeli are dated to the 1390s by colophons (referring to completion of the scribe's work on the text), but seem in fact to have been painted only in the following decade (see Kanter, 1994b, pp. 229–48). Traditional assumptions that the illuminations in these books are the artist's earliest certain works have rendered an accurate appreciation of his panel paintings from this period all but impossible. Two other illuminated choirbooks by Lorenzo Monaco do reflect his style in the last decade of the fourteenth century— Cod. 13 from the Biblioteca Laurenziana, Florence (ca. 1392), and Cod. C 71 in the Museo Nazionale del Bargello, Florence (1396)—and these in turn permit a considerable number of panel paintings to be comfortably situated in the same period of time. Among these, the Perkins *Madonna of Humility* is most closely related to the surviving fragments of an altarpiece from the Carmine in Florence, first reconstructed by Federico Zeri (1964–65); a Madonna Enthroned with Six Saints in the Museo Horne, Florence (Eisenberg, 1989, fig. 224); a Madonna in Glory with Saints Peter and Paul in the Walters Art Gallery, Baltimore (Zeri, 1976, pp. 25–26, pl. 12); and a recently discovered Madonna and Child in the conservatorio di Santa Marta at Montopoli (De Marchi, 1998a, p. 408, fig. 223), all probably to be dated to the last half of the decade.

Lorenzo Monaco experimented with numerous compositional variations on the theme of the Madonna and Child throughout his career, often combining characteristics from different conventional types to produce novel images which he would then repeat with subtle alterations in more than one version. The theme of the Madonna of Humility is one with which he took particular liberties. In those centers where the subject was most popular, Siena and Northern Italy, the Madonna was usually shown seated on the ground in a garden or flowering meadow, with the Christ Child lying across her lap or suckling at her breast. In late-trecento Florence, the Virgin was commonly shown in glory seated on a floating bank of cloud rather than in humility seated on the ground, yet always in the same posture with one knee drawn up and the other leg folded beneath her. The Christ Child too was more often shown alert and in a gesture of benediction than asleep or suckling. Lorenzo Monaco first attempted this class of image in a devotional triptych of ca. 1392–93 in the Pinacoteca Nazionale, Siena. For the Perkins panel, he borrowed the Virgin's posture and the Child's attitude from the Siena painting, combined with a cushion and dais borrowed from images such as the Madonna and Child Enthroned in the Fitzwilliam Museum (in this case suppressing the throne but retaining the adoring angels at the sides) to create a new type of image. Within a very few years, by the turn of the century, he had arrived at a further refinement, eliminating all references to thrones or other architectural embellishment and to servitor angels in acts of reverence or adoration, in a *Madonna of Humility* now in a private collection (see Kanter, 1994b, p. 304, fig. 119) in which the Virgin is seated on a cushion directly on a marble pavement. This is the solution he adopted, with only minor variations and sometimes reinstating the angels, for nearly all the numerous examples of the subject he produced over the next quarter century. The Perkins *Madonna of Humility* remained a unique image, at once a moving expression of religious sentiment and a testament to a restless and highly inventive artistic imagination. [LBK-PP]

*Bibliography*: Sirén , 1905, pp. 165–66; Giglioli, 1906, p. 74; Van Marle, 1927, p. 127 n. 1; Zeri, 1988, pp. 30–31; Eisenberg, 1989, pp. 176–77, 185, 194 (with previous bibliography); Kanter, 1994b, pp. 303–4; Skaug, 1994, I, p. 284, II, no. 8.13.

# Gherardo Starnina

Florentine, documented 1387–1409,
died before 1413

**17**

*Saint Lawrence*
Tempera on panel, 59.6 × 33 cm
Assisi, Museo-Tesoro della Basilica
di San Francesco, Perkins Collection

Saint Lawrence is dressed in the vestments of a deacon and holds in his right hand the iron grill on which he was martyred by the emperor Valerian. In his left hand he holds a plate of coins, symbolizing the treasures of the church entrusted to him by Pope Sixtus II before his own execution, which Lawrence then distributed to the poor. When Valerian demanded that Lawrence surrender to him the treasure, Lawrence brought the poor before the Emperor and proclaimed "these are the treasures of the Church."

The pavement of painted tiles receding to the left on which Saint Lawrence stands permits the identification of three other saints who once stood alongside him in the lateral panels of a single altarpiece. Two of these, Saints Vincent of Saragossa and Stephen now in the Museum of Fine Arts, Boston (Kanter, 1994a, pp. 130–36), originally occupied the left side of the altarpiece. The tiles beneath their feet are identical to those in the Perkins Saint Lawrence except that they recede in the opposite direction. A Saint Anthony Abbott last recorded in 1976 on the Florentine art market (Sricchia Santoro, 1976, fig. 31) continues the pattern of the floor in the Saint Lawrence and must have stood alongside it on the right side of the altarpiece. Two further panels representing Saint John the Baptist and a Bishop Saint associated with these by Syre (1979), Zeri (1988), and Fattorini (1997) come instead from a different altarpiece, as is indicated by the earlier style of the figures, the different viewing angle of their pavements, and the fact that these pavements contain five tiles receding in depth rather than four.

It has been shown (Kanter, 1994a) that two further panels in Boston, representing the prophets Isaiah and Jeremiah each seated between a pair of angels in adoration, once stood above the four lateral saints as spandrels, separating them from another tier of panels at the top of the altarpiece. The unusual construction of these spandrels and the existence of a related panel in the Museo di Palazzo Venezia, representing the prophet Hosea, led to the suggestion that the center panel of this altarpiece may have have been a painting of the Coronation of the Virgin in the Galleria Nazionale, Parma. It now appears that the Hosea is too large to have been accommodated above the Parma Coronation, so the latter can have been the center of this altarpiece only if the Palazzo Venezia Hosea comes from a different structure, which is possible but not demonstrable. It has more recently been proposed that the Parma Coronation may either have been the central pinnacle of the great *Death and Assumption of the Virgin* altarpiece by Gherardo Starnina from Lucca (Fattorini, 1997) or an independent processional standard (De Marchi, 1998b; Filieri, 1998). For the present, there is insufficient evidence to resolve the argument, but new discoveries about the provenance of the Parma Coronation imply that if it could be shown to have been part of the same altarpiece as the Boston and Perkins Saints, they would all have been painted for a church in or near Lucca.

Whatever the complete reconstruction of the altarpiece from which it came, there is general agreement that the Perkins Saint Lawrence must have been painted by Starnina after that artist's return to Florence from Spain, where he had been working for several years, around 1404 (Syre's contention that the Perkins panel is an early work painted in the 1380s cannot be seriously maintained). The lyrical gothic style that Starnina brought back with him from Valencia had a decisive influence on his Tuscan contemporaries, notably on Lorenzo Monaco and on a painter of a slightly younger generation, Giovanni dal Ponte. The coincidence of their works appearing alongside Lorenzo Ghiberti's own experiments with this international, courtly taste created a powerful and attractive alternative to the more conservative trends among Florentine artists, as exemplified by the studios of Niccolò di Pietro Gerini, Bicci di Lorenzo, Mariotto di Nardo, or Lorenzo di Niccolò. The immense popularity of Starnina's style outlived his death around 1413. It was only seriously challenged by the advent of Masaccio and the maturing of Fra Angelico in the late 1420s. [LBK-PP]

*Bibliography*: Syre, 1979, pp. 121–24; Zeri, 1988, pp. 32–35 (with previous bibliography); Kanter, 1994a, pp. 132–36; Fattorini, 1997, p. 60.

# Lorenzo di Niccolò
Florentine,
active between 1391 and 1412

**18**

*Saint Nicholas of Bari and Saint John Gualbert*
Tempera on panel, 153 × 82 cm,
overall; 118 × 76 cm, painted surface
Assisi, Museo-Tesoro della Basilica
di San Francesco, Perkins Collection

Framed by an elegant piece of Gothic architecture, this picture represents Saint Nicholas of Bari, dressed in bishop's robes with his miter and cross, and Saint John Gualbert, founder of a Benedictine order at the abbey of Vallombrosa in Tuscany. Both figures are standing. Saint John Gualbert is wearing the habit of a Benedictine monk: he holds a book in his right hand and a cross in his left. Three golden balls are tucked into the fold of Saint Nicholas's robe, in reference to the miracle in which he provided the dowry for three impoverished young women. In the upper part, the bust of a praying angel is set in a tondo.

As Federico Zeri has rightly pointed out (1988, pp. 24–25), the picture must have been the left-hand panel of a triptych. The right-hand panel would have depicted two more saints, while a representation of the Virgin and the Child was certainly placed in the middle. As the other elements of the altarpiece have not been found, however, this has to remain in the realm of hypothesis.

The picture is in a good state of preservation with the exception of the gold ground, part of which has been lost. Perkins assigned it to Lorenzo di Niccolò and argued that the work dates from the first decade of the fifteenth century. This attribution to the Florentine painter has been unanimously accepted by the critics (Van Marle, 1923, p. 643; Berenson, 1963, p. 121; Zeri, 1988, pp. 24–25).

Lorenzo di Niccolò—documented in Florence from 1391 to 1412 and erroneously considered the son of Niccolò di Pietro Gerini, with whom he painted numerous pictures before coming under the influence of Spinello Aretino—was one of the most interesting exponents of the late Gothic manner in Florence, of which this picture is a completely typical example.

The work was stolen along with several other pictures from Perkins's villa during the Second World War. Found in Vienna by Roberto Siviero in 1948, it was restored to its rightful owner. [GM]

*Bibliography*: Van Marle 1923, pp. 632–46; Berenson, 1963; Zeri, 1988.

## Bicci di Lorenzo
Florence, 1373–1452

**19**

*The Virgin and Child with Saint John
the Baptist and Saint John the Evangelist*
Tempera on panel, 45 × 32 cm
Assisi, Museo-Tesoro della Basilica
di San Francesco, Perkins Collection

The attribution of this panel to Bicci di
Lorenzo in Perkins's handwritten catalogue (now in the archives of the general curia of the Friars Minor Conventual
in Rome), has been accepted by Federico Zeri (1988, pp. 40–41) who assigned
the work to the mature period of Bicci's
career (1420–1430).

The panel represents the Virgin, probably seated and supporting the Child
with her left hand. He is sitting upright
on her left leg. Mary's left hand looks as
if it should be holding a flower—invisi-
ble or perhaps effaced—while the lower
part of the Child's naked body is covered with a piece of precious gold cloth.
At the sides and on a smaller scale, we
see the upright figures of Saint John the
Baptist, pointing at the Savior, and Saint
John the Evangelist, holding a book in
which he is writing. The four figures
have gilded haloes with inscriptions. On
the Virgin's nimbus we can read "AVE
MARIA GRAT.(IA)," i.e. the first words that
the angel addressed to Mary. The haloes
of the two saints bear the same inscription, "SCS IHOVANE." There are no letters
on the Child's aureole, just ornamental
motifs. The work has been damaged,
and this is most apparent in the lower
part of the representation of the saints,
where clumsy retouches and areas
where the paint has lifted off are visible.
The gold of the ground, on the other
hand, is relatively well-preserved. In the
eighteenth century the painting was
given a glass case, probably to protect it
when it was displayed in a shrine or
shown to the faithful.

Bicci di Lorenzo, the son of Lorenzo di
Bicci, took over his father's workshop in
the early years of the fifteenth century.
His first known work is dated 1414.
[GM]

*Bibliography*: Petrucci 1987, p. 58; Zeri
1988.

## Tommaso di Cristofano Fini, called Masolino da Panicale

Panicale in Valdelsa 1383–
Florence 1440

**20**

*Madonna and Child*
Tempera on panel, 66 × 42 cm
Assisi, Museo-Tesoro della Basilica
di San Francesco, Perkins Collection

The attribution of the work to Masolino by Perkins was later accepted by Federico Zeri (1988, pp. 88–89), in spite of some doubts. The painting displays the characteristics of elegance and delicacy typical of the Tuscan artist, whose principal works can be seen in the Florentine church of Santa Maria del Carmine (Brancacci Chapel), in the Roman church of San Clemente, and at Castiglione Olona.

The picture represents the Virgin standing and holding the naked and blessing Child in her arms. While the Child's gaze is directed toward the observer, the Virgin's is turned slightly to the right. In addition, unlike the Child, the Virgin has no halo, which may have blended in with the gilded background of the picture or disappeared over the course of the many changes made to the work. The retouches and restorations have considerably altered the original organization of the painting, in which, according to Zeri, the image of the Virgin must have been painted at least three-quarters or even full length.

The picture has undergone many alterations, both to the support as well as to the upper part. It was probably rectangular at the beginning and may have formed the central part of a polyptych. In addition to the patches of wear, the gold of the ground has lifted off and been scratched away in places. [GM]

*Bibliography*: Zeri 1988, pp. 88–89.

# Fra Angelico
Florentine, ca. 1400–1455

**21**

*Saint Anthony of Padua*
Tempera on panel, 12.5 × 9.5 cm
Assisi, Museo-Tesoro della Basilica
di San Francesco, Perkins Collection

The identity of this saint, wearing a Franciscan habit and carrying a red book and a cross, has been controversial. The name of Saint Antoninus inscribed across the background of the panel must be a slightly later addition to the painting, since Antoninus, who was Bishop of Florence and in any event a Dominican not a Franciscan, died only in 1459, four years after Angelico's death, and was canonized in 1522. Carl Strehlke (1994, p. 341) preferred to consider the inscription original and identified the figure as Anthony of Padua. This identification had earlier been rejected by Zeri (1988, p. 87), since Saint Anthony is almost invariably shown beardless, and although he frequently carries a book he is almost never portrayed carrying a cross. Zeri suggested instead that the saint may be Francis himself, presuming that when the inscription was added changing his identity to Antoninus (probably in the later fifteenth century), traces of the stigmata on his hands and sides would have been painted out without, however, troubling to change the color of his habit. This explanation is less plausible than that the figure is an unusual representation of Saint Anthony of Padua (who is portrayed bearded and holding a book and a cross in the Franciscan Tree tapestry included in this exhibition), since no evidence of careful or deliberate damage from the cancellation of stigmata is apparent on the panel.

It is clear that the Perkins Saint is a fragment, but the exact nature of the structure of which it formed part is not obvious. Probably it was part of the frame of a larger painting. Several frame fragments by Fra Angelico survive, most of them showing full-length standing saints cut from the buttressing pilasters of large altarpieces. Four of these, now in the Musée Condé, Chantilly, and the Fondation Rau, Marseilles, were re-

moved from the frame of Angelico's triptych of the Madonna and Child with Saints painted in the early 1420s for the high altar of San Domenico, Fiesole, a painting that was completely rebuilt and partly repainted by Lorenzo di Credi in 1501 and finally dismantled after 1792. Two small tondi with saints now in the Metropolitan Museum of Art, New York, and the National Gallery, London, both with a putative provenance from San Domenico, Fiesole, are sometimes thought to have come from this altarpiece as well. Alternatively, they may be identified with two small panels inventoried in the sacristy at San Domenico in 1769 (see Strehlke, 1994, pp. 340–41), and therefore have come from a different altarpiece or tabernacle frame in that church. Strehlke has pointed out a number of similarities between the London and New York roundels and the Perkins Saint, especially in the decorative treatment of their gilt surrounds and the presence of inscriptions across their backgrounds, suggesting that they may have originated from the same complex. The fact that the Perkins Saint was renamed Antoninus may indeed imply that he was originally to be found in a Dominican establishment, possibly in the environs of Florence, making Strehlke's theory highly plausible.

The Perkins Saint is painted on a slightly smaller scale than the New York and London roundels: presumably it would have stood in a narrow, vertical framing element whereas the two roundels may have filled the more ample space of spandrels. Also, it is painted with a darker, more nearly monochrome palette, and is less well preserved than the two larger panels. Comparisons between them, therefore, cannot be conclusive, but it is necessary to agree with Strehlke that all three panels appear to be later than the high altarpiece from San Domenico, which is still deeply imbued with impressions of the International Gothic style of Lorenzo Monaco and Angelico's youthful colleague, the illuminator Battista di Biagio Sanguigni. The sophisticated modelling in light and

shadow and the convincing rendering of bone structure and drapery volumes in these panels instead betray the influence of Masaccio's completed labors in the Brancacci Chapel, and resemble in style the greatest masterpiece of Angelico's early career, the *Coronation of the Virgin* altarpiece from San Domenico, Fiesole, now in the Louvre. Whether these fragments might once have formed part of the frame of the *Coronation of the Virgin* or simply have been painted as part of another, more modest commission of approximately the same date, ca. 1429, is impossible to know for certain. [LBK-PP]

*Bibliography*: Boskovits, 1976, p. 36; Zeri, 1988, p. 87; Strehlke, 1994, p. 341; Spike, 1996, p. 193, no. 2.

S̄ ANT                                                  ŌINVS

## Benozzo Gozzoli (?)
Florentine, 1420/22–1497

**22**

*The Holy Face*
Ink and tempera on parchment
mounted on panel, 39.5 × 28.5 cm
Assisi, Museo-Tesoro della Basilica
di San Francesco

This image of the head of Christ, crowned with thorns and bleeding from His wounds, is presented with an uncompromising directness and immediacy. The Savior is shown full-face and situated so close to the picture plane that His halo is cropped by the frame at the sides of the panel. His brow is creased in pain and His eyes are suffused with blood. The drama of this powerful image of suffering is softened only slightly by the decorative treatment along the borders of the gilt halo or the elegantly scripted lettering both in the nimbus and at the throat of Christ's tunic. These inscriptions read: IHESUS CRIXTUS REX [IUDEO]RUM (Jesus Christ King of the Jews, the title of mockery nailed to the top of the Cross at the Crucifixion); and REX REGHUM ET DOMIN[US DOMINATIUM] (King of Kings and Lord of Lords, from 1 Timothy 6:15).

The Assisi *Holy Face*, which is first recorded in an inventory of relics in the sacristy of the Lower Church of San Francesco in June 1600, has long been recognized as a near replica of a similar image in the Museo Civico Giovanni Fattori at Livorno. The paintings share every aspect of their iconography, including the inscriptions and the peculiar cropping of the haloes, and it can only be assumed either that one deliberately reproduces the other or that both reproduce a common, much-venerated prototype that no longer survives. The existence of a third related image, in the Pinacoteca Nazionale at Perugia, introducing slight variations in such details as the inscriptions, suggests that all three probably copy a lost prototype and perhaps not through direct contact by the respective artists so much as through workshop drawings.

The Livorno *Holy Face* was first recognized by Roberto Longhi (1928) as the work of no less an artist than Fra Angelico, and though this attribution has received less attention than it deserves, the painting has recently come to be admired as a singular example of his late style (De Marchi, 1990, pp. 104–7; Boskovits, 1994, pp. 386–87 n. 25; Spike, 1996, p. 237, no. 83). It is very likely that it was painted shortly after the Frate's return to Florence from Rome in 1450, and it may therefore reproduce an icon he might have encountered during his sojourn there (the painting was donated by a devout parishoner to the church of Santa Maria del Soccorso in Livorno only in 1837, its earlier provenance is unknown). The Assisi *Holy Face* appears to be Florentine as well, despite attempts to assign it to the Umbrian masters Benedetto Bonfigli (Zocca, 1936) and Bartolomeo Caporali (Farnetani, 1978). Pietro Scarpellini (1980) catalogued it as "Umbrian (?)," but noted that an attentive examination left even its Umbrian origin in doubt. Mario Salmi (1921) first suggested that it might be a replica by Benozzo Gozzoli of his master's (i.e. Fra Angelico) original at Livorno, an opinion repeated by Van Marle (1929) and more recently accepted and supported by Padoa Rizzo (1992), Acidini Luchinat (1994), and Cole Ahl (1996).

If by no means certain, it is indeed possible that the Assisi *Holy Face* was drawn by Benozzo Gozzoli, but not likely as early as Anna Padoa Rizzo and Diane Cole Ahl propose, the early 1450s. This date was in part suggested because it represents the period in which Gozzoli was active close to Assisi, at Montefalco, but it does not take into account the possibly later date of Angelico's supposed model nor does it fit satisfactorily within the internal development of Gozzoli's style. There is no reason why so small and portable a devotional object such as this need have been painted in the immediate vicinity of Assisi (it could easily have been presented to the Basilica as a gift from a pilgrim), although Boskovits (1994) suggested that both it and Angelico's original may have been painted there or in nearby Perugia. If the Assisi *Holy Face* is by Benozzo

Gozzoli, it could most comfortably be dated, on the internal evidence of style only, to the early or middle 1460s, between the frescoes in the Palazzo Medici (1459–60) and those in San Gimignano (1464–65) and Certaldo (1467), rather than to any earlier moment.

A Florentine origin for the Assisi *Holy Face* may also be indicated on iconographic grounds. The specific source informing the imagery of the painting has been identified as the mystic *Revelations* of Saint Bridget of Sweden (ca. 1304–1373), including the prominence accorded the crown of thorns, which Saint Bridget described as reaching down to the center of Christ's forehead, and as causing blood to flow in such profusion that it filled His eyes and ears. Saint Bridget's *Revelations* became an influential source for painters throughout Italy but especially in Florence, where the first, and principal, house of the Bridgettine order, known as the Order of the Holy Savior, was founded at Santa Maria del Paradiso in the Pian di Ripoli in 1391. The *Revelations* may also have inspired Saint Antoninus, archbishop of Florence, in one of the passages in his *Opera a ben vivere* (part III, chap. xi, p. 149, cited in Boskovits, 1994, p. 386) that bears directly on an image such as the Assisi *Holy Face*: "…cogli occhi della mente, più che con quelli del corpo, considerate la faccia sua. Prima, alla corona delle spine, fittegliele in testa, insino al celabro; poi gli occhi, pieni di lacrime e di sangue; la bocca, piena di fiele e di bava e di sangue; la barba, similmente piena di bava e di sangue e di fiele, essendo tutta sputacchiata e spelazzata; poi la faccia, tutta oscurata, e sputacchiata, e livida per le percosse delle gotate a della canna, e tutta sanguinosa."

Devotional images of the Redeemer conflating the traditional types of the Salvator Mundi (Christ triumphant and blessing) with the Man of Sorrows (Christ suffering), resembling the Assisi and Livorno paintings in a number of essential details, proliferated in Florence in the last quarter of the fifteenth century, as examples by Botticelli (Bergamo,

Detroit, Cambridge), Cosimo Roselli (Città di Castello), Jacopo del Sellaio, and others may testify. Many of these were painted in relatively ephemeral media, such as tempera on linen, suggesting that they are the surviving members of a once much larger class of object. The Assisi *Holy Face* is itself painted on parchment mounted on panel, a practice also familiar in Siena from devotional images of Saint Bernardino painted to satisfy the enormous demand created by the rapid dissemination of his cult (see examples in the Museum of Fine Arts, Boston, and the Robert Lehman Collection, Metropolitan Museum of Art, New York). It is possible that Fra Angelico's and Benozzo Gozzoli's paintings are two of the earliest images of this class in Florence, perhaps more faithful to their original prototype but responding to the same spiritual demands among devout Florentine patrons. [LBK-PP]

*Bibliography*: Salmi, 1921, p. 170; Van Marle, 1929, p. 143; Zocca, 1936, p. 166; Farnetani, 1978, p. 8; Scarpellini, 1980, pp. 55–56; Padoa Rizzo, 1992, p. 41; Acidini Luchinat, 1994, p. 15; Cole Ahl, 1996, p. 207, cat. 1 (with previous bibliography).

## Stefano di Giovanni, called il Sassetta
Sienese, 1395–1450

**23**

*Saint Christopher*
Tempera on panel, 72.5 × 23.5 cm
Assisi, Museo-Tesoro della Basilica
di San Francesco, Perkins Collection

Saint Christopher ferrying the Christ Child across a river on his shoulder is an image frequently encountered in Italian painting of the Renaissance. As the patron saint of travellers, invoked for protection against illness or sudden death, he is often portrayed on the wings of portable triptychs for private devotion or near entrances of churches and public buildings. In Siena, he figures prominently in a fresco decorating the antechapel of the Palazzo Pubblico, painted by Taddeo di Bartolo in 1408, as a replacement for an earlier image of the saint on the same site (Solberg, 1991, II, pp. 950–60). Many of these representations, especially in Sienese painting, closely follow a single compositional formula, suggesting that they may derive from a famous but now lost example probably of the early fourteenth century. Saint Christopher is shown striding along a river bed, with fishes and eels swimming about his ankles. He is dressed regally—in the case of Sassetta's painting he wears an ermine-lined cloak with jewelled clasps at the throat and shoulder—with the skirt of his tunic tucked above his knees into his belt. He leans heavily on a staff with one hand and looks up over his opposite shoulder at the Christ Child on his back. In the Perkins panel, the Child wears garments of silver, now largely corroded to black and red bolus preparation, and holds a globe symbolizing the weight of the world in His right hand. Saint Christopher's staff is topped with palm fronds, largely worn away where they overlap the gold ground, symbolizing his pending martyrdom.

The Perkins Saint Christopher was first recognized by Federico Zeri (1963) as a fragment of Sassetta's most complex and influential altarpiece, painted for the high altar of San Francesco in Borgo San Sepolcro between 1439 and 1444. The back side, facing the monk's choir, of this large double-sided structure celebrated the life and miracles of Saint Francis, with eight scenes from his legend (now in the National Gallery, London, and the Musée Condé, Chantilly) flanking a large image of Francis in Glory adoring the virtues of Chastity, Poverty, and Obedience and trampling the vices of vanity, pride, and avarice (Villa I Tatti, Florence). The predella recounted four episodes (three of which are now in the Musée du Louvre, Paris, and the Berlin Museums) from the legend of the Beato Ranieri, a much-venerated Franciscan friar entombed beneath the high altar block itself. The front face of the altarpiece featured a monumental image of the Madonna and Child enthroned with a choir of angels (Musée du Louvre, Paris) flanked by full-length images of Saints John the Baptist, John the Evangelist, Anthony of Padua, and the Beato Ranieri (Musée du Louvre, Paris, and Villa I Tatti, Florence), with a predella showing scenes from the Passion (Detroit Institute of Arts).

Smaller panels showing the Crucifixion (Cleveland Museum of Art), the Annunciation (Robert Lehman Collection, The Metropolitan Museum of Art, New York) and numerous figures of saints filled the pinnacles and pilasters of this altarpiece. Among these, the Perkins Saint Christopher is known to have stood at the bottom of the buttressing pilaster at the right-hand side of the front of the altarpiece. Directly above it stood a Saint Stephen in the Pushkin Museum, Moscow. The same positions on the left-hand pilaster were occupied by (at the top) a Saint Lawrence also in the Pushkin Museum and (at the bottom, opposite the Perkins Saint Christopher) a Saint Michael the Archangel (lost; see Banker, 1991, and Gordon, 1993, for a complete reconstruction of the altarpiece based on a document detailing Sassetta's iconographic program). Only two other panels, out of sixty in total originally painted, are known to survive today—a Saint Matthew in the Cini Collection, Venice, and a Saint Augustine in a private collection, New York—making the survival of a panel such as the Perkins Saint Christopher all the more precious and fortunate.

Sassetta is commonly, and correctly, regarded as the founder of the Sienese Renaissance school of painting, the first great artist in that culturally rich but rigorously conservative center to grapple with many of the same problems of narrative and representation being explored in Florence by such painters as Masaccio, Fra Angelico, Fra Filippo Lippi, and Domenico Veneziano. In some instances he is credited with anticipating the discoveries of his Florentine counterparts, especially in the techniques of rendering natural phenomena, but Sassetta never lost the sense of whimsy and decoration that distinguish the paintings of his more eccentric or even reactionary Sienese contemporaries such as Giovanni di Paolo or Sano di Pietro. The tension between these two strains in his art grew more pronounced towards the end of his career and is nowhere more visible than in the panels of the Borgo San Sepolcro altarpiece, his late masterpiece and one of the greatest paintings produced anywhere in Italy in the fifth decade of the fifteenth century. [LBK-PP]

*Bibliography*: Zeri, 1963, pp. 38, 41, 44 n. 17 (reprinted in Zeri, 1992a, p. 50); Zeri, 1988, pp. 102–5 (with previous bibliography); Christiansen, 1988, p. 84; Banker, 1991, pp. 32–33 n. 58.

# Giovanni di Paolo
Sienese, 1399–1482

**24**

*Saint James*
Tempera on panel, 15.2 × 11.5 cm
Assisi, Museo-Tesoro della Basilica
di San Francesco, Perkins Collection

In keeping with the pioneering tastes of Mason Perkins and of his numerous American clients in the early part of the twentieth century, the Perkins donation to the Sacro Convento di San Francesco is rich in paintings from the Sienese school. Many of these are small, delicate examples of the work of the greatest masters, not the least of which is this beautiful, almost miniaturist image of Saint James by that most eccentric of all fifteenth-century painters, Giovanni di Paolo.

Saint James is here shown half-length, facing three-quarters to the right, wearing a red tunic and brown cloak and holding a pilgrim's staff in his left hand. Along with his brother, John the Evangelist, James the Greater was one of Christ's earliest disciples. Following an eighth-century Spanish legend, Saint James was thought to have preached the gospel in Spain, where his remains were supposedly brought to rest following his martyrdom in Jerusalem. By the eleventh century the site of his putative burial, Campostela, had become one of the principal pilgrimage centers in Europe, with the result that the figure of the saint became associated with pilgrims and his image invoked as protection for travelers in general.

The Perkins panel has been trimmed slightly at the sides and more dramatically at the top and bottom. Originally the saint was portrayed full-length, probably standing on a tiled or faux-marble pavement, while the fragmentary arcs of punch tooling visible at the top corners of the panel once continued upward to complete an ogival or trilobe arch above his halo. This arch was surrounded by a raised border of *pastiglia* decoration, which was in turn surmounted by a smaller, triangular painting of the Archangel Gabriel, today preserved in the Musée du Petit Palais at Avignon. The association of these two

fragments was first noted by Federico Zeri (cited in Laclotte and Mognetti, 1976), who further identified a companion panel to the Perkins Saint James representing Saint Christopher, formerly in a private collection in Paris. On the analogy of the Perkins and Avignon panels, the Saint Christopher would also have been surmounted by a triangular gable, in this case representing the Virgin Annunciate, though if this fragment survives it has not yet been identified. Both completed panels originally functioned as wings of a portable triptych, a form of devotional painting exceedingly popular throughout Tuscany but especially in Siena in the trecento and early quattrocento. The central panel of this triptych, probably representing the Madonna and Child or the Crucifixion, has not yet been identified. An approximate idea of the appearance of the complete work may be gleaned from a beautifully preserved example by Giovanni di Paolo, probably from the early-1430s, now in the Los Angeles County Museum of Art (Dabell, 1996, pp. 111–17), or from a later triptych in the Pinacoteca Nazionale, Siena (Torriti, 1990, p. 226 n. 178).

An inordinate number of portable triptychs from Siena contained an image of Saint Christopher on one wing. In the last third of the trecento, these were usually paired with an image of Saint Anthony Abbott, presumably because both saints were commonly invoked for protection against disease. Anthony Abbott was known as the healer of men and animals and was the patron of an order of hospitalers, while an inscription beneath the image of Saint Christopher on a fourteenth-century Florentine triptych in the Walters Art Gallery, Baltimore (Zeri, 1976, p. 16), where he is not coincidentally paired with an image of Saint Anthony Abbott, reads: XPOFORI SANCTI SPETIEM QUICUMQUE TUETUR ILLO NAMQUE DIE NULLO LANGUORE TENETUR [Whoever contemplates the image of Saint Christopher will not be taken by any illness during that same day]. Christopher was also invoked for protection against sudden death and

was known as the patron saint of travellers. It is in this guise that his association with the Perkins Saint James, patron of pilgrims, is particularly appropriate on the wings of a small devotional tabernacle intended to be folded closed for portability.

All scholars who have discussed the Perkins Saint James have recognized it as an early work by Giovanni di Paolo, whose exceptionally long and prolific career is still subject to heated debates over matters of dating and attribution. Laclotte considered it and its companion fragments in Avignon and Paris to be contemporary to a remarkable group of narrative panels in Siena and Otterlo generally thought to have formed the predella to the Fondi altarpiece of 1436. A comparison to these panels is in fact meaningful, but dating them to the mid-1430s on the basis of a presumptive association with the Fondi altarpiece is incorrect. Zeri more accurately observed "non è da escludere una data verso il 1430, o anche qualche anno prima." In fact, the most telling similarities of the Saint James to other panels by Giovanni di Paolo are all with the surviving fragments of the Pecci altarpiece of 1426, now dispersed to Castelnuovo Berardenga, Baltimore, and Berlin. The Pecci altarpiece was Giovanni di Paolo's first major public commission in Siena, followed within a year by another major altarpiece for the Branchini family (Norton Simon Collection, Pasadena). The Perkins Saint James, or more appropriately the triptych of which it formed part, together with such works on a similar scale as a Madonna and Child and a Saint Michael in the Pinacoteca Vaticana, represents the class of domestic painting which secured the young artist's reputation at that time.
[LBK-PP]

*Bibliography*: Laclotte and Mognetti, 1976, no. 88; Laclotte, 1983, p. 320; Zeri, 1988, pp. 106–7 (with previous bibliography); Moench-Scherer, 1992, p. 58.

115

## Sano di Pietro
Sienese, 1406–1481

**25**

*Saint Bernardino in Glory*
Tempera on panel, 42 × 27.5 cm
Assisi, Museo-Tesoro della Basilica
di San Francesco, Perkins Collection

Fra Bernardino degli Albizzeschi (1380–1444) was the most dynamic and influential preacher in the cause of the reform movement of the Franciscan Observance in the early-fifteenth century. His charismatic personality and spirited message of a return to the principles and ideals of moral purity embodied by Saint Francis generated an enormous and devoted following throughout central Italy, but nowhere more than in his native Siena. Crowds thronged the churches and piazze to hear his public sermons on subjects touching all aspects of the everyday lives of his listeners. Miracles were attributed to him even before his death in 1444, and the cause of his canonization, vigorously espoused by the Sienese, was accomplished by Nicholas V in 1450.

Within months of Bernardino's death, official images of him were commissioned from important artists to promote his cult. Most of these follow the portrait painted by Pietro di Giovanni d'Ambrogio, dated 1444, in the Church of the Osservanza at Siena, which established not only the characteristic sallow, sunken-cheeked features of the saint but also the iconographic prototype showing him holding an open book and the sunburst monogram of the Holy Name of Christ. Bernardino's devotion to the Holy Name was legendary, and virtually all images of him include the monogram as his distinguishing attribute, either as a luminous apparition held before him in one hand or engraved in gold on a tablet held up for the veneration of the populace, as in a panel by Sassetta or his workshop in the Pinacoteca Nazionale, Siena (n. 205, misattributed to Vecchietta). Other variations show him treading on three bishop's mitres, symbolizing bishoprics he refused during his ministry, or floating above a terrestrial globe supported by angels.

No artist is more inextricably associated with the cult of Saint Bernardino than Sano di Pietro. Sano, a conservative and immensely prolific artist who, with Giovanni di Paolo, all but monopolized the market for altarpieces and small devotional panels in Siena in the middle decades of the fifteenth century, became the unofficial chronicler of Bernardino's life and miracles, and the principal supplier of the nearly insatiable public demand for commemorative images both before and after his canonization. Pavone and Pacelli (1981) list some twenty surviving independent images of Saint Bernardino by Sano di Pietro, and three times that number of altarpieces or Madonna and Child panels that include him as an attendant figure. The earliest of these was painted in 1445 or 1446 for the Compagnia della Vergine beneath the hospital of Santa Maria della Scala in Siena, and is now preserved in the Chapterhouse of the Cathedral there (Mallory and Freuler, 1991; Christiansen, 1991; Freuler, 1994). It includes an unusual detail—two angels bearing the saint aloft on a cloth of honor—that is also found in the Perkins Saint Bernardino and in only three other known images: another small panel by Sano sold at Sotheby's in Florence, April 4, 1986; a panel by Priamo della Quercia dated 1450 (Pinacoteca Civica, Volterra); and a panel by Giovanni di Pietro in the Fioratti collection, New York (Strehlke, 1988, pp. 268–69). Elsewhere when portraying Bernardino in Glory, Sano shows the two angels holding the saint directly by his habit at the knees. Strehlke related the inclusion of the cloth of honor to a ceremony first enacted in the Piazza del Campo, Siena, on June 14, 1450, in which an effigy of the saint was lifted to "paradise" on a mechanical device with music-making angels. The Compagnia della Vergine panel and some, if not all, of the others predate this ceremony, however, and it is likely that the cloth of honor was instead meant to emphasize the holiness of Bernardino's person. It is conceivable that the Perkins panel was painted for a member of the Compagnia della Vergine who may have asked for it to repeat the image of the saint on the hospital altarpiece. Sano himself was a member of this confraternity.

The Perkins Saint Bernardino, which is preserved with its original frame and in excellent condition, is of exceptionally high quality and is certainly to be considered among the finest of Sano di Pietro's small-scale images of the saint. It is most plausibly datable around 1449, by comparison to the predella and pilasters of the Scrofiano altarpiece of that year, which raises the possibility of its having been painted before Bernardino's canonization (many of the haloes appearing in other paintings of Saint Bernardino made prior to 1450 were added only after his canonization, but it is unclear whether all of them were added or whether the practice of distinguishing between Saints and Blessed was less rigorous than it is sometimes now thought to have been). Of particular delicacy are the two angels with their fluttering gold and red-glazed draperies and carefully delineated wings, reminiscent of the equally refined angels hovering above the Virgin of Humility in a small panel by Sano di Pietro now in the Museo Civico at Montalcino. This painting has been shown by Christiansen (1988, pp. 87–88) to be a replica by Sano of a lost painting by Sassetta, and the same question may profitably be asked of the Perkins Saint Bernardino (and perhaps of the Compagnia della Vergine panel) as well. Sassetta was commissioned to paint an image of Saint Bernardino for the hospital church of Santa Maria della Scala, a site of great public prominence, in January 1445 (Gallavotti-Cavallero, 1985, p. 187), but this painting, which must certainly have had an enormous influence in its time, is not known to survive. [LBK-PP]

*Bibliography*: Pavone and Pacelli, 1981, pp. 6, 28; Zeri, 1988, pp. 110–11 (with previous bibliography); Strehlke, 1988, p. 268.

# Matteo di Giovanni

Sienese, active by 1452–died 1497

**26**

*The Nativity with Saints Dominic and Catherine of Siena*
Tempera on panel, 67 × 47 cm
Assisi, Museo-Tesoro della Basilica
di San Francesco, Perkins Collection

The scene of the Nativity takes place in a deep rocky landscape, before a manger built into the mouth of a cave with a lean-to shed roof above and at the right the ruins of a classical basilica, symbolic of the destruction of the old order and its replacement by the new. The Virgin and Saint Joseph kneel in adoration of the Christ Child, lying naked on a golden aureole on the ground. Behind Saint Joseph at the left kneels Saint Dominic, holding a book, a quill pen, and a portable ink pot, and behind the Virgin kneels Saint Catherine of Siena, in the habit of a Dominican nun, holding an open book and a stalk of lilies. God the Father appears in glory in the sky above, blessing the scene on the ground before Him. Behind Him is an angel sending word of the birth of Christ to two shepherds walking in the middle distance.

The Perkins Nativity is typical of a category of small domestic altarpieces that became popular in Siena in the last three decades of the fifteenth century, substituting a narrative subject for the traditional Madonna and Child with Saints or Angels. Commonly executed on this scale, though sometimes a bit larger, examples are known by nearly every major master of the period: Francesco di Giorgio, Matteo di Giovanni, Liberale da Verona, Benvenuto di Giovanni, Pietro Orioli, Bernardino Fungai, Guidoccio Cozzarelli…, only Neroccio de' Landi seems not to have contributed to the growing market for these paintings. The Perkins Nativity, as was noted by Zeri (1988, p. 114), owes a particular debt to an earlier image of the subject, probably painted around 1471 or 1472, by Francesco di Giorgio, now owned jointly by the National Gallery of Art, Washington, and the Metropolitan Museum of Art, New York (see Kanter, 1988, pp. 320–22),

which introduces an apparition of God the Father, steeply foreshortened in a gilt mandorla, blessing the scene below, conflating the symbolism of the Nativity with the Incarnation.

For all of its known history, the Perkins Nativity has been attributed to Guidoccio Cozzarelli (1450–1516), a follower of Matteo di Giovanni through the 1480s who later shifted his stylistic allegiance to another of Matteo's onetime assistants and followers, Pietro Orioli (1458–1496). Cozzarelli was so able and devoted an imitator of Matteo di Giovanni that their works are still frequently confused, notwithstanding such specialized studies as Bernard Berenson's of 1918, aimed exclusively at distinguishing between the two artists. A case in point is the Perkins Nativity, which has, presumably, been considered too sketchy and loose in handling to be an autograph work by Matteo. It is, however, entirely typical of Matteo di Giovanni's nervous, wiry style, with his angular, crisp draperies, tense postures, and sharply characterized, bony facial types, so different from Guidoccio's usual soft, rounded, and inadequately animated figures. A signed Nativity by Matteo formerly in the Henschel collection, Cassel (Pope-Hennessy, 1950, fig. 7), provides an analogy for the Perkins painting in most of its details of composition, iconography, and figure type (except for that of the beardless and grimacing Saint Joseph).

Dating Matteo di Giovanni's small-scale devotional works, the great majority of which represent the Madonna and Child rather than narrative subjects, can only be approximate, based on similarities in figure style to his altarpieces. The closest comparisons to the Perkins Nativity may be found in the Celsi altarpiece of 1480 now in the Museo dell'Opera del Duomo in Siena, and in the Saint Barbara altarpiece of 1479 in San Domenico, Siena. Some of the features common to these works appear as early as 1476, in Matteo's altarpiece for the Placidi chapel in San Domenico, but this date seems precocious for the Perkins Nativity. Neverthe-

less, it may have been the coincidence of two important altarpiece commissions for the Sienese Dominicans which led to his painting this more modest Nativity for a Dominican or Dominican Tertiary patron, probably around or just before 1480. [LBK-PP]

*Bibliography*: Zeri, 1988, pp. 114–15 (with previous bibliography).

# Niccolò di Liberatore da Foligno
## (called Niccolò Alunno)
Umbrian, ca. 1430–1502

**27**

*Gonfalone della Peste*
Tempera on linen, 175.5 × 125 cm
Kevelaer, Priesterhaus

*Gonfaloni*, or processional banners, are known through documents of the fifteenth century to have been commissioned in great numbers, primarily by lay confraternities but also by municipal corporations. Frequently these were double-sided, sometimes painted on panel but more often on linen (for lighter weight and greater ease of portability), and invariably intended to be carried in procession through the streets of a town on major feast days or in times of crisis, such as plague or war. Due primarily to the fragility of their medium and the physical exigencies of their use, however, surviving examples are comparatively rare, and few among these are preserved in uncompromised condition. The present example has suffered less than most, but has been subjected to several restorations in the past, most recently by H. Holtmann in 1926, that have covered minor flaking losses with heavy corrective and now largely discolored overpainting. Some of these have been adjusted in watercolor or dry pastel for the present exhibition, to return the *gonfalone* more nearly to its original legibility and beauty.

Niccolò Alunno's *Gonfalone della Peste* represents the Virgin and six saints interceding on behalf of the town of Assisi for deliverance from the plague. At the top, Christ the Redeemer, bearing the stigmata of His sacrifice and carrying the standard of His victory over death, is seated on a mandorla of seraphim in a gesture of judgment or blessing. Two adoring angels kneel on clouds at either side, the innermost pair holding arrows symbolizing the plague as divine vengeance. In related images, these arrows are cast down at the earth below either by angels or by Christ Himself: the angels holding the arrows at rest in this instance are undoubtedly emblematic of the cessation of pestilence. Below and before the angels on the left is the Virgin, dressed in white and crowned as

Queen of Heaven, beseeching Her Son for mercy on behalf of the town of Assisi portrayed across the bottom of the banner. Assisi is also represented by six protector saints as advocates interceding on her behalf. Saints Sebastian and Roch at the far left and right, respectively, are the saints traditionally invoked for relief from the afflictions of illness and especially the plague. Alongside Saint Sebastian at the left are Saints Clare and Francis, while opposite them on the right are the Bishop martyrs Saint Rufino and Saint Vittorino, patrons of Assisi.

The *Gonfalone della Peste* was first mentioned by Fra Ludovico da Pietralunga around 1570, in his detailed description of the Basilica of San Francesco at Assisi (cited in Gnoli, 1911, p. 63), when it was to be seen mounted as an altarpiece in the chapel of Saint Louis of Toulouse (now the chapel of Saint Stephen) in the Lower Church. Fra Ludovico called it a "tavoletta cioè confalone," and his clear description of its subject leaves no doubt that this is indeed the painting to which he was referring, while the language that he used to identify its author, drawn directly from Vasari's *Lives of the Painters*, suggests that this is also the painting referred to by Vasari as a "tavola" (panel) painted by Niccolò Alunno for San Francesco (Vasari-Milanesi, III, p. 510; Lunghi, 1993, p. 10). The painting was sold (or given) to Johann Anton Ramboux, presumably on one of his two visits to Assisi in 1820 or 1835, and it was in his collection in Cologne (no. 202) that it was mentioned by Crowe and Cavalcaselle (1866), A. Rossi (1872), and Frenfanelli Cibo (1872). With the dispersal of the Ramboux collection in 1867 all trace of the *Gonfalone* was lost, until it was rediscovered a quarter century later at the Priesterhaus at Kevelaer by Paul Perdrizet (1908) and subsequently photographed and published by Umberto Gnoli (1911).

For Gnoli, the chief interest of the *Gonfalone della Peste* was less artistic—he considered only the animated and expressive head of Saint Francis to be worthy of note—than historic and topographic: the image of Assisi painted across the bottom of the banner is the earliest known complete view of the town. Allowing for minor artistic license in emphasizing, for example, ecclesiastical structures over common houses, it is also a remarkably accurate view of Assisi, portraying the medieval city with its expanded ring of fortified walls (completed in 1316) still intact and the Rocca Maggiore at the summit of the hill in the form in which it was completed by Pope Pius II in 1460, a *terminus post quem* for execution of the painting. The unmistakable profile of the Convent and Basilica of San Francesco, with its wall of arched buttresses, dominates the hillside at the left. The *campanile* (bell tower) of San Francesco is shown not with its present flat roof but with a steeply pitched attic that was pulled down in the sixteenth century because it attracted lightning. Other *campanili*, notably those of S. Chiara at the right, the Benedictine abbey of S. Pietro in the lower center, and the Cathedral directly below the staff of Saint Rufino, are also shown with steeply pitched attics that no longer exist (the Cathedral is also shown, inappropriately, with a lanterned dome remarkably similar to that designed for it in the sixteenth century by Galeazzo Alessi, possibly to be understood as an early "restoration" to the *Gonfalone*). Absent, however, is the escarpment of the infirmary on the west end of San Francesco, built by Sixtus IV in 1472, a probable *terminus ante quem* for the painting. Within this period of twelve years, Gnoli pointed out, Niccolò da Foligno was active in Assisi in 1468, when he painted a *Gonfalone* for the Compagnia di San Gregorio now in Karlsruhe (Santi, 1976, pl. V) and around 1470, the presumed date of his altarpiece in the cathedral of San Rufino. Although the San Rufino altarpiece is now believed to date from 1462 (Lunghi, 1993), Gnoli's proposal to date the *Gonfalone della Peste* to the end of that decade is convincing on stylistic grounds.

Gnoli's assessment of the artistic merits of the *Gonfalone della Peste* were somewhat harsh. They were not accepted by Francesco Santi (1976), nor do they bear up to scrutiny of the painting itself. Except for the coarse repaints and a few patches along old tears, the dry tempera surface of the painting is beautifully preserved, if sunken a bit in the thinner, darker pigments at the top, and the gilding is intact. The heads of the angels and seraphim are all fully legible in substantially their original form and reveal Niccolò da Foligno at the height of his very considerable powers of expression, while the panoramic view of Assisi is rendered with uncanny accuracy. The draperies of all the figures, though stiffened by repainting, are drawn and modelled with an astonishing rapidity and freedom of gesture, and the weave of the unprimed cloth support is expertly used for texture and ground color throughout. Fifteenth-century linen *gonfaloni* were not painted with the layers of translucent oil glazing with which panel paintings of the time were finished and to which they owe much of their effects of modelling and detail. They are meant to be judged by a different aesthetic, one in which Niccolò da Foligno's *Gonfalone della Peste* stands out for originality of conception and quality of execution. [LBK-PP]

*Bibliography*: Vasari (Milanesi ed.) III, 1878, p. 510; Crowe and Cavalcaselle, 1866, III, p. 127; Frenfanelli Cibo, 1872, pp. 83, 116; Rossi, 1872, p. 259; Perdrizet, 1908, p. 118; Gnoli, 1911, pp. 63–70; Gnoli, 1923, pp. 210, 212, 215; Berenson, 1968, p. 296, pl. 654; Omelia, 1975, p. 41 n. 32; Santi, 1976, p. 21, pl. VIII; Nessi, 1982, p. 360; Scarpellini, 1982b, pp. 37, 42, 135, 215–19; Todini, 1989, I, p. 243; Lunghi, 1993, pp. 10, 43; Merzenich, 1995, p. 310 n. 62.

## Francesco di Gentile

Marchigian, active last third
fifteenth century

**28**

Triptych: *Madonna and Child with
Music-making Angels*; *Christ at
the Column*; *Saint John the Baptist*
Tempera on panel, 66.5 × 39 cm,
center; 66.8 × 19.5 cm, wings
Assisi, Museo-Tesoro della Basilica
di San Francesco, Perkins Collection

This beautifully preserved painting,
fully signed by its author, "Franciscus
Gentilis me pinxit" (Francesco di Gentile painted me), is remarkable from a
number of points of view, not least of
which is the elaborate carpentry of its
frame. The carved and gilt Gothic ornament surrounding the Virgin and Child
in the center panel and creating architectural niches for the standing figures
in the wings is in fact so flamboyant
that Zeri (1988) was induced to suggest
that Francesco di Gentile may not have
designed this structure *ex novo* but
rather that he might have been commissioned to repaint a triptych made
earlier in Flanders. While the vocabulary of this ornament is indeed Flemish, its disposition and quality are typ-
ically Marchigian, strongly resembling
such large-scale monuments as the
carved wooden choir stalls by Giovanni di Stefano da Montelparo in San
Domenico at Fermo or those by Giovanni di Matteo da Maltignano and his
sons Paolino and Francesco in the
Duomo at Ascoli Piceno, both of 1448.
It is not unreasonable to suggest that
this frame may have been carved by
one of these, or by another of the documented *tagliatori* active in the Marches at this period, such as Corrado Teutonico, who was responsible around
1490 for the frame on the high altarpiece in San Medardo, Arcevia, later
painted by Luca Signorelli. Giovanni di
Stefano da Montelparo carved a number of frames for altarpieces by Carlo
and Vittore Crivelli and Niccolò Alunno (Crocetti, 1989–90). Unfortunately,
the frame maker of the Perkins triptych did not sign his work alongside
the painter, even though the two
artists' contributions compete with
each other for attention. The painted
decoration of classicizing candelabra
in gold against a red ground appearing
on the outsides of the wings may well
have been added (or renewed) in the
sixteenth century.

Another unusual aspect of this triptych
is the iconography of the wings. Single
figures of standing saints are frequently
encountered on the wings of folding
triptychs. Often these are the name
saints of the painting's original owner,
or saints of special devotion to the owner, such as patrons of a confraternity, or
Saint Christopher, protector of travellers.
However, a devotional icon such as the
image of Christ bound to a column, ab-
stracted from its narrative context by the
absence of His tormentors, is hardly ever
encountered on a triptych wing, as it is
here. Saint John the Baptist in the right
wing is less unusual except that he is here
portrayed embracing a Crucifix, again a
rarely encountered iconography.

Little is known about the painter
Francesco di Gentile. Although a certain number of works by him are
signed, none are dated and it has not
yet been possible to determine a
chronology for him or a sense of the
development of his style. It is possible
in this case only to hazard a guess that
the Perkins triptych may be a relatively
early work, perhaps painted shortly after 1470. The figure types in the center
panel are still strongly reminiscent of
much earlier examples by Gentile da
Fabriano, and the composition of the
Mother and Child group derives either
from Madonnas of the 1460s by Giovanni Bellini or their Mantegnesque
prototypes. The figures in the wings
also recall Giovanni Bellini in their
poses, whereas other, presumably later
paintings by Francesco di Gentile depend instead on the numerous altarpieces and devotional panels painted
by Carlo Crivelli for patrons throughout the Marches. It is in part the naive-
ly charming Bellinesque or Mantegnesque classicism of this painting
blended with the ornately flamboyant
Gothic architecture of its frame that
makes it an object of such appealing
and mysterious beauty. [LBK-PP]

*Bibliography*: Zampetti, 1969, p. 36;
Zeri, 1988, pp. 124–25 (with previous
bibliography).

123

# Anonymous Umbrian
# or Roman Master

Last quarter fifteenth century

**29**

*The Stigmatization of Saint Francis*
Tempera on panel, 83 × 59.4 cm
Assisi, Museo-Tesoro della Basilica
di San Francesco, Perkins Collection

This large devotional panel, or perhaps small domestic altarpiece, was commissioned by a certain Donna Costanza Micheli, undoubtedly as a votive offering or to secure indulgences for the soul of her brother Stefano, as we are informed by an inscription with the date 1488 (? or 1483, the last digit is damaged and unclear) across the bottom. A coat of arms—presumably of the Micheli family—also appears at the bottom of the panel, but neither these nor the names of the donors are recognizable from documents of the period. The panel illustrates the miracle of Saint Francis receiving the stigmata at La Verna on September 17, 1224, as described in the biography of the saint written in 1263 by Bonaventure of Bagnorea, the *Legenda Maior*. Saint Francis kneels before a vision of the Crucified Christ with the wings of a Seraph. Red rays emanating from Christ's wounds imprint their marks on Francis's hands, feet, and side. Brother Leo is seated reading at the left, unaware of the occurrence of the miracle before him, and behind the two figures the wilderness of La Verna is symbolized by a rugged mountainous landscape with a church, a fortified town, and wild deer grazing on the hillside.

Despite its precarious condition—the legibility of the surface has been severely impaired by abrasion and by paint losses along a vertical split in the panel through its center—the Perkins *Stigmatization of Saint Francis* has long been recognized as a beautiful and, partly because it is dated, important image in the history of central Italian painting. Roberto Longhi (1927) attributed it to Antoniazzo Romano, an attribution defended by Federico Zeri (1988) who compared it to several small-scale narrative panels he considered to be key works by Antoniazzo from the decade of the 1480s, including a predella of the Nativity in the Metropolitan Museum of Art, New York, and a Saint Francis Adoring the Crucifix in the Kress Collection at Bucknell University (Lewisberg, Pennsylvania). This opinion has not otherwise been widely accepted, as a number of recent authors have attempted to sift through the unusually large number of paintings attributed to Antoniazzo Romano seeking to define his personality more narrowly. Roberto Cannata (1982, p. 32 n. 12), for example, attributed both the Metropolitan Museum and Kress Collection panels to a "Master of Tivoli," an artist largely active around Rome whom he found to be significantly more accomplished than Antoniazzo, and stated without further precision that the Perkins Stigmatization could not be by Antoniazzo either. Anna Cavallaro (1992, p. 251) also believed that none of the paintings grouped together by Zeri were by Antoniazzo. The Perkins panel she labelled simply "scuola Umbro Romana." The very material difficulty of identifying a clear artistic personality for Antoniazzo Romano is linked to the nature of artistic production in Rome in the late quattrocento, where individuality of style was far less highly prized than was adherence to iconographic or compositional prototypes of particular veneration. The large corpus of works assigned to Antoniazzo is in fact exceptionally heterogeneous in style, possibly indicating a large and fluid workshop organization or perhaps the freedom with which other studios candidly imitated his paintings, not unlike the situation in early sixteenth century Venice among the followers of Giovanni Bellini. Within this large group of paintings, however, the Perkins Stigmatization stands out for its high quality and its evident dependence on Umbrian examples by Pietro Perugino and his circle. Antoniazzo Romano was intimately familiar with Perugino's work, easily available in Rome after 1480, but he does not seem to have internalized the lessons of Perugino's art as completely in any of his other works as did the artist of the Perkins Stigmatization. This painter has not yet been recognized as a concrete personality, nor is it clear whether he was active in Rome or, more likely, Umbria, a question that archival research into the identities of the panel's donors might help to resolve. [LBK-PP]

*Bibliography*: Longhi, 1927, p. 256 n. 13; Cannata, 1982, p. 32 n. 12; Zeri, 1988, pp. 118–19; Cavallaro, 1992, p. 251, cat. no. 120 (with previous bibliography).

HOC OPVS FECIT FIERI DNA CONSTANSIA MIHAEL ANIMA STEFANI FRATRIS SVI AÑO DNH 14 8 B

## Umbrian Master
First half sixteenth century

**30**
*Double-sided Processional Cross*
Oil on shaped wooden panel,
41 × 35.5 cm, recto and verso
Assisi, Museo-Tesoro della Basilica
di San Francesco

The three upper extremities of this cross have three cusps while the lower one has only two, so that it could be set on a base or a staff. On the front is represented the Crucifixion on Mount Golgotha—identified by the skull and crossbones—with a tablet above Christ's head bearing the inscription "INRI" in red letters. On the left of the transverse arm we see the Virgin with her hands joined in prayer and, on the right, Saint John. At the top, the Eternal Father with a long white beard has his hands raised in the typical attitude of prayer.

On the back the iconography is more or less identical, except for a few variations in the poses of the Virgin and John, while the Father has his right hand raised in prayer and is resting the palm of his left hand on the terrestrial globe, as if the artist wanted to underline his role as Salvator Mundi.

The still Gothic form of this piece seems to have been inspired by the processional crosses made of embossed metal that were produced in large numbers by the goldsmithries of the time. This model, which first appeared at the end of the thirteenth century, remained in use in Umbria up until the sixteenth century and even later.

The pictorial language adopted by this Umbrian painter already displays a Mannerism of the very first generation: in fact, while this work is most reminiscent of the art of Perugino (the grief-stricken figures of the Virgin and Saint John), it is also possible to discern not just a firsthand knowledge of Raphael (the treatment of the Eternal Father at the top), but also of the contributions made by Tuscan culture. Thus this processional cross may have been painted by an artist—and imitator of the style of Pinturicchio and Raphael—belonging to the circle of the Perugian painter Berto di Giovanni, and it is even possible that it was executed by the latter. This last hypothesis appears to find support in the representation of the Eternal Father at the top, which bears a striking resemblance to the Saint John on Patmos by Berto di Giovanni, now in the Pinacoteca Civica of Perugia. [PL]

*Bibliography: Il Tesoro della Basilica,* 1980, pp. 60–61, pl. LXII–LXIII.

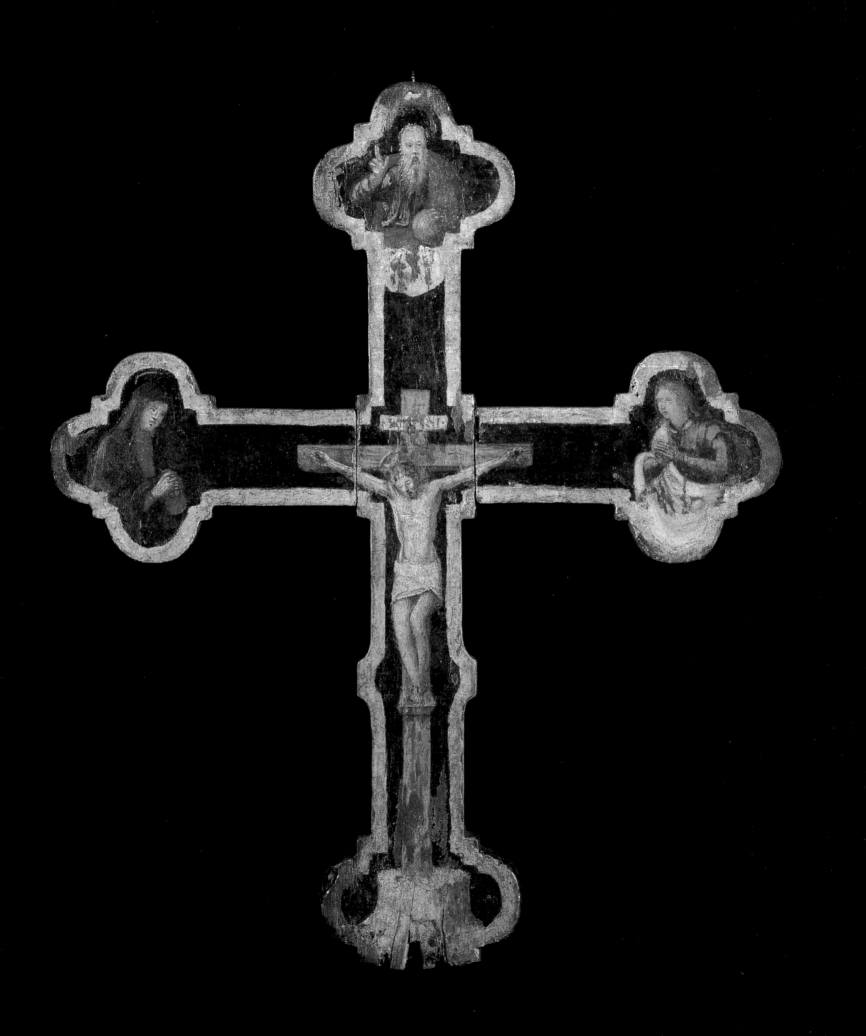

# MANUSCRIPTS

## Italian

Second quarter thirteenth century

**31**

*Franciscan Breviary*
Parchment, 27 × 19 cm, 388 ff.
Assisi, Biblioteca Conventuale-
Comunale, MS 694

The manuscript is devoid of miniatures, and has no decorative elements of particular interest. Only the initials and headings are painted in red. The binding is modern.

The text of the volume, on the other hand, is especially important, in so far as it represents the first draft of the Franciscan breviary. The use of the breviary, a liturgical book par excellence that contains the prayers said by clergy and monks and which is still read from today, was imposed by Saint Francis on all the Friars Minor, after the approval of his rule in 1223 by Pope Honorius III.

The type of breviary chosen by Saint Francis for his order made no reference to any of the breviaries in use in the dioceses of the various monastic orders at the time, but drew directly on the breviary utilized at the papal court in Rome, as is made clear by the inscription on the codex: "breviarium ordinis fratrum minorum secundum consuetudinem sancte romane ecclesie."

The minuscule Gothic book hand, clear and elegant, belongs to the tradition of the thirteenth century. The fact that in the litanies of the saints no mention is made of Francis—canonized as we know in 1228—or of any other Franciscan saint allows us to date this manuscript to the first few decades of the thirteenth century. [GM]

*Bibliography*: Abate, 1960, pp. 47–227; Cenci, 1981, p. 370.

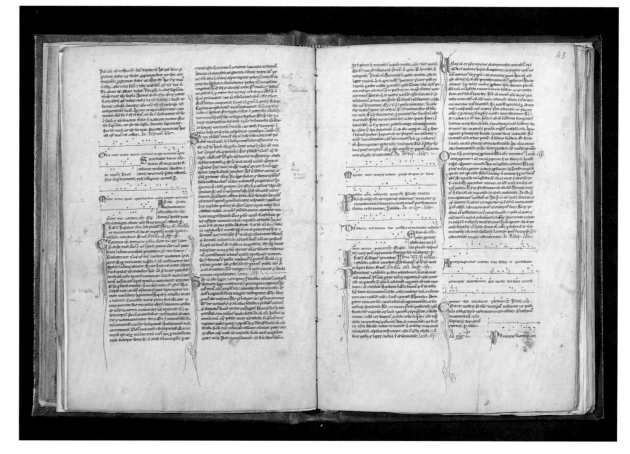

**French**
Second quarter thirteenth century

**32**

*Antiphonary and Gradual*
Parchment, 210 × 150 mm, 242 ff.
Assisi, Biblioteca Conventuale-
Comunale, MS 695

Known as the Reims Gradual, because
of its supposed provenance, it is made
up of two distinct parts, which may
originally have been bound in two different volumes: the first (ff. 1–55) is a
gradual with the ordinary of the Mass;
the second (ff. 56–239) an antiphonary
for the various liturgical feast days.
It was undoubtedly produced in France
and probably donated to the Basilica of
San Francesco in the second half of the
thirteenth century, to be used for liturgical purposes, by Cardinal Matteo
Rosso Orsini, appointed protector of
the Order of Friars Minor by his uncle
Nicholas III in 1278. Orsini, who had
pursued his theological studies at the
University of Paris, where he may have
come into possession of the manuscript, displayed particular generosity to
the Basilica in Assisi, donating tapestries, liturgical objects and various
manuscripts: Cenci (1981, p. 11), has
identified at least ten manuscripts that
used to belong to him in the library of
the Sacro Convento. Folio 1 bears a note
referring to ownership by the cardinal:
"Iste liber est domini Mathei sancte
Mary in Porticu diae. card." The manuscript must date from sometime between 1228, the year of Francis's canonization, owing to the presence of two se-
quences for the saint's feast day, and
1234–35, owing to the absence of feast
days devoted to saints canonized after
Francis, such as Saint Dominic (1234)
and Saint Elizabeth of Hungary (1235).
The manuscript has a very rich decoration, much of which has unfortunately
disappeared as a consequence of the sys-
tematic removal of all the illuminated
letters, around sixty in number, which
may have happened in the seventeenth
century.
The manuscript is important not just
for its liturgical texts, but also and above
all for the music it contains, comprising
a vast repertoire of Gregorian melody

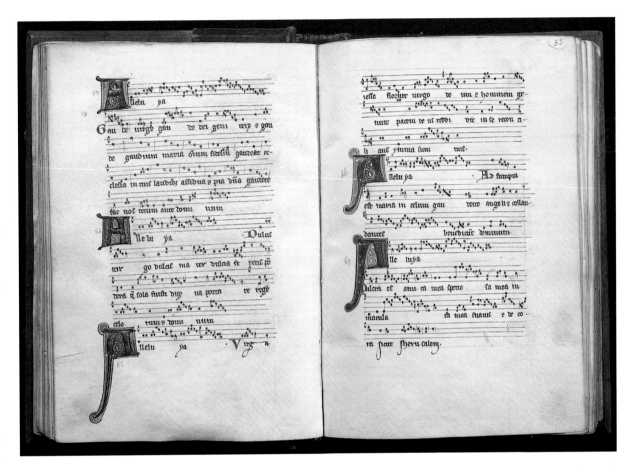

and polyphonic compositions for two
and three voices that are among the oldest to have come down to us. It has been
the subject of several thorough studies.
[GM]

*Bibliography*: Alessandri, 1911, pp.
245–60; Seay, 1957, pp. 10–35; Cenci,
1981, p. 11; Assirelli and Sesti, 1990, pp.
194–201.

# Paris

ca. 1235–45

**33**

*Bible accompanied by a Gloss*
Parchment, 46.5 × 32 cm, 111 ff.
Assisi, Biblioteca Conventuale-
Comunale, MS 11

This codex, comprising two books of the Maccabees as well as glosses drawn from patristic texts, is one of seventeen surviving volumes of a Bible now divided between the library of the monastery in Assisi and the Vatican Apostolic Library (Mercati, 1924) where they arrived at the time of the purchase of the Rossiano collection.

According to an undocumented tradition, this Bible had been donated by Saint Louis, king of France. There appear to be good grounds for this belief, however, since various volumes of the work, to be precise manuscripts 3 and 7, seem to have been drawn up by the author of the Missal, Epistolary and Evangeliary in the monastery, three works that were produced on the orders of Louis IX and sent from Paris for liturgical use in the Basilica of San Francesco (Assirelli, 1988, p. 112).

This Bible, certainly the most important group of illuminated books conserved in Assisi, did not—according to the inventory of 1381—originally take the form in which we know it today. This book, for example, was once bound together with two others: MS 4 and the second part of MS 5. The entire Pentateuch was probably contained in two large volumes.

As has been pointed out, this Bible was produced in Paris over a relatively long period of time (from at least the third to the fifth decade of the thirteenth century). It is ornamented, but the decoration is limited to illuminated initials. In the present manuscript we find one large initial, to be precise the "D" of *Dominus* (f. 1*v*) which is decorated with two curious intertwined snakes on a gold ground at the beginning of the prologue to the Book of the Maccabees (where a dedication to Saint Louis can also be found). There are two more initials with illuminated scenes on a gold ground, to be precise the "E" of *Et factum* where the siege of a city is represented (f. 2) and the "F" of *Fratribus*, which depicts a messenger delivering a letter to a group of seated Jewish elders (f. 74). These iconographic choices are indicative of Parisian scriptoria where, at the beginning of the thirteenth century and in university circles, profound changes were taking place in the approach to the drafting and illustration of biblical manuscripts, in particular through the abandonment of large, full-page miniatures in favor of historiated initials (often just one at the beginning of the books of the Old and New Testament). [GM]

*Bibliography*: Mercati, 1924, pp. 83–127; Branner, 1977; Assirelli, 1988, pp. 105–30.

laborare ꝫ tendo. ꝑ ꝰ cuius est nīe ut qui in uia moꝝ dedat uelle ipsū
me bono ope faciat ꝗ sūmmare. de quo ꝯppḃa ait. ipe est dñl oīꝵ inuo
camiḃ se in ueritate. ꝫ nos delinq̄t omnes qui spānt inse. diuinitas do
mini nři ihū xpi dñi nos huic incolumes ꝫ regis dei curatem amantes
ad nřoꝛ salutem custodiat. ꝫ post huir uite cursum ad uitam eternam
beatitudinem puenire concedat.

R̄euerentissimo ꝫ oīm caritatis ofō dignissimo. Gerold sacri pa
latij archidiachono. Rabanus uilis seruoꝛ dei seruus in xpo sa
lutem. Memini me ī palatio uangionum ciuitatis ꝯstitutū
tecum habuisse sermonem de eminentia sc̄ē scripturaꝝ ꝫ de difficultate di
uinaꝝ historiaꝝ in quiḃ nō solum pauci scita loca ꝙ uarietate trꝝ ꝫ si
cū punctuaꝝ obscur ꝫ est sensus quint ꝑ proposita siḡ ꝫ occultus est ī
tellectus. ꝫ ꝙ eodem ꝯmitarios in libros regum tuiꝑ a nob editos ue
nabilis abbatis huil diuino tradideram. tu quid puntatem meam exhorta
tus es q̄ tenui in libros paliporū atꝙ machabeoꝝ ꝯmitarios uiꝑ uestigia
maioꝛ pati studio ꝙderem. Frā eiuimū potui ꝑ posui libri expositnem
Lodoico regi editam dedi. Setꝗ sitis uero tue scitati tradendam reseruia
ui. ut petitio tua sialꝫ una. neꝙ haberes me suggillandi. ꝙ te rogan
ti nollem q̄ facere ꝙ aliis ḡtis ꝯtulim. ꝑ inde q̄ iam ꝯfestūs opus habes
uiꝗ eo sicut decet seruum xpi cum ꝯsone uisoꝝ ꝫ ꝙ solus imperta
ueris ad plimoꝝ utilitatem puenire facias. Decrto q̄ uolo scitatem
tuam scire ꝙ nōm opus ideo ꝑtim dedi uina historia. ꝑtim de ioseph.
iudeoꝝ historici traditione. ꝑtim ū de aliaꝝ ḡentium historijs ꝯtextuī
ut q̄ ū ꝯt ḡentis iudee ac principum eius. ꝫ aliaꝝ ḡentiū sibi inxpo
libro ꝗstio sit ꝫ multoꝛ libꝛoꝛ collatione uitas cāe hystorie pateat
ꝫ sensus narrationis est. lectoꝛi uia dioꝛ fiat. Tu si quid in memorato
ope ꝫ gratum atꝙ utile inueneris largitoꝛi ofm bonoꝛ inde ḡratias
reꝑras. Si quid ā rephensibile in eo esse ꝑ spo̅eū nře institutati ꝫ im
pitie deputes ꝫ ꝑ clementem iudicem ueniam imperte nob per la
catas oꝛones festines. Et eꝙ optimo largitoꝛi digni honoꝛem ꝫ fragili
opificia oportunū ꝙ feret solatium fraternitatem tuam diuina maiestas
ꝑ spis successib pollentem ꝫ eterne beatitudinis gaudia. ꝑ merentem
omi tempoꝛe nři memoꝛem ꝯseruare dignetur.

E̅t fr̄m est post
qḿ ꝑcussit a
lexander philip
pi rege macedo
qui primū regnauit in grecia.
egressus de terra cechim ꝑ
cussit darium regem psaꝝ
ꝫ medoꝝ ꝫ ꝯstituit prelia mul
tā. cur dicat. ꝫ frā est. cum nō sit sermo au hec ꝙ incipit. sub uingi

Initium libri machabe
oꝛ simile est ꝑrincipio
libri ezechielis ꝓphe. Ubi
scriptum est. et fr̄m est ī
tricesimo anno in cir
to milesit. Et. Unde pmū
nobis ꝙ oritur cur is
qui ad huc nichil dixerit. ita
exorsus est dicens. Et frā
est postqḿ ꝑcussit alex
ander ꝫ reliqua. Tam q̄
sermo ꝙ iunctionis est
samus q̄ nō iungitur ser
mo subleqnt ī sermoni
precedenti. Sin ꝙ michil

# Umbrian

ca. 1230–57

**34**

*Bible*
Parchment, 400 × 280 mm, 306 ff.
Assisi, Biblioteca Conventuale-
Comunale, MS 17

The manuscript, drafted for the Sacro Convento of Assisi in an Umbrian scriptorium, contains the text of the Holy Scriptures, from the book of Genesis to the book of Job. The rest was contained in a second volume that vanished long ago, as we are told by a note at the bottom of the flyleaf: "Prima pars Biblie, Secunda parte non reperitur amplius hoc anno 1753…"

According to a well-attested oral tradition, the Bible used to belong to the Blessed Giovanni da Parma, sixth minister general of the order (1247–55) and predecessor of Saint Bonaventure, who was a fervent disciple of Joachim of Fiore and a supporter of the extreme tendency within the order known as the Spirituals. This would explain the simplicity of the volume's decoration, devoid of gold grounds and with just a few figures in the illuminated letters. One of the most interesting letters is to be found on f. 5v, in the incipit of the book of Genesis: in the letter "I" of *In principio*, running the entire length of the folio, appears the figure of the Creator, under the image of Christ, along with those of Adam and Francis, enclosed in small architectural aedicules set one above the other. In some interpretations, Francis was considered not just an "alter Christus," as indicated by the stigmata clearly visible on both his hands and feet, but also a mediator of the reconciliation between God and human beings. The presence of the halo above his head means that the volume must have been produced after 1228, the year of his canonization.

The volume is perhaps the oldest of the Gothic manuscripts in the library of the Franciscan monastery in Assisi. In fact it is given first place in the inventory of the private library of the Sacro Convento, drawn up in 1381, which states that it was used for spiritual readings during the monk's meals in the refectory. [GM]

*Bibliography*: Assirelli and Sesti, 1990, pp. 82–89; Ciardi 1982b, pp. 331, 333–34; Frugoni, 1993, p. 110.

inuidos, nuc te depor desideri. kmc
ut qd tantu op me subur fecistu. et
a genesi exordiu cape orationib; iu
ues: quo possi eode spu quo scrip
ti sut libri. in latinu eos trasferre
sermone.

N PRINCIPIO creauit
ds celu ⁊ tram. tra aut erat
inanis ⁊ uacua. Et tenebre
erat sup facie abissi. ⁊ sps
di ferebat sup aquas. Dixitq;
ds. fiat lux. et facta e lux.
Et uidit ds luce qd eet bona:
⁊ diuisit luce a tenebris.
Appellauitq; luce die: et
tenebras nocte. factuq; est
uespe ⁊ mane. dies unus.
Dixitq; ds. fiat firmamtu i
mecho aq̄r. ⁊ diuidat aqs
ab aquis. Et fec ds firmamtu.
diuisitq; aquas q̄ erat sub
firmamto. ab hiis q̄ erat sup
firmamtu. Et factu e tta.
uocauitq; ds firmamtu ce
lu. et factu e uespe ⁊ mane
dies scds. Dixit uo ds. Con
greget aq̄ q̄ sub celo sunt
in locu unu: ⁊ appareat ari
da. factuq; e tta. Et uocauit
ds arida tra. ⁊ gregatiōesq;
aq̄r; appellauit maria. Et
uidit ds qd eet bonu. ⁊ ait.
Germinet tra herba uirēte
⁊ faciente sem. et lignu po
miferu. facies fructu uixta

gen suu: cui sem insemetipo sit sup
terra. Et factu e tta. Et ptulit tra
herba uirete. ⁊ afferente sem uixta
gen suu. lignuq; facies fructu. ⁊ ha
bes unuqdq; sente secm specie sua.
Et uidit ds qd eet bonu: factuq; est
uespe ⁊ mane. dies tci. Dixit aut ds.
fiant luminaria in firmamto celi:
⁊ diuidat die ac nocte: ⁊ sint in signa
⁊ tepora. ⁊ dies ⁊ annos. et luceat in
firmamto celi. et illuminet tta. Et
factu e tta. fecitq; ds duo magna lum
inaria. luminare mai ut peet diei.
⁊ luminare mi ut peet nocti. ⁊ stel
las. ⁊ posuit eas in firmamto celi. ut
lucerent sup tta. Et peet diei ac nocti:
⁊ diuiderent luce ac tenebras. Et uidit
ds qd eet bonu. Et factu e uespe ac ma
ne. dies quart. Dixit ⁊ ds. Producant
aq̄ reptile aie uiuetis: ⁊ uolatile sup
tta. sub firmamto celi. Creauitq; ds cete
grandia. ⁊ omē aiam uiuete atq; mo
tabile. q̄ pduxerat aq̄ in species suas.
⁊ oē uolatile secm gen suu. Et uidit
ds qd eet bonu. benedixitq; eis dicēs. Cre
scite ⁊ mltiplicamini. et replete aq̄s
maris. auesq; multiplicent sup tta.
Et factu e uespe ⁊ mane. dies qntus.
Dixit q̄q; ds. pducat tra aiam uiue
tē in genere suo. iumenta. ⁊ reptilia. ⁊
bestias tre. secm species suas. factuq;
e tta. Et fec ds bestias tre uixta specie
suas. ⁊ iumenta. ⁊ oē reptile tre i ge
nere suo. Et uidit ds qd eet bonu. et
ait. faciam hoiem ad imagine ⁊ sim
ilitudine nram. ⁊ psit piscib; maris

# Paris

Mid-thirteenth century

**35**

*Missal said to be of Saint Louis*
(*Ordo Missalis fratrum minorum
secundum consuetudinem romane curie*)
Parchment, 33.5 × 23.8 cm
Assisi, Museo-Tesoro della Basilica
di San Francesco

The cultural ties between the Franciscan
Order and France had been particularly
close right from the outset. They were
initiated in 1219 with the arrival of several friars in Paris and their immediate
insertion in the city's religious and in-
tellectual life. The principal teaching
posts at the Parisian *studium*, as the university was then called, were soon entrusted to the Franciscans and Queen
Blanche of Castile decided that the education of her son, the future King Louis
IX, should be placed in the hands of
four friars, two Dominicans and two
Franciscans.

Under such circumstances, it is evident
that the production of books, and consequently of illuminations as well, was
strongly influenced by the iconographic
preferences of the order. Franciscan
monasteries were essentially commissioners of manuscripts, rather than pro-
ducers in their own right.

Manuscripts written and illuminated in
France began to flow into the library of
the Sacro Convento of Assisi very early
on. The majority of them are now in the
city's Communal Library, but the treasury of the Basilica still conserves three
precious manuscripts, the missal said to
be of Saint Louis, an evangeliary and an
epistolary. These are listed in the inventory of 1338—"Item unum missale no-
tatum cum evangelistario et epistolario,
de lictera parisiensi" (Alessandri and
Pennacchi, 1920)—along with numerous other manuscripts that cannot all
be identified.

The decoration of the missal consists of
two full-page miniatures, fourteen historiated letters and numerous ornamented letters. The full-page miniatures represent the Crucifixion (105*v*)
and the Christ of the Apocalypse in a
mandorla, flanked by the four symbols
of the Evangelists (106*r*). At the corners

of the latter's frame are set four shields with figures of the Evangelists writing, while the shields surrounding the Crucifixion depict two angels bearing incense at the top and two scenes from the life of Moses at the bottom (*Moses Marking the Houses of Jews with the Tau Cross before the Tenth Plague* and the *Adoration of the Brazen Serpent*).

Already linked to Parisian manuscripts from the mid-thirteenth century (Hertlein, 1965), the manuscript has been more precisely placed through the studies carried out by Branner (1977). He has dated the execution of the missal to 1255–56 on the basis of comparisons with contemporary Parisian production, especially the manuscripts that he found grouped under the expression "Ste. Chapelle Main Line," in reference to the manuscripts produced for the chapel founded by Louis IX and in particular its celebrated evangeliary (Paris, Bibliothèque Nationale, MS Lat. 17326). One highly intriguing but not demonstrable hypothesis is that the manuscript had been commissioned directly by the king of France and was intended for use in services held at the high altar of the Lower Church of Assisi (Ciardi, 1980; Assirelli, 1982).

While the decoration of the missal is not particularly rich, it still arouses admiration by the evident solemnity of its organization and by the extreme care taken over the execution, making it one of the finest examples of illumination produced in Paris around the middle of the century. Two different miniaturists appear to have been responsible for the decoration: one painted the Crucifixion and the Christ of the Apocalypse, while the other probably did all the historiated letters (Branner, 1977). [AT]

*Bibliography*: Fratini, 1882; Marinangeli, 1914b; Alessandri and Pennacchi, 1920; Gnoli, 1921-22; Kleinschmidt, I, 1926; Zocca, 1936; Haseloff, 1938; *Mostra storica*, 1953; Hertlein, 1965; Branner, 1977; Ciardi, 1980; Assirelli, 1982; Dal Poz, 1994.

**36**

*Epistolary*
Parchment, 29.9 × 19.9 cm
Assisi, Museo-Tesoro della Basilica
di San Francesco

Listed for the first time in the inventory of 1338 (Alessandri and Pennacchi, 1920) along with the missal said to be of Saint Louis and an evangeliary, this manuscript is decorated with eight historiated letters and 211 ornamented letters.

The historiated letters, while fairly simple from the viewpoint of their composition, are executed with extreme care. Although the writing of the manuscript has to be attributed to the same hand as that of the missal, the style of the illumination is quite different. In Branner's view (1977), the manuscript must date from 1255–56 and is related to the so-called "Prat Atelier" group of manuscripts. Hertlein (1965) distinguishes the work of two different artists in the manuscript, which he dates to around 1270. He believes one of them to have been the author of the illustrations in the third volume of a Bible now in the Communal Library of Assisi (MS 3) and the other, who executed the majority of the illuminated letters, to be the one responsible for the decoration of the book of Genesis in the same Bible. [AT]

*Bibliography*: Marinangeli, 1914b; Alessandri and Pennacchi, 1920; Gnoli, 1921–22; Kleinschmidt, I, 1926; Zocca, 1936; Haseloff, 1938; Branner, 1977; Ciardi, 1980; Assirelli, 1982; Dal Poz, 1994.

**Paris**
Mid-thirteenth century

**37**

*Evangeliary*
Parchment, 19.5 × 13 cm
Assisi, Museo-Tesoro della Basilica
di San Francesco

This manuscript containing passages
from the Gospels for liturgical use has a
decoration—similar to that of the Missal

of Saint Louis—consisting of ornamented letters drawn with a pen.

There are a total of 196 ornamented
initials (traced in red and blue), making up a fairly lavish set of decorations, something that is relatively rare
for a codex which undoubtedly originally accompanied the other two liturgical books that are associated with it

in the treasury of Assisi. [AT]

*Bibliography*: Marinangeli, 1914b; Gnoli,
1921–22; Kleinschmidt, I, 1926; Zocca,
1936; Hertlein, 1965; Ciardi, 1980;
Assirelli, 1982.

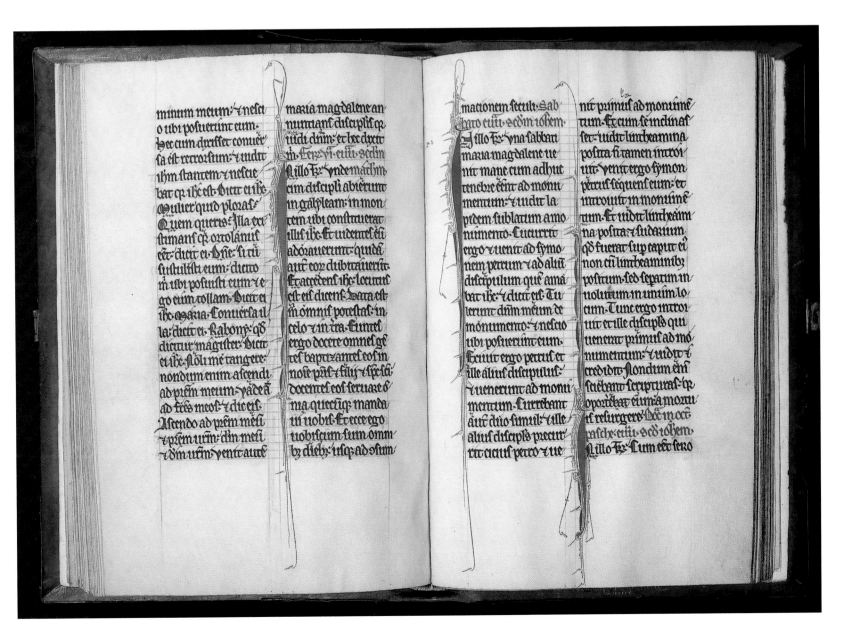

## Master of Saint Francis
Umbrian, active third quarter
thirteenth century

**38**

*Crucifixion*
Tempera and gold leaf on parchment,
175 × 140 mm
T. Robert and Katherine States Burke
Collection

The small, yet monumentally conceived image of the *Crucifixion* illustrates the introductory text for the Canon of the Mass, "Te igitur." On the reverse of the leaf is the conclusion of the Preface of the Mass: "...Suplici confessione di/centes. Sanctus. Sanc/tus. Sanctus. Dominus/ Deus Sabaoth. Pleni sunt..." The missing initial "T" of the "Te igitur" is represented by the imposing blue Cross, which occupies the full height and width of the composition. Flanking the powerful, moving image of the suffering Christ, streams of blood shown pouring from the wounds in His chest, hands, and feet, are on the left the swooning Virgin supported by two Holy Women, and on the right the young Saint John the Evangelist with Saint Francis standing slightly behind him. Filling the corners above the arms of the Cross are two mourning angels. The generously applied gold-leaf, which covers the entire background of the composition, and the rich palette, ranging from warm earth tones and pale blues and lavenders to brilliant reds, greens, and oranges, suggest that this fragment was originally part of an expensively produced book for an important patron or religious institution.

Sandra Hindman (1998), who published this cutting for the first time, convincingly attributed it to the Master of Saint Francis, the anonymous author of a cycle of frescoes with scenes from the life of Saint Francis in the Lower Church in Assisi. On the basis of the inclusion of Saint Francis among the cast of figures usually present at the Crucifixion, Hindman also proposed that the original missal might have been made for the Basilica of Assisi itself. This iconographic motif appears to be entirely without precedent in thirteenth century representations of the subject, where if Francis is present at all, it is as

a diminutive figure kneeling at the foot of the Cross. The saint as a full participant in Passion scenes is found mainly in paintings from the late fourteenth century onwards, beginning with Agnolo Gaddi and Lorenzo Monaco (Palladino, 1996). Before that time, such a composition is known only in the present image and in a *verre eglomisé* roundel in Paris (Louvre, OA 5966), possibly also painted in Assisi, perhaps by a follower of Puccio Capanna (Hueck, 1991; Cerri, 1992).

Both the palette and modeling of the figures in this illumination find a close point of reference in the work of the Master of Saint Francis, specifically as reflected in the processional Crucifix unanimously attributed to the artist in the National Gallery, London. Like the London Cross, the Crucifixion in the present cutting reflects a different stage in the artist's development than his only known dated work, the monumental Cross in the Galleria Nazionale in Perugia, inscribed 1272; a phase marked by overstated decorative concerns, rounder body proportions and elaborately rendered, billowing draperies. The chronological relationship of the London Cross to that in Perugia remains a subject of debate even in most recent studies, divided between those who situate it at least a decade later in the 1280s (Davies and Gordon, 1988; Bomford, 1989) and others who instead place it earlier, sometime in the 1260s (Boskovits, 1973b; Gordon, 1984; Romano, 1994).

A date before 1272 for the illuminated Crucifixion, and by extension for the London Cross, is suggested by a comparison of this cutting with a comparable scene of the Crucifixion in a missal dated 1273 from the Cathedral of San Rufino in Assisi (Assisi, Archivio Capitolare, MS 8). Although inexplicably referred to by Hindman (1998) with an attribution to the Master of Saint Francis, this missal has generally been considered not so much in relation to the Master's work, as to that nucleus of manuscripts produced for the Basilica of Assisi between around 1280 and 1290, which betray in equal measure the

persistent legacy of the art of Giunta Pisano and the new style of Cimabue and the team of Roman artists working in the Upper Church of Assisi in the last quarter of the thirteenth century (Todini, 1982; Sesti, 1990). These Roman or Cimabuesque elements, discernible above all in the statuesque quality of the figures and expressively dramatic gesture of Saint John the Evangelist in the San Rufino Missal, are completely absent from the Crucifixion cutting, in which plastic and naturalistic concerns are secondary to decorative ones, such as the elegant arabesques of the figures' draperies and the almost abstract arrangement of the three Holy women, one on top of the other, with the body of the third disappearing completely behind the other two—a compositional detail derived perhaps from the London Cross, where it was actually determined by the requirements of the narrow space.

The identification of this cutting, the only known surviving example of the Master of Saint Francis' activity as a manuscript illuminator, lends new support to arguments (Bigaroni, 1975; Sesti, 1990) for the existence of an active scriptorium in the Library of the Convent of Assisi involved not only in the writing but also in the illumination of manuscripts. As many of the larger historiated miniatures in the surviving books from the Convent have been excised, we cannot know precisely to what extent major artists involved in the decoration of the Basilica, such as the Master of Saint Francis, were also active as illuminators. That the Master of Saint Francis might have been at the head of such a workshop in the 1260s is now a realistic possibility, though it must remain a question open to debate. [LBK-PP]

*Bibliography*: Hindman, 1998, no. 12, pp. 32–33.

141

# Umbrian

ca. 1280

**39**

*Antiphonary*
Parchment, 52 × 38 cm, ff. 315.II
Assisi, Biblioteca del Sacro Convento, cantorino 2, MS 1

This large manuscript, used for liturgical chants, contains the antiphons for the period from the first Sunday in Lent until the feast of the Birth of Mary (September 8). Produced in Umbria, the book has a rich decoration, though unfortunately thirty of the initial letters were partly repainted by a clumsy hand at an unknown date.

The manuscript comprises a large number of initials ornamented with geometric and plant motifs traced in blue and red. Numerous other initials are illuminated with phytomorphic motifs forming compositions of vine shoots and lanceolate leaves of different colors, in which blue, purple and gray predominate. Three initials are historiated: the initial "I" of *Iste* (f. 258v) encloses the scene of a martyrdom with a saint kneeling as he is beheaded by his executioner; on the two levels of the "A" of *Absterget* (f. 267v), Christ is represented in the upper part and the assembly of saints in the lower part.

The most interesting image in the work is undoubtedly that of the initial "F" of *Franciscus* (f. 235r) where the artist has depicted the miracle of the cripples in front of the saint's tomb at Assisi. The illumination is divided into two levels: above, we see a fine work of architecture in the shape of a dome supported by columns forming arches from which hang three oil lamps; below, under a tre-foil arch from which three more oil lamps are suspended, the saint, his feet bare and his head circled by a golden halo, is dressed in his brown frock. He is lying on a high catafalque, carved directly out of the rock, at whose base sit the three cripples.

Of all the illuminated antiphonaries that were probably produced in Assisi in the years 1280–90, this is the only one to have come down to us (Assirelli and Sesti, 1990, p. 117). The style of the principal artist who played a part in the execution of the book—called the "Master of the Assisi Choir Books"— matches that of various manuscripts produced in the Bologna region (Ciardi, 1982a, p. 351) and bears a resemblance to the manner of the "Master of the Treasury," author of the panel representing *Saint Francis and Four Posthumous Miracles* (Scarpellini, 1980b, pp. 37–38).

Various miniatures that may have been removed from the book have been found at different times, although the experts do not agree over their attribution. Filippo Todini (1985, p. 327) considers one detached folio, formerly in the Von Nemes collection, to come from the Assisi codex. Another four illuminated initials are in the Germanisches Nationalmuseum in Nuremberg (Lunghi, 1985, p. 595). More recently, four more illuminated initials from this antiphonary have been identified (Labriola, 1997, p. 108). [GM]

*Bibliography*: Scarpellini, 1980b, pp. 25–61; Ciardi, 1982a, pp. 349–50; Todini, 1985, pp. 317–35; Assirelli and Sesti, 1990; Labriola, 1997.

## Master of the Assisi Choirbooks
Umbrian or Roman, active last quarter thirteenth century

**40**
*Four Cuttings from an Antiphonary*

**40/1**
Initial P with *Christ Blessing and a Prophet*, 16.8 × 11.4 cm

**40/2**
Initial S with the *Misfortunes of Job* (?), 13.5 × 9.8 cm

**40/3**
Initial P with *Saint Paul Preaching*, 24.5 × 12 cm

**40/4**
Initial F with *Saint Francis Preaching*, 33.8 x 11.2 cm

Tempera on parchment
Nuremberg, Germanisches Nationalmuseum

These four illuminated initials are reasonably presumed to have been cut from a single choirbook on the basis of their common figure style and closely similar decorative borders. The initial P with Saint Paul preaching is commonly misidentified as a sermon of Saint John the Evangelist, but the text preserved alongside the inital leaves no doubt of its actual subject: "vas electionis Paulus" [You are the chosen vessel, Paul], from the Commemoration of Saint Paul on June 30. The initial F is presumed to show a sermon of Saint Francis, although the tonsured figure does not wear a knotted rope belt nor does he bear signs of the stigmata. The subject of the initial S is generally described as the Misfortunes of Job, in reference to Job seated on a dunghill outside the walls of a city and mocked by his friends, as in a similar initial by the Master of the San Lorenzo Choirbooks in an antiphonary in the Museo dell'Opera del Duomo in Orvieto (Todini, 1989, II, fig. 209). The apocryphal Book of Job forms the gospel readings for the first two weeks in September, and it is possible therefore that the initial began the responsory "Si bona suscepimus de manu Dei, mala autem quare non sustineamus?" [We accept good things from God; and why should we not accept evil?], repeated at matins throughout that period. It could also represent the Parable of Dives and Lazarus, the gospel reading for Thursday of the second week of Quaresima, although no antiphons in modern use for that day begin with the initial S. The initial P with Saint Paul and the initial F with Saint Francis have been pasted into a collage with other decorative fragments presumably cut from the same book, completed with panels of modern decoration to fill out the rectangular field.

One of these four cuttings, the initial F with Saint Francis preaching, was first brought to the attention of modern critics by Miklos Boskovits (1983), who attributed it (without reference to any of its three companions in Nuremberg) to one of the most important Italian illuminators of the late dugento, the Master of the Deruta-Salerno Missals. Boskovits argued for a Roman rather than Umbrian or Tuscan origin (as had been proposed in the past, see Toesca, 1927, p. 1094; Bologna, 1955, pp. 23–25, 76–77) for this master, in recognition of the provenance of his recognized manuscripts from places as widely removed as Umbria, the Kingdom of Naples, Rome, and Siena, and his familiarity with the work of Cimabue earlier than the Assisi frescoes (Cimabue is documented as resident in Rome from 1272).

Acknowledging similarities between all four of the Nuremberg initials and the work of the Master of the Deruta-Salerno Missals, Elvio Lunghi (1986) nonetheless assigned them to a distinct artist who had been isolated shortly before by Todini (1982, pp. 162, 189) as the Master of the Assisi Choirbooks, the author of the few remaining illuminations in the fragmentary antiphonaries from the Basilica of San Francesco at Assisi (Assisi, Biblioteca Comunale, MS 1). Todini later (1989), expanded his own and Lunghi's attributions to include cuttings formerly in private collections in Munich, Paris, New York, and London. For Todini and Lunghi, this painter was as dependent on the style of Cimabue's frescoes in the Upper Church of San Francesco as he was on the example of the Master of the Deruta-Salerno Missals, representing a brief moment of supremely Gothic elegance in the last decade of the thirteenth century. The only scholar to have addressed this problem more recently, Ada Labriola (1997), seems to concur in maintaining a separate identity for the painter of the Assisi antiphonaries but stresses nevertheless his strong ties to the Master of the Deruta-Salerno Missals. For Labriola, the Nuremberg initials may be related to the early style of the Deruta Master, probably still in the 1270s, while other initials in the group more closely resemble his later work in the 1290s.

The stylistic and decorative connections among the cuttings united by Todini and Lunghi are so compelling that it is difficult to envision their having been executed over a period of as many as two decades. It is in fact possible that all of them were executed for a single set of antiphonaries destined for use in the Basilica of San Francesco, but codicological analyses of the surviving volume of the antiphonary (cat. no. 39 in the present exhibition) are not yet detailed enough to allow any of them to be inserted in their proper sequence there. It is also difficult to state with confidence that the author of these illuminations, who for clarity and convenience should retain the designation Master of the Assisi Choirbooks, was a wholly independent artist or whether he might have been a member of a larger scriptorium headed by the Master of the Deruta-Salerno Missals, or if such a scriptorium might represent a native Umbrian trend in manuscript illumination developing in the cosmopolitan atmosphere of the "Cantiere d'Assisi" rather than a Roman or other extra-Umbrian phenomenon. The question of dating the Assisi choirbooks to the 1270s, 1280s, or 1290s is equally difficult to resolve. Umbrian manuscript painting developed in close rapport with monumental painting of the same period, but it is not yet clear whether it assumed a purely derivative role or whether it was just as often the source of innovations that appeared shortly afterwards in paintings on panel or in fresco. [LBK-PP]

*Bibliography*: Bredt, 1903, nos. 32, 34; Boskovits, 1983, pp. 261, 271 n. 8; Lunghi, 1986, pp. 595, 614; Todini, 1989, I, p. 116; Labriola, 1997, p. 108.

40/1

40/2

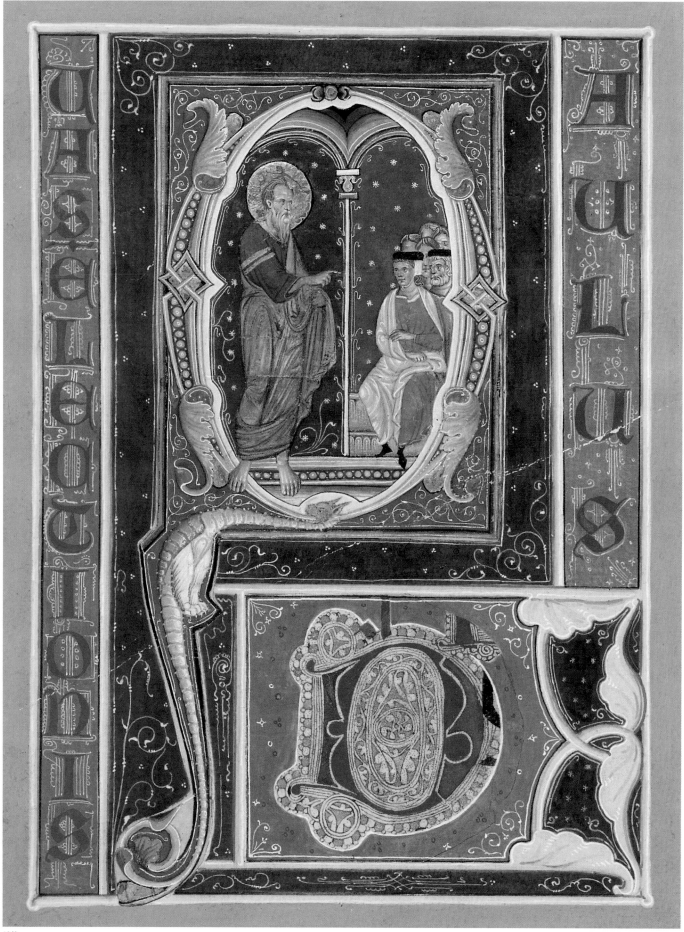

40/3

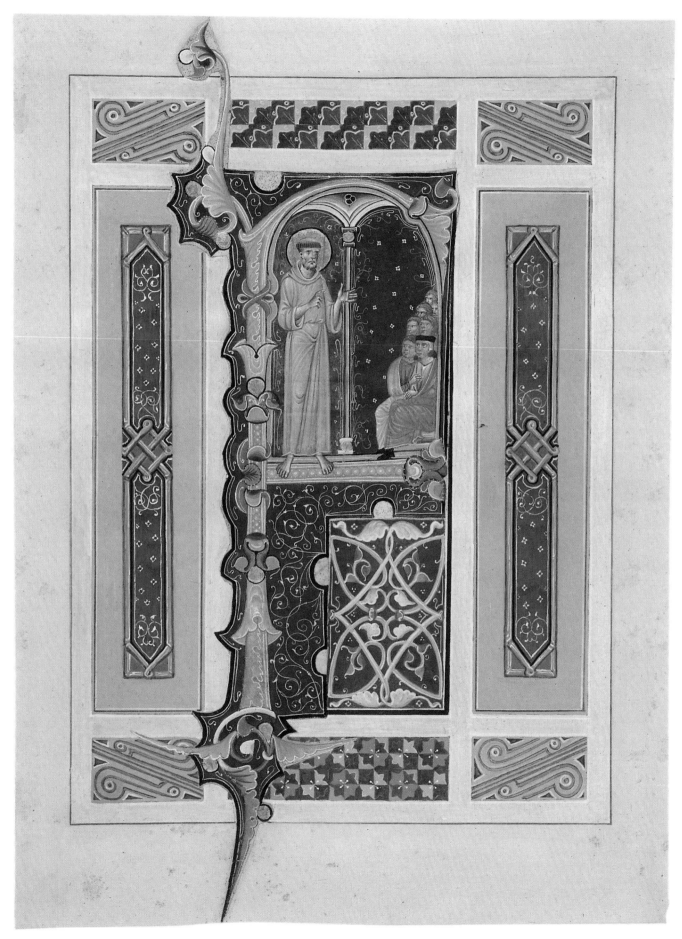

# John Pecham

Last third thirteenth century

**41**

*De Perspectiva*
Parchment, 16 × 11 cm, 179 ff.
Assisi, Biblioteca
Conventuale-Comunale,
MS 673

This book of miscellanea contains the first part of the *Tractatus de perspectiva*, along with other texts by Pecham and by several Parisian scholars of the thirteenth century.

The Friar Minor John Pecham, who was the first Franciscan to be appointed archbishop of Canterbury and then primate of England, taught theology at the university of Paris from 1269 to 1271–72.

The author of numerous texts of a theological and spiritual character, Pecham also took a great interest in science, as testified by this precious *Tractatus de perspectiva* in which the monk describes his studies on optics (Pecham—who died in 1292—was not the only Minorite of the thirteenth century to investigate scientific subjects). [GM]

*Bibliography*: Lindberg, 1970; Cenci, 1981, pp. 229–30.

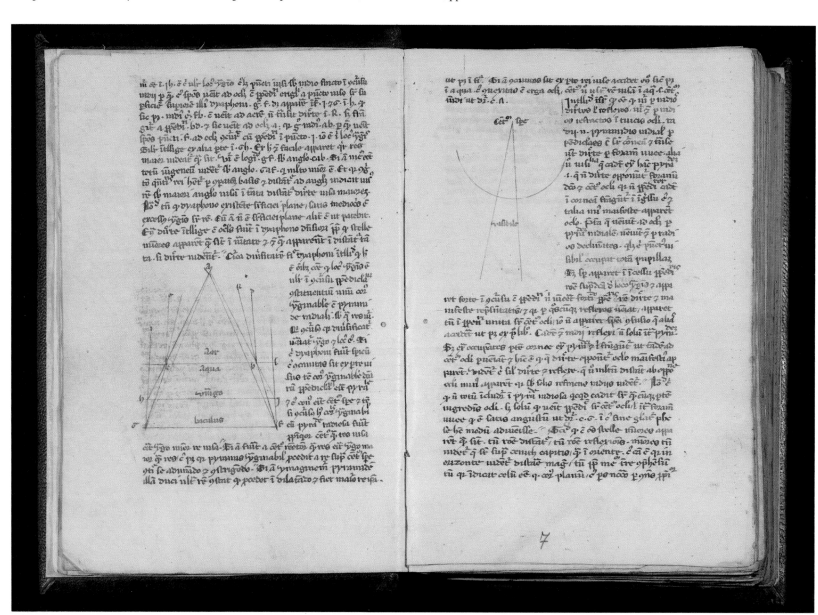

# Umbrian (?)
Fifteenth century

**42**

*Lexicon*
Parchment, 21.1 × 16 cm, 71 ff.
Assisi, Biblioteca Conventuale-Comunale, MS 665

This manuscript—to which the title *Liber qui interpretatur unumquodque verbum* was added in the sixteenth century—contains a lexicon, that is to say a dictionary of Latin.

The work—intended for personal use—may be the same manuscript as the one mentioned in the inventory published by Alessandri (1906, p. 148 n. 110). This book used to belong to the friar Girolamo da Assisi, and entered the monastery library on his death.

The manuscript, laid out in two columns, is devoid of illustrations or decorations, apart from the fact that the initial letters of each entry and of the explanations that follow are written in red ink. [GM]

*Bibliography*: Alessandri, 1906; Cenci, 1981.

# TEXTILES

43

*The Franciscan Tree*
Tapestry in wool and silk,
445 × 333 cm
Assisi, Museo-Tesoro della Basilica
di San Francesco

Of all the paraments donated to the sanctuary by Sixtus IV during his pontificate, the only ones to have survived are this tapestry and the altar frontal representing Saint Francis Displaying His Stigmata. Unfortunately it is impossible to establish whether the work was commissioned for the purpose by Sixtus IV or whether he simply passed on to the Basilica a gift that had been made to him. The highly unusual iconography of this work, intended to exalt the Franciscan Order, must have been devised by a scholar or clergyman.

This type of image, inspired by Saint Bernardino's treatise entitled *Lignum Vitæ*, consists of a symbolic representation of the Cross as a living tree, and therefore with branches, leaves and flowers. The iconography is also connected with the historic and heraldic theme of the "Genealogical Tree," in this case that of the Franciscan Order, depicted here in a hierarchy that is in itself symbolic.

At the center of the tapestry we see Francis receiving the stigmata from Christ, set against the background of a tent with an inscription. Out of this tent emerge the roots and trunk of the Franciscan Tree, whose foliage bears flowers on which the figures of Franciscan saints are seated. On the left we see: Saint Elzear holding a wreath of white and red roses that evokes the rosary and a sword symbolizing his aristocratic origins; Saint Clare holding the monstrance that she used to drive the Saracens out of Assisi; and Saint Louis of Toulouse with his royal crown and cope adorned with the French *fleur-de-lis* (an allusion to the fact that the saint renounced the throne of Naples to enter the Franciscan Order). On the right, Saint Elizabeth of Hungary is holding the cloak that she gave to a pauper in one hand and the three crowns symbol-

izing her royal status as virgin, wife, and widow; Saint Anthony of Padua clasping a processional cross and a book representing the divine word that he used to repulse the demon, depicted here in the form of a horned lion; and Saint Bernardino of Siena with the radiant "Signum Christi" and three episcopal miters corresponding to the three bishoprics that he turned down out of humility. At top center and above the figure of Saint Francis, the Virgin is surrounded by a glory: she is holding an apple, the forbidden fruit of the Garden of Eden that symbolizes the fall of humankind. Seated on Mary's lap, the Child is clutching a pomegranate, Christian emblem of the Resurrection. As if to establish a direct link between the pontiff, Saint Francis and the Virgin and Child, Sixtus IV is portrayed in the middle of the bottom row, against a blue background strewn with flowers. At the foot of the pope's figure, we see the coat of arms of the della Rovere family with the crossed papal keys. On either side of Sixtus IV stand Nicholas IV and Alexander V—two Franciscan pontiffs—and alongside them Saint Bonaventure (who had not yet been canonized) and Cardinal Pierre d'Auriole, doctors of theology. The *millefleurs* decoration is intended to evoke the Garden of Christ, a memory of the lost Earthly Paradise and prefiguration of the Celestial Paradise to come.

The iconographic program of this tapestry—which seems at first sight to be a celebration of the Franciscan Order—also conveys a message of religious politics that could only be understood by a small number of people. By way of a response to the discords that were tearing apart the Franciscans, in fact, the tent (inscribed with the words "Tres. ordines. hic. ordinat") in which Saint Francis is located constitutes an allusion to a spiritual unity whose roots lie in the figure of the saint himself, just as the pomegranate whose rind protects a multitude of seeds evokes the union of a large number of people under a single authority.

In order to assert the primacy of the

Franciscan Order in the diffusion of the cult of Mary—at that time the principal prerogative of the Dominicans, who professed devotion to the rosary—the artist has depicted Saint Elzear with a wreath of white roses (joyful mysteries) and red roses (sorrowful mysteries) embodying the original form of the rosary. The representation of the Virgin and the Child at the top of the Franciscan Tree is also intended to exalt the Marian cult. There is yet another political message concealed in the image: the presence of the Franciscan pope Alexander V—elected in 1409 but only recognized in France, England and certain regions of Germany and Italy—is meant to provide a definitive legitimization of his status.

In addition, the work is imbued with a subtle numerological symbology based on the numbers three (the Trinity)—there are three Franciscan popes, doctors of the Church, divine images and saints in each of the two series—and fifteen—corresponding to the *Pater* of the rosary and the stations of the Passion—for this is the total number of figures. Neither the records relating to the execution of this tapestry nor its preparatory cartoon have come down to us, but it is likely that it was made in Brussels: at the end of the fifteenth century, in fact, the most precious such works were being produced by Flemish factories and it is believed that other *millefleurs* tapestries, such as the *Tapestry of Philip the Good* (Historisches Museum, Bern) or the series of the *Lady and the Unicorn* (Musée National du Moyen-Âge et des Thermes de Cluny, Paris), were woven in this city.

As for the date, some conclusions can be drawn directly from the tapestry, which could not have been made before 1471, the year Sixtus IV was made pope, nor after 1482, the date of the canonization of Saint Bonaventure, who is represented here not among the saints but among the doctors. [PL]

*Bibliography*: *Il Tesoro della Basilica*, 1980, pp. 161–65, pl. CCII–CCIX; Viale Ferrero, 1982, pp. 125–26.

153

**Florentine Workshop, design by Antonio di Iacopo d'Antonio Benci, called Pollaiuolo**
Florence ca. 1431–32–Rome 1498

and **Francesco Botticini**
Florence 1446–1497

**44**
*Altar Frontal of Sixtus IV*
1476-78
Velvet, bouclé gold yarn and appliqués of knot and open stitch embroidery (gold and silver thread and polychrome silk), 84 × 380 cm, altar frontal; 29 × 370 cm, gilt frieze
Assisi, Museo-Tesoro della Basilica di San Francesco

This parament is made up of two elements that can be used independently of one another: an altar frontal made of cloth with embroidered applications and a gilt frieze adorned with embroidered figures and a fringe of gilded silver. This work was part of the set of sumptuous paraments donated by the Franciscan pope Sixtus IV to the Basilica of San Francesco, of which this altar frontal and a Flemish tapestry representing the *Franciscan Tree* are all that survive.

It can be stated with certainty that this altar frontal was offered to the sanctuary during the 1470s, but it is impossible to come up with a more precise date. In fact, even though this work is already listed in the inventory of the sacristy drawn up in 1473, it is evident that the entry, written in a different hand, was added later. It is very likely that the parament was donated either in 1476 (the date of the 250th anniversary of the death of Saint Francis), or in 1478 (the year in which the 250th anniversary of the saint's canonization was celebrated). A document in the monastery archives, also dated 1476, declares: "to the

guardian and friar Agnolo [di Gaspare Sanfiordi], four florins for going to Florence to ask for the parament of the high altar to be made for Count Gironimo [Riario], nephew of Sixtus IV."

The gold ground of this magnificent and seamless piece of weaving has a sumptuous decoration of bouclé, gilded and silvered motifs, standing out against the surrounding red velvet. Pope Sixtus IV della Rovere is represented in the middle, kneeling with his hands joined in prayer before Saint Francis, who is displaying the stigmata on his right hand and holding a cross in his left. Above, between the two figures, we see a sun symbolizing the divine light and twelve small flames that may be an allusion to the twelve apostles. It is possible that this iconography refers to a visit paid by Sixtus IV to Assisi, during which Saint Francis appeared to him as he was walking around Assisi, a story that is related in a nineteenth-century document. However, Father Palumbro thinks that the Sistine-Franciscan iconography

is based on the common practice of representing the donor at the feet of his patron saint. This hypothesis is supported by the fact that Sixtus IV's baptismal name was Francesco and that up until the beginning of his pontificate he had attributed everything that had occurred in his life and the progress of his career in the Church to the intercession of Saint Francis.

The faces—which were applied to the cloth afterward—are embroidered (knot stitch for the faces, open stitch for the saint's hair) to a design made with pen and ink on very fine silk. At the sides, a woven decoration presents a symmetrical pattern of oak branches with leaves and acorns, while a ribbon at the center is inscribed with the words: "SIXTUS / IIII. PONT / MAXIMUS." The outer frame consists of a branch stripped of leaves with a ribbon winding around it.

The design of the altar frontal was first attributed to Pollaiuolo by Venturi (1906), who discerned significant stylistic affinities between the figure of Saint

Francis and that of Saint James in the panel painting executed for the church of San Miniato. Further support for this attribution is provided by a comparison with the paraments made for the baptistery of San Giovanni in Florence—now in the Museo dell'Opera del Duomo—commissioned by the Calimala guild from a group of embroiderers who came from all over Europe and based on preparatory drawings by Pollaiuolo.

As far as the execution is concerned, a document of 1477 tells us that the consuls of Florence had decided that the "embroiderers of the guild, that is to say Coppino (from Malines) and Paolo (from Verona), could make and embroider two faces for the pope," while the foliage is generally attributed to the Florentine weaver Malocchi.

The gilt frieze, framed by an oak branch adorned with acorns, has fifteen compartments and is embroidered with knot and open stitches. The compartments at each end are rectangular and enclose two angels supporting the coat of arms

of the della Rovere family. Inside the other compartments (square this time) are represented, starting on the left, Saint Catherine of Alexandria, Saint Anthony of Padua, Saint Gregory the Great (but, according to Marinangeli, Saint Sixtus the Second), Saint Francis, Saint John the Baptist, Saint Peter, the Virgin and Child, Saint Paul, Saint John the Evangelist, Saint Benedict, Saint Louis of Anjou, Saint Bernardino of Siena and Saint Clare. The author of the preparatory drawings for the frieze appears to have been Francesco Botticini, an artist belonging to the Pollaiuolo circle.

The iconographic program of the altar frontal reflects the rule of the time, which placed the Franciscan Order under the protection of the papacy: while the saints embroidered in the compartments are arranged in a descending hierarchical scale (from the center toward each end), the fact that the figures of Saint Francis (standing) and Sixtus IV (kneeling) are the same size tends to underline the importance of the pope in

his capacity as the supreme representative of divine authority.

Over the centuries, the work has undergone modifications: the short sides of the altar frontal and the gilt frieze have been cut; the two pieces of fabric—originally independent as the altar frontal was supported by a frame placed in front of the altar while the frieze was hooked onto the cloth—are now attached to the same lining and thus form a single parament; finally, during the restoration carried out in 1939, the figures of Saint Francis and Sixtus IV were brightened up with a few touches of paint. [PL]

*Bibliography*: *Il Tesoro della Basilica*, 1980, pp. 81–85, pl. XCIV–XCIX; Varoli Piazza, 1991; Cuoghi Costantini and Silvestri, 1991, pp. 103–5; Magro, 1991, pp. 47–53; *Tesori vaticani*, 1993, p. 287.

## Tuscan Workshop
End of sixteenth century

**45**

*Miter*

Silk, polychrome silk thread, gems, pearls, small silver rings, height 30 cm
Assisi, Museo-Tesoro della Basilica di San Francesco

The miter is the headdress worn by the pope, cardinals, and bishops at formal liturgical celebrations and its usage seems to have spread in the West after the year 1000. Originally, the miter consisted of a rounded bonnet but, over the course of the centuries, its form has undergone various modifications: thus it has developed from a sort of turban squashed in the middle to form two horns (first rounded and then pointed) to the headgear with points at right angles that is still in use today. The strips of cloth, also called "lappets," that hang from the back of the miter were already present in ancient miters, but their practical function has been lost and they have become purely decorative.

This miter consists of two stiff panels covered with red silk, held together by a gusset lining and by two lappets. On each side, a cord covered with gold thread runs along the outer edges and marks the internal subdivision. This takes the form of an upside-down "T" adorned with rosettes—decorated and alternating with precious stones—embroidered on the gold ground. At the sides, the cloth—to which a reticulated ground of gold thread has been applied —is entirely covered with a pattern of multiform flowers and leaves embellished with precious stones. This kind of miter, called *pretiosa* owing to the care lavished on its decoration, was only used for the highest functions.

As for the date of the object, a number of Tuscan fabrics from the second half of the sixteenth century, such as the hanging of the Pentecost now in Casentino (1574) and the embroidered and painted altar frontal in the Museo dell'Opera del Duomo in Florence (second half of sixteenth century), have a similar decoration made up of phytomorphic motifs. This type of design and work indicates that the miter was made at the end of the sixteenth century, while the fineness of the execution suggests a major Tuscan center of production, perhaps Florence.

Despite the loss of gems and appliqués, this miter has retained all of its splendor. [PL]

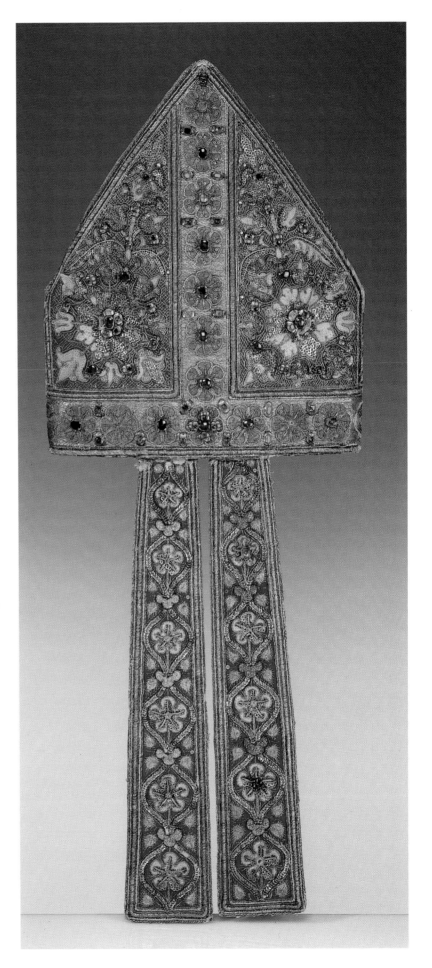

# RELIQUARIES

## Parisian Workshop

Late thirteenth century–early fourteenth century

**46**

*Reliquary of the Seamless Robe*
Cast, embossed, chased and gilded
silver, 28.5 × 24 × 9.5 cm, front
Assisi, Museo-Tesoro della Basilica
di San Francesco

This reliquary, enshrined in an architectural setting, consists of slender columns supporting three trefoil arches surmounted by an openwork trefoil and crowned with a tympanum adorned with lions rampant and pinnacles. Inside the lateral arches are set statuettes of Saint Francis and Saint Clare, at whose feet one and two nuns respectively kneel in prayer. The central arch, larger than the others, has a grating adorned with quatrefoils—and surmounted by a bust of the Risen Christ sculpted in the round—through which the relics can be seen. Two silver plaquettes occupy the rear of the reliquary. A Christ in Majesty with two angels at the sides holding a censer is depicted on the upper plaquette, while a Nativity is represented on the lower plaquette: Mary is lying down and, at the foot of the bed, Saint Joseph seems to be pointing at the crib with the Child wrapped in swaddling clothes, under the muzzles of the ox and the donkey.

This object, which was already listed in the inventory of 1338, was donated to the Basilica of San Francesco by "Domina Johanna regina uxor quondam Phylippis regis Francie": this may have been Queen Joan of Navarre, wife of Philip IV, or Joan of Burgundy, wife of Philip V. The shrine holds a large number of relics, but the most important of them is the Seamless Robe, a symbolic allusion to the unity and indivisibility of the Church. The fact that the work was a royal commission is demonstrated by the material used (gilded silver rather than copper) and by the simple and sober style that shows the relics off to advantage. In addition, the reliquary has an architectural structure which has often been compared with that of the Sainte-Chapelle, and may therefore have been made by a Parisian goldsmith working for the court.

As for the date, the fantastic animals with the head of a dog and the body of a dragon that support the rectangular base were used widely in the art of the Northern France from the second half of the thirteenth century onward. The form and the chased decoration of this reliquary, which resembles a Gothic tabernacle, provide confirmation of this date. The front face, on the other hand, is a perfect example of the type of reliquary "with statuettes" that was common at the beginning of the fourteenth century, while the modeling of the figures and their arrangement to create an illusion of depth suggest that this piece was made in the closing decades of the thirteenth century. [PL]

*Bibliography*: Liscia Bemporad, 1980, pp. 94–95, pl. C–CII; *L'Art au temps des rois maudits*, 1998, pp. 193–95.

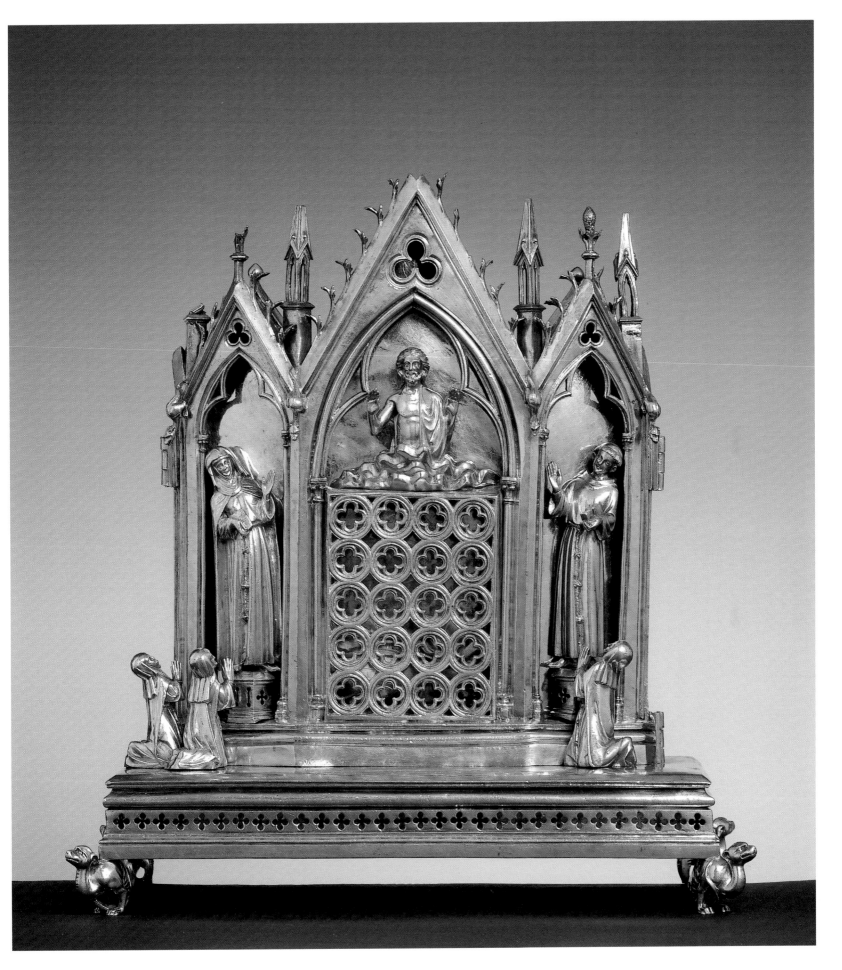

**Parisian Workshop**
Late thirteenth century–early
fourteenth century

**46**

*Reliquary of the Seamless Robe*
Cast, embossed, chased and gilded
silver, 28.5 × 24 × 9.5 cm, back
Assisi, Museo-Tesoro della Basilica
di San Francesco

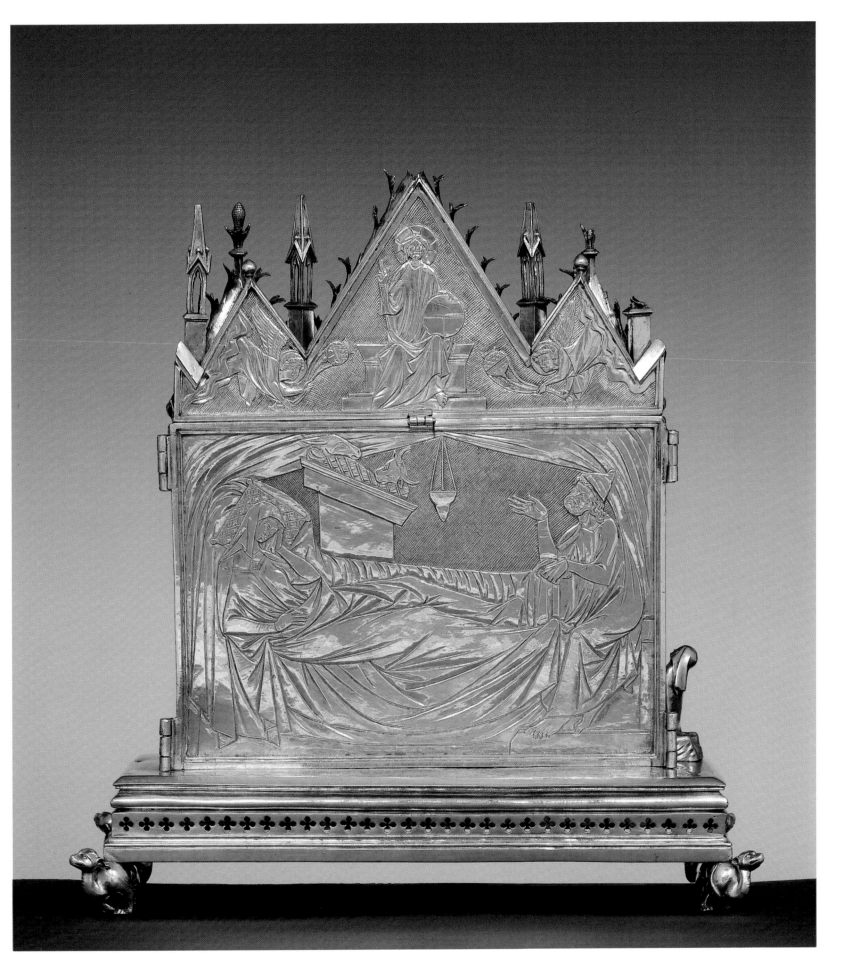

163

# Roman Workshop
ca. 1278–81

**47**

*Reliquary of Saint Andrew's Finger*
Gilded, engraved and chased silver,
rock crystal, red gemstones (garnets?),
39.2 × 21.5 × 12.6 cm
Assisi, Museo-Tesoro della Basilica
di San Francesco

The reliquary of Saint Andrew's finger
was donated to the Sacro Convento by
Pope Nicholas IV (Girolamo Masci,
1288–92), the first pontiff to be elected
from the Franciscan Order, as part of a
major program of commissions and donations undertaken on behalf of the
monastery in Assisi (in this connection
see the account of Guccio di Mannaia's
chalice elsewhere in this catalogue). It
may have been part of the group of diverse objects and precious ornaments
donated on the occasion of the promul-
gation of the bull of May 14, 1288,
which authorized the provincial minister and guardian of the Assisi monastery
to use, "de discretorum fratrum ejusdem ecclesie Sancti Francisci consilio,"
the profit from alms to "facere conservari, reparari, aedificari, emendari, ampliari aptari et ornari Ecclesias Sancti
Francisci de Assisio et Sanctae Mariae
de Portiuncola" (*The Registers of
Nicholas IV*, 1886–93, vol. I, p. 13 n. 74).
The bull was accompanied by a summary giving a list of the objects, but this
has unfortunately been lost.
The work can be recognized from a description in an article of the inventory
of 1338: "In primis una capsa de argento deaurata plena multis reliquiis, orna-
ta lapidibus pretiosiis cum cristallis in
modum portarum: super quam est una
crux de argento deaurata in qua est
lignum vere crucis coopertum cristallo;
quam misit dominus Nicholaus papa
quartus, de ordine minorum" (Alessandri and Pennacchi, 1920, p. 13). In the
following inventory, a more precise description of the relics is given: "de digito
sancti Petri et sancti Pauli apostolorum,
de stola sancti Jacobi et multe alie sancte
reliquie sunt ibi" (Alessandri and Pennacchi, 1920, p. 44).
The reliquary is a casket in the form of a
parallelepiped with a lid shaped like a
truncated pyramid. The main face of the
casket is adorned with six semicircular
blind arches bordered with an alternating series of rock crystals and red cabochons. Six more arches are engraved on
the opposite face. The smaller sides are
decorated with two engraved arches
framing figures of saints: Saint Francis
and Saint Pudentiana on the right, Saint
Anthony and Saint Agnes on the left.
Two cabochons of rock crystal are set on
the upper face of the lid. The front face
is adorned with four small blind arches
like those on the faces of the casket, also
bordered with rock crystals. Four
shields are engraved on the other three
faces—one on each of the small faces
and two on the main face—in which
symbols of the Evangelists are set. The
box is closed longitudinally by a long
clasp decorated with engraved patterns
and terminating in two lily motifs.
At the center of the lid is set a support
for a cross, whose rock crystal stem is
bordered with acanthus leaves. A relic of
the Holy Cross was originally lodged in
a cruciform space in the middle. The
ends of the arms, with a three-lobed
profile, are adorned on the front with
four settings from which the stones have
been lost, while the back is engraved
with the four symbols of the Evangelists, like those on the lid.
The reliquary, of very high quality, is in
fact quite unique in thirteenth-century
goldsmith's work. The presence of a
stamp with keys in a shield refers, in all
likelihood, to a workshop active in
Rome: a similar hallmark can be seen on
a small plaque added in the second half
of the fourteenth century to the silver-
plated cover of the icon of the Savior re-
puted to be of miraculous origin in the
Sancta Sanctorum (Bulgari, 1958, I, p.
3). Two other hallmarks are set on the
shaft of the cross: a star superimposed
on a Latin cross and another on a Greek
cross.
Although there seems to be no doubt
that the reliquary formed part of the
donation of Nicholas IV, it is far from
easy to establish the date of its manufac-
ture. In fact the work displays a certain,
underlying archaism that contrasts, for
instance, with the new Gothic tendencies and innovative use made of translucent enamel in the other sumptuous
piece of gold work donated to the Sacro
Convento d'Assisi by Nicholas IV, to
mention once again the chalice of Guccio di Mannaia, which was probably
made around 1290.
It has been pointed out in this regard
(Hueck, 1982b) that the presence of the
images of Saints Pudentiana and Agnes
on the reliquary might serve to date its
commission by Nicholas IV to some
time before 1288, the year of his election
to the Holy See, and after 1278, the year
in which he was appointed cardinal
deacon of the Roman Basilica of Santa
Pudenziana by Nicholas III and took up
permanent residence in Rome. The period of time over which the reliquary
may have been executed could be even
further limited by the fact that the future pope was appointed cardinal bishop of Palestrina in 1281 and gave up the
title of Santa Pudenziana.
The rendering of the engraved figures,
as well as of the shields with symbols of
the Evangelists on the lid, is characterized by a feeling of solidity and volume
that is reminiscent of the classical tendencies to be found in Roman figurative
art during this period. Thus it does not
seem over bold to propose a typological
reference to the paintings of the Sancta
Sanctorum (ca. 1280), and in particular
to the figures of the saints situated in
the lunettes of the mosaics of the
chapel, as well as to the frescoes on the
ceiling with symbols of the Evangelists.
Moreover, from an iconographic viewpoint, independent figures of saints and
of martyrs had served for centuries as
the focal points in the decoration of the
apses of Roman churches, and the
"new" Franciscan saints, Anthony and
of course Francis himself, were soon to
join them, at the behest of Nicholas IV.
Within the framework of the program
of figurative renovation of the apses of
San Giovanni in Laterano (1291) and
Santa Maria Maggiore (1296), Nicholas
in effect had the figures of the two saints
of the order, canonized just over half a
century earlier, added to the traditional
iconography of the apsidal mosaics.
The architectural structure of the reliquary of Saint Andrew's finger is influenced to some extent by Northern
European models, chiefly from France
and the region of the Meuse, represented in Rome by numerous treasures in
the city's main basilicas; on the other
hand, its relations with the contemporary production of Byzantine gold-
smiths are of little significance.
The large size of the rock crystal cross
set on the lid is unusual, indeed almost unique in the output of the thirteenth century. The trefoil extremities
of its arms are derived, without any
doubt, from French gothic works produced in the second half of the thirteenth century. [AT]

*Bibliography*: Kleinschmidt, 1915;
Alessandri and Pennacchi, 1920; Zocca,
1936; Bulgari, 1958; Liscia Bemporad,
1980; Hueck, 1982b; Ciardi, 1991.

## Workshops in Limoges and Umbria
Mid-thirteenth century
and mid-fourteenth century

**48**

*Reliquary of Saint Francis's Robe (then of the Companions of Saint Ursula)*
Gilded and embossed copper, gilded and engraved glass, rock crystal and other gemstones, champlevé enamels, 27 × 37 × 21.1 cm
Assisi, Museo-Tesoro della Basilica di San Francesco

This reliquary in copper, called the reliquary of Saint Ursula, takes the form of a parallelepiped with a faceted lid. The front of the casket has three openings shaped like gemeled windows with trefoil arches. They hold transparent panes of glass through which the interior is visible. Three medallions are set on the front part of the lid. The central medallion is made of gilded and engraved glass. Two rock crystals are mounted on the smaller sides, while three more rock crystals are set on the top of the lid. Beads of crystal and jasper once ran along the other edges, but most of them have been lost. The medallion of gilded glass is decorated with the Stigmatization of Saint Francis and the seraph has the features of the crucified Christ. There is an almost horizontal break in the glass cover. On the base of the reliquary, five copper plaquettes are decorated with champlevé enamels, three of them adorned with a cross and vine shoots. The other two are illustrated with scenes (*The Magi before Herod* and *The Journey of the Magi*; *The Adoration of the Magi*).

The presence of relics at Assisi connected with the martyrdom of Saint Ursula and her companions is attested since 1317: they had been brought back from Cologne by a friar who had gone there expressly to obtain them. This relic—according to the treasury inventory of 1338—was the head of one of the eleven thousand Virgins killed along with Ursula. A new relic (also the head of one of the saint's companions) is mentioned in the inventory of 1473. The inventory of 1566 records the presence of five heads: two of them set on their respective busts while the others were located in the reli-

quary of Saint Gereon. In 1624, reference was made to the transfer of the heads that had been kept with the remains of Gereon to the reliquary reproduced here, a reliquary that had up until then contained "the robe worn by Saint Francis at his death" (*Libro degli Inventari* s. B, n. 38, c. 12r). In 1797, the two heads set on busts were also placed in this casket.

The principal studies devoted to this reliquary raise the problem of the contemporaneity of the different parts of the object, and more particularly the gilded glass of the lid and the enameled plaquettes of the base. While the plaquettes—made in Limoges around the middle of the thirteenth century—are elements of another reliquary that had been broken up and then used at an unknown date to reinforce the base of this piece, this is not the case with the gilded glass of the lid, which is a simplified revival of the early Christian technique of gilded glassware. Whereas that type of glass consisted of a gold leaf placed between two thermally welded discs of glass, here the upper sheet of glass has merely been placed on top to protect the decoration underneath. According to some experts, this medallion—whose style looks more polished and sophisticated in relation to the simplicity of the reliquary—must have been produced later (between the first and the second half of the fourteenth century, while the reliquary itself was made between the end of the thirteenth century and the very beginning of the fourteenth) and then applied to the lid that we see today. Gnoli (1921–22, p. 428) holds that the reliquary and medallion date from the same period and attributes them to two different artists (he believes that the reliquary was made in Assisi and the medallion in Siena). More recently, Liscia Bemporad (1980, pp. 99–100) has proposed an Umbrian provenance for both elements, and suggests that they might be the work of a single workshop influenced—as far as the gilded glass is concerned—by the iconographic repertory provided by the numerous works of art in the Basilica.

Reasons of an iconographic character lead us to think that the reliquary and medallion had been designed from the outset for Francis's robe. One notes, in fact, the force of the relationship established between the saint's humble garment (the one "in which he died," as it is described in the inventory of 1624) visible through the openings of the reliquary, and the gilded glass which shows us Francis wearing the habit while he receives the stigmata—a mysterious evocation of Jesus's "death of the cross" (Phil. 2:8). And it is no coincidence if, in the iconography chosen for this scene, the image of Christ Crucified has replaced that of the seraph. So this reliquary, like the order's other contemporary sources, was intended to encourage the faithful to meditate on the intimate union between the saint from Assisi and the dying Christ, so that the robe—offered for veneration—is presented as a sort of holy shroud that once wrapped Francis's body, touched by grace. [UU]

*Bibliography*: Kleinschmidt, 1915, I, p. 276; Gnoli, 1921–22, pp. 428–30; Zocca, 1936, p. 130; Hertlein, 1965, pp. 57–58; Liscia Bemporad, 1980, pp. 98–100.

**Parisian Workshop**
ca. 1260–70

**49**

*Reliquary of the Holy Thorn*
Partially gilded, embossed, engraved
and chased silver, rock crystal,
13.5 × 6.5 cm
Assisi, Museo-Tesoro della Basilica
di San Francesco

A gilded band around the circular base
of this reliquary bears the following inscription: "spinone de sacros(an)c(t)a
corona domini." From the base it rises
in a smooth, funnel-shaped shaft, interrupted at the center by a cluster adorned
with six studs. These are decorated with
round plaquettes inlaid with simple
geometric patterns in niello. The reliquary is fixed directly onto the shaft and
consists of an almond-shaped frame
containing a rock crystal, hollowed out
to hold the thorn.
The history of this object is interesting:
while not mentioned in the inventory
of 1338, the reliquary is to be found in
the list of relics possessed by the
monastery in 1350. In this connection,
it is said that "sanctus Ludovicus res
Francie per manus fratris Bonaventura
generalis ministri misit isti conventui
pro reverentia s(an)c(t)i Francisci"
(Kleinschmidt, 1915, I, p. 27). Owing to
its simplicity—and despite the importance of the relic—it was not included
in any other inventory, apart from that
of 1624.
It also received little study and its erro-
neous dating (to the fourteenth century) was not corrected until 1965, when
Hertlein finally succeeded in recon-
structing the history of the reliquary in
a convincing manner (cf. Hertlein,
1965, pp. 58–63, whose conclusions are
cited in Liscia Bemporad, 1980, p. 96).
Hertlein based these conclusions on the
inventory of 1350, which associated the
reliquary with a gift made by Saint
Louis, king of France, to the Basilica of
San Francesco, and concluded that the
reliquary must predate the death of
Saint Bonaventure in 1270. It is also essential to compare this object with a
reliquary of the Holy Thorn in the Swiss
abbey of Saint-Maurice-d'Augaun. This,
recorded as a donation by Saint Louis in
1262, is identical—right down to the inscription—to the one in the Museum-
Treasury (the sole difference lies in the
precious stones that ring the mount).
At the time of his voyage to Constantinople, Louis IX had obtained from
Baldwin II of Jerusalem what was said
to be Christ's crown of thorns. It was for
this crown that the king had had the
Sainte-Chapelle built in Paris, and he
had also removed some of the thorns
and sent them to various places (there is
another of them in Assisi). The expert's
conclusion was as follows: the reliquary in Assisi came from the same
Parisian workshop as the Swiss reliquary and was made around the same
time. It is also likely that the object was
brought to Assisi by Saint Bonaventure
when he returned from his journey to
the French capital a few years later.
[UU]

*Bibliography*: Kleinschmidt, 1915, I, p.
280; Gnoli, 1921–22, p. 438; Zocca,
1936, p. 132; Hertlein, 1965, pp. 58–63;
Liscia Bemporad, 1980, p. 96.

**French Workshop**
Mid-fourteenth century

**50**
*Reliquary of the Hair of Saint Catherine*
Cast, chased and engraved silver, ivory,
and pearls, 20 × 8 × 5 cm
Assisi, Museo-Tesoro della Basilica
di San Francesco

This composite reliquary is made up of
several parts that are quite distinct from
one another. The small ivory casket,
pierced by trefoil openings through
which the relics can be seen, stands on a
base with geometrical mouldings supported, at the corners, by four baboons.
On the lid is set a slightly flattened node
decorated with acanthus leaves, from
which rises a spiral stem. On top of the
stem stands a crystal container in the
form of an ampoule. A band running
around the base of the cylindrical shrine
bears the inscription "de capillis sancte
caterine" in black enamel lettering. The
shrine is crowned by a small cupola
adorned with pearls and set on an openwork drum.
This object is cited for the first time in
the inventory drawn up in 1430. Originally the lantern must have had an
enamel decoration that has now been
lost. The small ampoule holding another relic and suspended from the stem
by metal wires was added in 1700,
along with several others that have
since vanished.
This work—given to the Basilica by
Cardinal Tommaso Orsini—must date
from the first half of the fourteenth century, as is clear from a comparison with
the reliquary of the Holy Thorn in
Monreale Cathedral, offered by King
Philip III of France. The similarities between the two objects suggest that the
reliquary was made in a workshop that
had close ties with the French court, as-
similating its taste and style. [PL]

*Bibliography*: *Il Tesoro della Basilica*,
1980, p. 101, pl. CX.

**51**

*Reliquary of Saint James*
Gilded, embossed, chased and engraved
silver, turquoise, amethysts,
49 × 15.5 cm
Assisi, Museo-Tesoro della Basilica
di San Francesco

This work is a perfect demonstration of
the vast range of architectural drawings
from which artists took the inspiration
for their reliquaries and monstrances,
producing small and imaginary
"caprices" that were much more fanciful
than the buildings actually constructed.
This reliquary, which still holds a fragment of the skull of Saint James the
Greater, may once have housed other
relics that more closely matched the
iconography (of scenes from the Passion) represented on the pyx.
Above the rounded foot, engraved with
arcs and small foliated scrolls, is set a
node made up of six rhomboidal bezels.
Its corners are adorned with flowers
while a rosette is set inside. Above the
node, the stem resumes its conical shape
and is decorated with the same patterns
as on the foot.

The small hexagonal temple stands on
slender round and hexagonal columns
crowned with crenelated turrets supporting trefoil arches. The pediments
are adorned with lions rampant along
the outer cornice and an amethyst and
an agate at the top. Each pediment is also decorated with busts in relief, set just
above the rise of the arch. The pyramidal roof rests on a drum pierced by windows with two lights, while the pinnacle
has been lost. The temple houses a
cylindrical pyx made of silver: in the
middle, this has an engraved arch framing a medallion depicting the Crucifixion at the top and a plaquette representing the Flagellation at the bottom.
This work, certainly produced by a
French goldsmithry, can be dated not
on the basis of its form—employed by
craftsmen over a relatively long period
—but by means of the plaquette, in
which the handling of the drapery and
the disposition of masses in the bodies
are typical of the mid-fourteenth century. [PL]

*Bibliography: Il Tesoro della Basilica,*
1980, pp. 103–4, pl. CXII.

## French and Umbrian Workshop

Second half fourteenth century
and ca. 1430–40

**52**

*Reliquary of Saint Blaise*
Embossed and chased silver,
gilded copper, translucent enamels,
31 × 12.5 cm
Assisi, Museo-Tesoro della Basilica
di San Francesco

The multifoil and mixtilinear base of
the reliquary has a border adorned
with beads. The smooth surface is divided into six crescents to which enameled rosettes are applied. The circular
stem is interrupted by a large node
adorned with gadroons on its top and
bottom, decorated in turn with enamel
rosettes. In addition, the band around
the middle is inscribed with the words
"+ DIGITUS BEATI BLASII +". The upper
part of the stem is decorated with floral
enamels, while the base of the reliquary
itself is covered with pointed and projecting leaves arranged to form a chalice. The reliquary is shaped like a
hexagonal aedicule and has large openings in the form of Gothic arches
through which the glass cylinder containing the relic can be seen (the openings are supported by slender wreathed
columns with Doric capitals surmounted by small flowers). The intrados of
the arches is trefoil while the extrados
forms a tympanum bordered with rows
of little flowers. Above the arches rises a
hexagonal spire with lions rampant on
the ribs and, at the top, a socket holding
a blue stone.

The reliquary is mentioned for the first
time in the inventory of 1430, where the
compilers noted the absence of the foot,
a piece of information that had vanished from the new inventory of the
treasury made in 1473. The object is referred to again in the inventory of 1624,
with the addition of another relic, one
of Saint Blaise's teeth, while the inventory of 1700 mentions yet another, this
time a piece of the saint's throat. Later, a
larger reliquary that has now been lost
was used to house the relics of the venerated miracle worker, of which many
had been accumulated in the meantime.
With the exception of the base, a stylistic examination of the reliquary allows
us to assign it, with a minimal margin of
error, to the fourteenth century, as is apparent from the lavish decoration of the
little temple and the abundance of plant
and geometrical motifs. This is rightly
emphasized by Liscia Bemporad (1980,
p. 102), who carries out a careful analysis of the studies devoted to this piece.
The absence of the foot mentioned in
the inventory of 1430 shows that it must
have been replaced (probably not long
afterward), perhaps because it had been
broken at the time the inventory was
drawn up or shortly before. The style of
the new foot supports this date. [UU]

*Bibliography*: Gnoli, 1921–22, pp. 435,
438; Kleinschmidt, 1926, I, p. 280; Zocca, 1936, p. 132; *Il Tesoro della Basilica*, 1980, pp. 102–3.

## Umbrian and Venetian Workshop
Late-fourteenth century
and late-fifteenth century

**53**

*Reliquary of the Column
of the Flagellation and the Stone
of the Holy Sepulcher*
Gilded, embossed, chased and engraved
silver and copper, enamel, and niello,
32.5 × 12.4 cm
Assisi, Museo-Tesoro della Basilica
di San Francesco

This reliquary is made up of two distinct parts joined together at an unknown date, but in any case before 1566, the year when this object is mentioned for the first time—as we see it today—in the inventories of the treasury. The base is multifoil and mixtilinear and its edge is adorned with a decoration made of simple mouldings interrupted, in the middle, by a row of embossed beads. Above it stands the foot in the form of a truncated pyramid on a hexagonal base. After another series of mouldings, the stem is set on top of the foot: also on a hexagonal base, it is adorned with cross- and diamond-shaped enamels and has a large oval node at its center. This node, decorated with embossed foliage, has six projecting studs bearing enamel images of Christ in Pity, the Virgin and several apostles, including Saint Peter. The cylindrical body of the reliquary has a base in the shape of a truncated cone that rests on the stem: on its plinth, adorned with palmettes, stand six slender wreathed columns topped by Corinthian capitals that support a cupola, actually two small depressed cupolas (the smaller set on top of the larger), decorated with gadroons and enamels. The cupolas are surmounted by a small sphere and supported by a nielloed drum inscribed with the words:
"TU NOS AB HOSTE DEFENDE MALIGNO."
As has already been said, this reliquary was first mentioned in 1566 as the custodial of a fragment of the column of the flagellation and of the cord with which Christ was bound to it. It is not until 1700 that reference is made to the insertion of another relic: a fragment of the Holy Sepulcher in Jerusalem that had been donated to the Basilica.

Liscia Bemporad (1980, p. 105) has recently shown that the two parts of the reliquary do not date from the same period and come from different places. The base and the stem belonged to another reliquary, or more likely a chalice, as is stated in the inventory of 1566 ("tabernacolo […] con il piede di calice" [Tabernacle … with the foot of a chalice]: cf. *Libro degli Inventari* s B., n. 38, c 4r). The chalice had been made in Tuscany at the end of the fourteenth century, or perhaps in Umbria, a region strongly influenced by Tuscany: the enamels on the node are inspired by Sienese art. The form of the body, on the other hand, is typical of late fifteenth-century Venetian goldsmithry.
The inscription on the drum of the cupola, invoking divine protection against the devil, may have been linked to the thaumaturgical powers attributed to relics of the saints. Even though it may not have occurred until afterward, the insertion of the relic of the flagellation is perfectly in keeping with the meaning of the phrase: it is in effect Christ himself who, through the scourgers, has undergone attack by the wicked and is now able to offer us powerful protection against evil. The later addition of the relic of the Holy Sepulcher confirms this interpretation and evokes the whole story of the Salvation, i.e. the Passion, Death and Resurrection of the Lord: display of the tokens of the victorious sacrifice of Christ who has defeated the "enemy" forever will defend those who have stuck unswervingly to faith in him. [UU]

*Bibliography*: Kleinschmidt, 1926, I, p. 279; Gnoli, 1921–22; Zocca, 1936, p. 133; *Il Tesoro della Basilica*, 1980, p. 105.

**Venetian Workshop**
Fifteenth–sixteenth century

**54**
*Reliquary of Saint Vitus*
Partially gilded, embossed and chased
silver, 32.7 × 11.5 cm
Assisi, Museo-Tesoro della Basilica
di San Francesco

This reliquary—which houses a fragment of one of Saint Vitus' bones—stands on a rounded and profiled base. From this rises a foot adorned with embossed gadroons that terminates in trefoil arches crowned by a beaded cornice. The circular and gilded stem is decorated with an openwork motif of diamonds and four-leafed clovers, with a round node in the middle that is divided into segments. The cylindrical casing of blown glass is set in a mount made of metal strips while a cross whose arms end in swallowtails stands on a ribbed conical roof that has a gilded frieze adorned with lilies running round its base.

In this reliquary, the refinement of the bands of gilding and openwork (whose function is to conceal the joints) contrasts strongly with the rough-and-ready character of the mounting for the shrine, probably altered over the course of the centuries.

The motifs, such as the swollen gadroons, the openwork and the effect obtained through the contrast between the gold of the decorations and the silver of the structure, have led the experts to attribute this object to a Venetian goldsmithry, active between the end of the fifteenth century and the beginning of the sixteenth. [PL]

*Bibliography*: *Il Tesoro della Basilica*, 1980, pp. 108–9, pl. CXIX.

## Umbrian Workshop
Fifteenth century

**55**

*Reliquary of the Cross of the Blessed Giles*
Gilded, embossed, chased and engraved
copper, 37.8 × 12.6 cm
Assisi, Museo-Tesoro della Basilica
di San Francesco

The reliquary has the architectural form
of a temple, made up of semicircular
arches crowned with a pyramidal vault,
covered with scallops and surmounted
by a globe with a cross. The smooth
support of the reliquary is attached to a
hexagonal body decorated with leaves.
The stem, also adorned with leaves, still
has three of the six original studs, their
heads engraved with a tiny rose. The
multifoil base, bordered with beads, is
worked in *repoussé* with motifs of fes-
toons and pinecones, emphasizing its
division into six fillets. Inside the reliquary we can see a copper crucifix,
whose arms end in multifoil extremities, on which the figure of Christ is represented on a very small scale, adopting
a formula introduced by Giunta Pisano.
A parchment scroll placed at the base of
the cross bears the inscription "Crux B.
Egidij socij Beati Francescani."

This reliquary, which did not enter the
Basilica's treasury until the beginning of
the twentieth century, consists not only
of the assemblage of a base and a stem
that probably belonged to a chalice
from the beginning of the fifteenth century, but also of additions made in order to lengthen the stem and support
the body. The structure of the miniature
temple, based on the use of semicircular
arches, and the absence of ornamentation are suggestive of the innovations of
the Florentine Renaissance and lead us
to date the object to the end of the fifteenth century.

The crucifix enshrined in this reliquary
belonged, as the parchment scroll in-
forms us, to the Blessed Giles of Assisi
(d. 1261/2), the first companion of Saint
Francis, who was buried in a much-
venerated shrine beneath the high altar
of San Francesco al Prato, Perugia. [PL]

*Bibliography*: *Il Tesoro della Basilica*,
1980, p. 108, pl. CXVIII.

## Umbrian Workshop
Mid-fourteenth century

**56**

*Reliquary Casket*
Painted wood, 16 × 57 × 14.5 cm
Assisi, Museo-Tesoro della Basilica
di San Francesco

This rectangular casket has a lid with
four faces and an iron handle on the
top. The painted decoration of the lid
consists of an external border adorned
with a braid and a series of black medallions enclosing four gilded tondi, while
the inner band is decorated with coats
of arms. The ornamentation of the box
itself, on the other hand, has a distinctly
symmetrical pattern on the front and
sides, made up of more escutcheons alternating with peacock feathers, a motif
of Oriental origin that could be interpreted as a symbol of the Resurrection
of Christ. The rear part has a continuous decoration of vine shoots.

The coats of arms, which may have been
those of the Franciscan authorities, have
unfortunately not yet been identified,
but it appears that this casket might be
the one—listed in the inventory of 1370
—that originally contained the sandals
of Saint Francis.

The stylistic elements of this work indicate that it was made around the middle
of the fourteenth century, which would
explain its presence in the inventory of
1370. [PL]

*Bibliography*: *Il Tesoro della Basilica*,
1980, p. 104, pl. CXIII.

**French Workshop**
Fifteenth century
and seventeenth century or later

**57**

*Reliquary of Saint Rose*
Cast, chased and embossed silver,
cast and gilded brass, amethysts,
sapphires, height 42.6 cm
Assisi, Museo-Tesoro della Basilica
di San Francesco

The base of this composite reliquary,
standing on a rectangular pedestal with
feet in the shape of pommels, consists of
six spiral columns surmounted by multifoil arches that support a depressed
cupola.

Under the cupola we see a statuette of
the Virgin and Child in Majesty flanked
by two figures. The slender and cylindrical stem is set on top of the vault: at
the bottom it is decorated with mouldings, while further up it is engraved with
bunches of grapes set inside arches. On
each side of the stem, two statuettes
stand on a base in the form of an acanthus leaf.

The plate in the shape of a lunette,
which has a blue cabochon in a setting
at the point of junction with the stem, is
adorned with two gilded angels supporting an oval medallion with the gilded heads of winged cherubs on each
side. Below it is a cut amethyst in a bezel
housing a fragment of the heart of Saint
Rose. The lunette is crowned by a pyramidal pinnacle resting on four slender
spiral columns and containing a winged
cherub's head.

This reliquary—which is not mentioned in any inventory—underwent
several alterations at the time of the insertion of the relic of Saint Rose, a few
decades after the institution of her feast
day in 1690. In fact it was not earlier
than the seventeenth century that elements like the rectangular pedestal, the
acanthus leaves serving as a base for
the statuettes placed on each side of the
stem and the lunette with gilded angels
were added to the foot (characterized by
depressed arches in a style that is still
Gothic) and the stem, both datable to
the fifteenth century.

Despite its composite character, this object—undoubtedly made by a French
goldsmith—retains a certain unity of
style. [PL]

*Bibliography*: *Il Tesoro della Basilica*,
1980, pp. 105–6, pl. CXVI–CXVII.

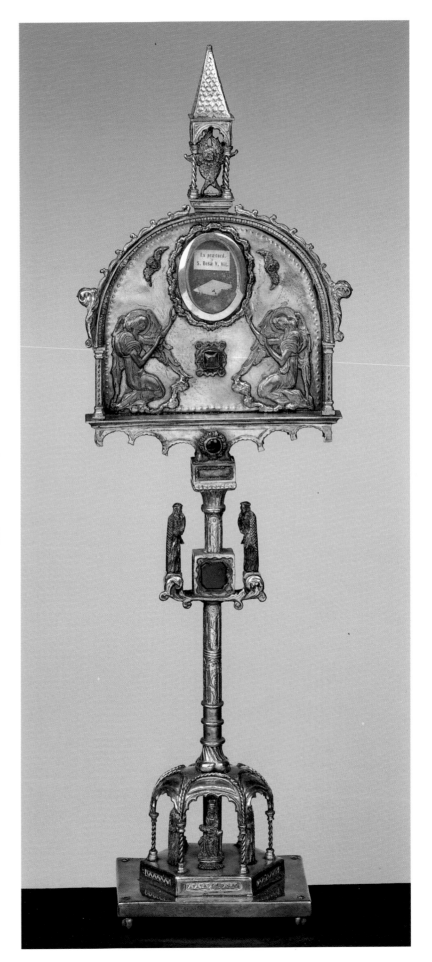

# CHALICES

# Guccio di Mannaia

Siena, documented from
1291 to 1318

**58**

*Chalice of Nicolas IV*
Silver cast by the lost-wax process
and then gilded, embossed, chased
and engraved; translucent enamels,
height 22 cm
Assisi, Museo-Tesoro della Basilica
di San Francesco

The chalice, donated to the Basilica of
San Francesco by Pope Nicholas IV
(1288–92), bears the only known signature of the Sienese goldsmith Guccio di
Mannaia, alongside the name of the
pontiff who had commissioned it:
"GUCCIUS MANAIE DE SENIS FECIT. / NIC-
CHO(L)AUS PAPE QUARTUS" runs the inscription on two lines, in gold reveal on
the enameled base of the stem. This is
the only signed work by the artist, but
numerous Sienese documents record his
activity as an engraver of seals between
1291 and 1318 (Machetti, 1929; Cioni
Liserani, 1979).
The chalice, which is of extraordinary
importance and quality, is described as a
"calix argenteus pretiosus, inauratus,
cum smaltis et figuris; quem misit dominus Nicholaus papa quartus de Ordine
Minorum; et in signum huius, dictus Papa est ibi figuratus et nomen suum de-
scriptum; et est ponderis XLV uncia-
rum" in the inventory of the Basilica
compiled in 1370 (Alessandri-Pennac-
chi, 1920, p. 11). In a later inventory,
dated 1430, a paten depicting the Last
Supper is mentioned along with the
chalice. This object, of which all trace has
been lost, must have accompanied the
chalice from the outset, given the coincidence of the weight (forty-five ounces)
with the one given in the first inventory
(Liscia Bemporad, 1980, p. 124).
The entry in the inventory also refers to
the fact that the pope who donated it to
the Basilica was portrayed on the work,
a sign that the importance of both the
object and the man who commissioned
it was clearly understood. In fact
Nicholas IV was a key figure in the history of the Basilica of Assisi and, more
generally, the order, as he was the first
Franciscan to ascend the papal throne,
in 1288. But even before that, from 1274

to 1279, he had been minister general of
the order and in that capacity had overseen the decoration of the transept of
the Upper Church, carried out by
Cimabue and his workshop at the behest
of Pope Nicholas III Orsini (1277–80).
During his pontificate, Nicholas IV devoted a great deal of attention to the
Basilica and monastery in Assisi, issuing
as many as eight bulls in the first year
alone, some of them expressly concerned with the funding and continua-
tion of the work on the Upper Church.
Guccio's chalice undoubtedly formed
part of this broad program of artistic patronage, given the complex and specific
character of the iconography used in the
enamels. Eighty of these (though two of
them have been lost) in vivid colors
adorn the stem and base of the cup. We
do not know the exact date of the chalice's execution, but it seems unlikely that
a work of such complexity should have
been made right at the beginning of
Nicholas IV's pontificate, in other words
prior to a definitive elaboration of the
ambitious plan of decoration for the
monastery in Assisi. Hence it is likely
that it was donated around 1290.
The enamels, arranged in ten rows of
eight plaquettes each, cover the whole
structure of the chalice, which is made
up of a foot with sixteen lobes and a
stem with eight faces—interrupted
halfway up by a more or less spherical
node—on which rests an ellipsoidal
bowl.
Starting from the foot, the enamels represent the Crucifixion, the Virgin, Saint
Francis, Saint Anthony, the Virgin and
Child, the donor Nicholas IV, Saint Clare
and Saint John the Evangelist, set in quatrefoil panels. However, the identification as the pope of the figure wearing a
miter and cope over the Franciscan habit
is not completely certain, though it does
seem highly plausible (Liscia Bemporad,
1980, p. 123), in view of the pontiff's
habit of having his portrait inserted in
the most important of the works that he
commissioned, such as the apsidal mosaics in the Roman Basilicas of San Giovanni in Laterano and Santa Maria Maggiore, and of the fact that this is the only

personage depicted without a halo.
The larger plaquettes on the foot alter-
nate with eight smaller ones depicting
the symbols of the Evangelists and four
other symbolic animals. A further eight
small and round enamels, set above the
quatrefoil ones, represent birds of prey
in bright colors. They are followed, on
the node, by the figures of four prophets
alternating with angels, and eight
medallions containing the images of
Christ and seven apostles, two of whom
can be recognized as Peter and Paul. The
stem of the chalice is decorated with
eight birds of prey that are set, above
and below the node, in panels bounded
by a trefoil arch. Finally, eight more angels are depicted on the ring around the
bottom of the bowl. Between the enamels, the surface of the chalice is covered
with a decoration of leaf and ribbon
motifs that surround the plaquettes.
The iconographic program appears to
turn on the theme of Christ's incarnation and death and on the propagation
of his message of salvation through the
Gospels and, from the perspective of
Franciscan spirituality, the preaching
and life of the saint from Assisi and of
his followers (Gauthier, 1972; Liscia
Bemporad, 1980).
The richness of the composition and
materials make this object a true turn-
ing point in the history of medieval
gold work. In fact it was to serve as a
fundamental model for the production
of chalices for decades to come. But
Guccio's creation presents some important innovations from the technical
viewpoint as well: it is the earliest surviving example of the use of translucent enamel, which is systematically
applied here for the color green, while
the other colors should be considered
semi-translucent.
The chalice in Assisi represents a fairly
clean break with the earlier Sienese tradition, although there do appear to be
some elements of continuity—though
only of a generically typological character—with the work of the goldsmith
Pace di Valentino, about a generation
older (Hueck, 1982).
From the stylistic point of view, the

enamels seem to anticipate the dominant tendencies in Sienese painting of
the following decades: the concentrated
and elegant lineation, a marked intensi-
fication of the expressions on some of
the faces and the predominance of a
vivid palette, on which the translucent
enamel bestows an incomparable bril-
liance. There can be no doubt that Guccio di Mannaia was strongly influenced
by the stylistic tendencies of the Gothic
figurative culture of the second half of
the thirteenth century, of which some
precious examples could be found in
Assisi, from the "ultramontane" frescoes
in the right transept and the Basilica's
stained-glass windows, most of them
executed by craftsmen from Northern
Europe, to the numerous French illuminated manuscripts, which had begun to
enter the monastery library around the
middle of the century. [AT]

*Bibliography*: Labarte, 1856; Molinier,
1891; Lisini, 1905; Gnoli, 1907; Marinangeli, 1914; Kleinschmidt, 1915; Alessan-
dri-Pennacchi, 1920; Machetti, 1929;
Zocca, 1936; Toesca, 1951; Rossi, 1957;
Bini, 1963; Hueck, 1969; Gauthier,
1972a, 1972b, 1973; Gardner, 1975;
Cioni Liserani, 1979; Leone de Castris,
1979; Liscia Bemporad, 1980 (with previous bibliography); *Gotico a Siena* (II),
1982; Hueck, 1982; Castelnuovo, 1983;
Leone de Castris, 1984; Cioni, 1987; Bellosi, 1985; Bellosi, 1989; Ciardi Dupré
dal Poggetto, 1991; Cioni, 1994; Taburet
Delahaye, 1994; Di Berardo, 1996 (with
previous bibliography).

**59**

*Chalice*
Gilded, chased and embossed copper,
gilded and engraved silver,
21.2 × 11.7 cm
Assisi, Museo-Tesoro della Basilica
di San Francesco

The multifoil and mixtilinear base with
a profiled border supports a hexagonal
foot engraved with a series of radiating
diamonds and trefoil arches (the same
decoration is found on the base of the
bowl). The foot extends to form a
hexagonal stem with mouldings and a
ribbed frame adorned with geometric
motifs. On this stands a node ornamented with embossed acanthus leaves
against a punched ground and six studs
representing the symbols of the Passion.
The medallions on the node were not
part of the chalice's original decoration.
In fact, while the images of Christ in
Pity and the Cross are chased and were
once covered with a layer of enamel, another technique was employed for the
hammer, nails, tongs, and crown of
thorns, which are engraved on a silver
ground. These medallions appear to
have been added over the course of the
nineteenth century as an inventory
drawn up in the eighteenth still mentions the absence of four studs. It may
also have been at this time that the ribbing was added to the stem. [PL]

*Bibliography*: *Il Tesoro della Basilica*,
1980, p. 126, pl. CXL–VI.

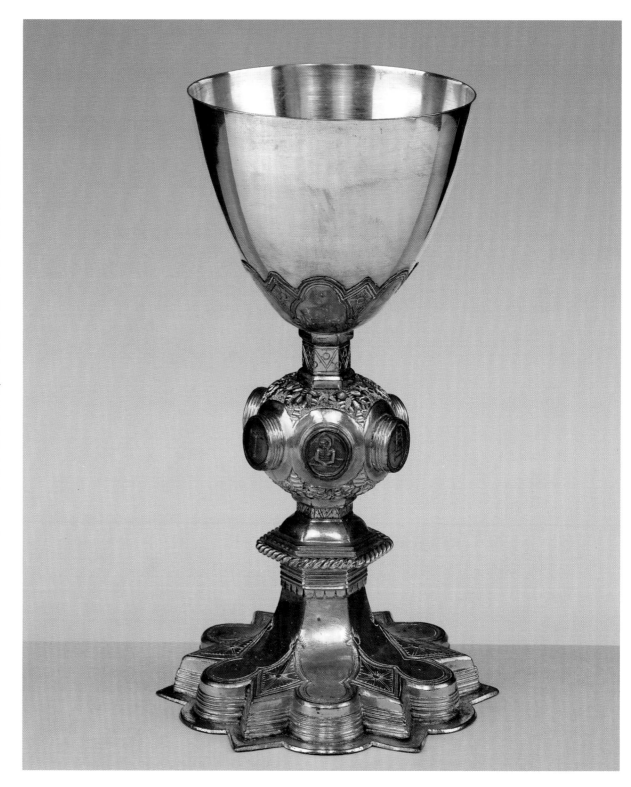

**Umbrian Workshop**
End fifteenth century

**60**
*Chalice*
Gilded, chased and embossed copper, embossed and partially gilded silver, 21.3 × 13.5 cm
Assisi, Museo-Tesoro della Basilica di San Francesco,

This chalice, which has now been restored to its original function, had been transformed into a reliquary and used to house a variety of relics, of which the most important was that of Saint Cecilia.

On a multifoil and mixtilinear base (adorned with cruciform motifs) stands the foot, divided into six sectors by fine ribs, each of which is adorned with two lanceolate leaves (with a tulip in the middle) that stand out against the punched ground. The upper part of the stem is decorated with mouldings and rhomboidal engravings. It concludes in a slightly flattened node with six settings that were once enameled and that are framed by acanthus leaves in relief. Inside the medallions (which can be divided into two groups), we find representations of the Man of Sorrows with the Virgin and Saint John on one side and on the other Saint Francis kneeling before the Cross flanked in turn by two Crosses. The base of the bowl, with a multifoil and mixtilinear border, has an engraved decoration consisting of rosettes inscribed in medallions alternating with diamonds.

The presence of the figure of Saint Francis leads us to suppose that this chalice was made expressly for the Basilica of Assisi and was therefore produced by a local workshop. [PL]

*Bibliography*: *Il Tesoro della Basilica*, 1980, p. 126, pl. CXLVII.

## Umbrian-Sienese Workshop
End fifteenth century–beginning
sixteenth century

**61**

*Chalice*
Gilded, cast and chased copper,
embossed silver, translucent enamel,
23 × 12 cm
Assisi, Museo-Tesoro della Basilica
di San Francesco

The mixtilinear, embossed and engraved foot is adorned with acanthus
leaves linked together at the base by a
band. The stem, with a hexagonal section, is decorated with mouldings and a
series of engraved rhombuses. It terminates in a large node, also ornamented
with leaves, on which are set six medallions of translucent enamel on a blue
ground containing the following representations: the Man of Sorrows, the
Virgin, Saint John, Saint Francis, Saint
Anthony and a coat of arms with a red
ladder on a gold ground. Higher up toward the bowl, the hexagonal stem is
decorated with a checked pattern. The
ornamentation of the socket in which
the bowl is set, bordered by a festoon, is
identical to that of the foot.
This object, which has features typical
of fourteenth century Tuscan design,
also shows the influence of decorative
models characteristic of Renaissance
art and the craftsman displays considerable skill in rendering the volume of
the figures depicted on the enameled
plaquettes.
The presence of Saint Francis and Saint
Anthony in the medallions seems to indicate that the chalice was commissioned for the Basilica of Assisi or a
Franciscan church. So it is likely that the
author of this work was an artist working in the Umbro-Sienese region. [PL]

*Bibliography*: *Il Tesoro della Basilica*,
1980, p. 128, pl. CL.

# SCULPTURE

## Roman or Umbrian Workshop
Mid-twelfth century

**62**

*Processional Cross*
Gilded, embossed and chased copper,
over a wooden core, 47.5 × 33 cm
Assisi, Museo-Tesoro della Basilica
di San Francesco

This is a Latin cross with rectangular extremities (the foot is connected to the stem by two diagonal elements). The front bears an image of Christ on the Cross that stands out from the metal surface. The figure of Christ is portrayed frontally with a serene expression, His eyes open and His head—framed by long hair—crowned with a cruciform halo. The loincloth is decorated with fine parallel lines and Christ's feet are nailed separately on a suppedaneum. There seems to be another small cross set above Christ's head, bearing the inscription: "ihs (vs) / na / zarenvs / [r]ex iv / de / o / rv(m)." The "r" of *iudeorum* is actually a "p," but this error may simply be a consequence of the influence of Byzantine language on the Western world, as the Latin "p" in fact corresponds to the Greek letter "rho." It is also worth noting the use of the long Greek "e" ("eta," written here as the Latin "h"), a practice that was actually very common, in the abbreviated name of Jesus.

The four rectangles that surround the cross contain representations of Mary and Saint John according to the canons of the Eastern Deësis (on the horizontal arms), an incense-bearing angel at the top and the Entombment at the bottom. The edge of the cross is adorned with small beads in relief.

On the back, the image of the Paschal Lamb is placed at the center: he has a cruciform halo and is holding the upright of his cross with his front right foot. The lamb is set inside a clypeus from which radiate four arms of a more or less rectangular shape. At the four ends we can distinguish the symbols of the Evangelists: the bull on the left, the eagle at the top, the lion on the right and the angel at the bottom. The first three are holding the Gospel while the angel—note his magnificent wings

that overlap on the lower arm of the cross—grasps a scroll inscribed with the word "liber," referring to the beginning of the Gospel according to Saint Matthew ("Liber generationis…," [The book of the generation of Jesus Christ] Matt. 1:1).

This cross was listed in the inventories of Assisi for the first time in 1430 and has been systematically mentioned ever since. But we know nothing of its provenance or whereabouts during the three centuries that separate its making from its entry into the treasury of the Basilica of San Francesco. The cross was produced by a Roman workshop—based in Umbria or Latium—and, owing to its resemblance to other works, such as the altar frontal of Celestine II at Città di Castello or a number of painted wooden crosses, has to be dated to around the middle of the twelfth century (cf. Liscia Bemporad, 1980, p. 116).

This cross adopts the Eastern iconography of a living Christ triumphant over death (which is why His eyes are open). His cross is actually His throne (the inscription contains the word "King"), in accordance with the theology of John, who saw Christ's crucifixion and death as a manifestation of His glory. This is also the significance of the poses of Mary and John, which express their veneration rather than the feelings of despair they convey in Western crosses representing the *Christus patiens*. As for the angel, he is serenely carrying out his liturgical duties, which entail censing the king's throne. At the bottom, the scene of the entombment does not show the Father engaged in burying His Son (cf. Liscia Bemporad, 1980, p. 115), but simply the figure of Joseph of Arimathea (cf. Matt. 27:59–60: "And when Joseph had taken the body, he wrapped it in a clean linen cloth, And he laid it in his own new tomb […]." A similar account of the episode can be found in the other Gospels). However, the "deposition" in the tomb of a Christ who looks almost like a child suggests a parallel with the nativity of Jesus, when Mary Theotokos, that is to say the Mother of God, "brought forth her firstborn son,

and wrapped him in swaddling clothes, and laid him in a manger […]" (Luke 2: 7). The Fathers of the Church saw this first "deposition" of the Child in the manger as a foreshadowing of the other "deposition," the one for which Jesus became incarnate and was born in order to save humanity. Thus, in Eastern iconography the crèche of the Nativity always has the shape of a tomb (Marinangeli even mistook this Deposition in the Tomb for a scene of the birth of Jesus). The back of the cross presents an explanation in eschatological and apocalyptic terms of what had already happened at the time of the crucifixion. The Paschal Lamb is not contained in a Host (as Marinangeli very curiously asserts) but in a "Greek" cross whose central point is expanded to form a clypeus

that contains an image of the *Agnus Dei*. The whole of the representation—surrounded by four animals—is in fact an explicit reference to chapter IV of Revelations where John has a vision of the Lamb seated on a throne surrounded by four beasts. Here, the artist has simply and explicitly represented the throne in the form of a cross, thereby establishing a mirror relationship with the other side of the object that to some extent undermines the traditional idea of back and front to which we are accustomed. [UU]

*Bibliography*: Gnoli, 1907, p. 433; Kleinschmidt, 1926, I, pp. 272–73; Gnoli, 1921–22, pp. 555–56; Sandberg-Vavalà, 1929, pp. 66–67; Zocca, 1936, p. 144; *Il Tesoro della Basilica*, 1980, pp. 115–16.

191

**Umbrian Master**
Thirteenth century

**63**
*Madonna and Child*
Wood, 95.5 × 20.5 × 18 cm
Assisi, Museo-Tesoro della Basilica
di San Francesco

The iconography of the crowned Virgin, seated on a throne, holding a globe in one hand and the Child in her arms, is referred to in the mystical literature of the twelfth and thirteenth century as the Regina Cœli.

The image of the Madonna with the Child in her arms came to the West through the mediation of Byzantine art. The oldest examples of this type of representation are to be found in the mosaics at Ravenna. The origin of the frontal disposition of the fully-dressed Child also lies in Oriental art. However, from the Gothic period onward, this iconography gave way to a more intimate version with the Child turned toward his mother. Moreover, it should not be forgotten that in the twelfth century, and to an even greater extent in the thirteenth century, the cult of the Virgin became so widespread and firmly established that it came to be known as "Marian idolatry."

This wooden sculpture, in which the figures have relaxed expressions and where traces of blue and red from the original polychrome decoration can still be made out, belongs to the Roman tradition of frontal Madonnas, dating from the twelfth and thirteenth centuries.

The frontal position and supple attitude of the Child leads us to date the work to the thirteenth century, while the somewhat coarse carving and the fairly stiff treatment of the drapery suggest that it was produced by an Umbrian workshop of perhaps minor importance. [PL]

*Bibliography*: *Il Tesoro della Basilica*, 1980, pp. 61–62, pl. LXIV.

**Sienese Sculptor** (?)
Second quarter fourteenth century

**64**
*Madonna and Child*
Marble, 26 × 26.7 cm
Assisi, Museo-Tesoro della Basilica
di San Francesco, Perkins Collection

The heavily-worn surface of this relief
makes it impossible to gain a complete
understanding of the sculpture, placed
by Federico Zeri (1988, pp. 46–47) in
the Sienese milieu and dated to the middle of the fourteenth century.
Set inside a trefoil canopy, supported by
two small and delicate columns, the
sculpture presents the bust of the Virgin
supporting the seated Child with her
left hand as He leans against her side.
The work, very likely made for a Marian
shrine, was possibly located out-of-
doors, which would help to explain the
degree to which the surface is weath-
ered. This process must have been accentuated by continual contact with the
hands and mouths of devotees, which in
some places, such as the Virgin's left arm
or the part of her cloak covering her
breast, has almost completely effaced
the modeling of the sculpture. [GM]

*Bibliography*: Zeri 1988, pp. 46–47.

**65**

*Two Angels*
Gilded, embossed, chased and engraved
silver, 11.3 × 5.9 × 6 cm
Assisi, Museo-Tesoro della Basilica
di San Francesco

Each of these two angels rests on an oc-
tagonal, irregular and profiled base. The
figures, kneeling with their hands
crossed on their breasts, have large
wings decorated with feathers, while
their full frocks are adorned with punch
marks in the form of rosettes. The taper-
ing faces, slit eyes and long, meticulous-
ly curled hair of the figures are to some
extent reminiscent of the *Pasquarella*
executed in 1412 by Nicolò Piczulo and
now in the parish church of Castelvec-
chio Subequo. This work, composed of a
Virgin and Child in Majesty flanked by
two angels, seems to offer a clue to the
use to which these figures were put. In
fact it is likely that the angels were
placed, partly as decoration but also as
symbolic guardians, on each side of a
cross, group of sculptures, or shrine.
Hence it is thought that they used to be
part of a reliquary in the treasury of the
Basilica that is known to have had two
angels on a casket containing the Virgin's Veil. It would have been when this
relic was placed in a tabernacle (1604)
that the angels began to be used separately.
A comparison with the Reliquary of
Saint Andrew—a work by Pietro di
Giovanni Vitale dating from 1433 and
now in Vetralla Cathedral—suggests
that these angels were made in Umbria
or Latium during the first half of the
fifteenth century. [PL]

*Bibliography*: *Il Tesoro della Basilica*,
1980, p. 128, pl. CLXXXVI.

# Umbrian Workshop (?)
Fifteenth century

**66**

*Seal of the Monastery of San Francesco of Assisi*
Engraved bronze, 7.7 × 4.3 cm
Assisi, Museo-Tesoro della Basilica di San Francesco

The bronze seal shown here is an important testimony to the history of the Franciscan monastery in Assisi. Consisting of a mandorla in bronze fitted, on the back, with a handle in the form of a volute, the seal presents an interesting iconography of Saint Francis. The scene is surrounded by a cordon (evoking the cord of the Franciscan habit) which, running parallel to the edge, separates it from the inscription: S[IGILLUM] SACRI CONVENTU / A ASISII ORDINIS M[INORUM]. Saint Francis is portrayed inside a Gothic aedicule made up of two slender columns supporting a trefoil roof with three spires. The saint is represented frontally and dressed in his traditional habit. His head is ringed with a halo and his hands are raised in the early Christian gesture of prayer. Around him, both inside and outside the aedicule, are set eight small angels (with winged heads). Below, in a smaller aedicule, a Franciscan friar is kneeling with his hands joined in prayer. In reality, this is the scene of Saint Francis's stigmatization, presented in an almost liturgical version as if it were intended for the altar of a church. The raised hands display the miraculous wounds and evoke the canonical position of the saint in this scene. As for the angels, they recall the seraph that appeared to Saint Francis, while the figure at the bottom is Brother Leo, who testified to the event before the community and was the first person to venerate Francis's stigmata, a sign of God's infinite love incarnated in Jesus, whom the *poverello* imitated in order to be imitated in turn. [UU]

*Bibliography*: Unpublished.

**67**

*Small Cross*
Carved olive wood, 13.5 × 8.3 cm
Assisi, Museo-Tesoro della Basilica
di San Francesco

The shaft of this cross has a square cross-section with blunted edges and is interrupted by three nodes: the two lower ones are cubical (though all the edges are smoothed) and engraved with a simple geometric pattern, while the upper node—on which the cross proper rests—takes the form of an irregular parallelepiped decorated in relief with palm leaves.

Each side of this small Latin cross—bounded by a grooved border which, on closer examination, turns out to be phytomorphic—is decorated with a series of six more or less rectangular scenes. The five scenes on the upper part (including the one situated at the crossing of the arms) are separated from the representation at the bottom by a grooved band that is an extension of the outer border. Each scene is set in an architectural structure with a semicircular, slightly flattened arch that is inflected at the top, supported by two slender spiral columns.

The scenes represented on the front are: at the center, the Crucifixion with the Virgin and Saint John at the Foot of the Cross; on the left, Christ's Descent into Limbo; on the right, the Entombment; at the top, two angels. Under the Crucifixion are set the figures of Saint Helen and Saint Constantine: the discovery of the True Cross is attributed to Helen and it was under the reign of Constantine that the church of the Holy Sepulcher—the Anastasis in Jerusalem—was built. The separate scene at the bottom contains the figures of two saints.

The scene at the center on the back represents the Nativity (to which we shall return at greater length). Above it, the Annunciation to Mary is identified, at the top, by the inscription ΕΥΑΓΓΕΛΙCΜΟC (the last two letters have been altered). Under the Nativity, the Visitation is dominated by a scroll with rolled-up ends bearing the inscrip-

tion Ο ΑCΓΙΑCΜΟC. This scene is remarkable for the beautiful and thickly-folded drapery of the robes, which converges on the center of the representation to symbolize the embrace. To the left and right of the central scene, two pairs of Evangelists are seated at stylized desks. The lower scene is occupied by the apostles Peter and Paul.

The two last scenes—those of the Evangelists and the two saints—pose the problem of the figures' identity. In Byzantine iconography inscriptions are obligatory, but here the space available to the artist was too small even for abbreviations. Thus he chose to place alongside each figure a pair of simple vertical marks (rather like a double iota) that, viewed from a distance, could resemble an inscription. In the lateral scenes on the back of the cross, the marks carved next to the Evangelists on the superimposed sides of the writing desks are paired, perhaps to convey an idea of the abbreviation of the term Ο ΕΥΑΓΓΕΛΙCΤΗΟC, straddling the name, also abbreviated, of each of the figures. Another mark is visible in the scene of the Annunciation between the faces of Mary and the angel, as if intended to evoke the dialogue that would have been resumed here.

The ingenious artist must have thought that he had clearly defined the figures by giving them the features laid down by tradition, but the owner of the cross apparently did not appreciate a method that smacked of illusion. We do not know at what stage he requested the addition of the missing inscriptions, in spite of the lack of space (they are carved, in a hasty manner, alongside the main figures, especially the ones that could easily be mixed up as in the series of Evangelists). Thus the Evangelist on the right—to the left of the Nativity—is identified by the abbreviated name of ΙΩ (ΑΝΝΗC); set above the halo on the right; the Evangelist on the left in the scene on the opposite side (to the right of the halo) is accompanied by the inscription Λ(ΟΥΚΑC). But the two remaining figures (Matthew and Mark) are indicated by an M which, given that it is the ini-

tial of both names, paradoxically prevents identification of the saints.

The two saints in the scene located at the bottom of the back of the cross are also identified by means of the same letter, but this time the physiognomy of the figures makes it easy to recognize Peter on the left and Paul on the right.

The scene of the Nativity—at the center of the reverse side—is identified by the scroll above it as Η ΓΕΝ(Ν)ΗCΙC Τ(ΟΥ) Κ(ΥΡΙΟ)Υ, a definition that seems worthy of a detailed description. In the middle, in a cave set in the side of a mountain (and carved in such a way as to suggest its depth), we see the figure of the Virgin lying on a linen-covered bed, her face turned outwards, the Child wrapped in swaddling clothes in a crib behind her. A ray of light descends from a triple circle (the divine Trinity) to touch the Child, forming an eight-pointed star: this is a representation of the mystery of the Divine Incarnation of Christ (light of light, morning star) that already alludes, through the number eight, to His Passion and glorious Resurrection (at the dawn of the eighth day). At bottom right, the image of Joseph, portrayed from behind, indicates that he is unconnected with the mystery of the birth of the Son of God. On the opposite side we see the episode of the wet nurse washing the newborn Child as related in the Apocryphal Gospels, which bestows a real sense of humanity on Jesus. The shortage of space does not prevent the artist from inserting, on the right of the mountain, the Annunciation to the Shepherds (though there is only one of them here) and representing—in suggestive miniature—two of the Magi who have seen the Star. [UU]

*Bibliography*: Gnoli, 1921–22, p. 431; Kleinschmidt, 1926, I, pp. 274–75; Zocca, 1936, pp. 147–48; *Il Tesoro della Basilica*, 1980, pp. 120–21.

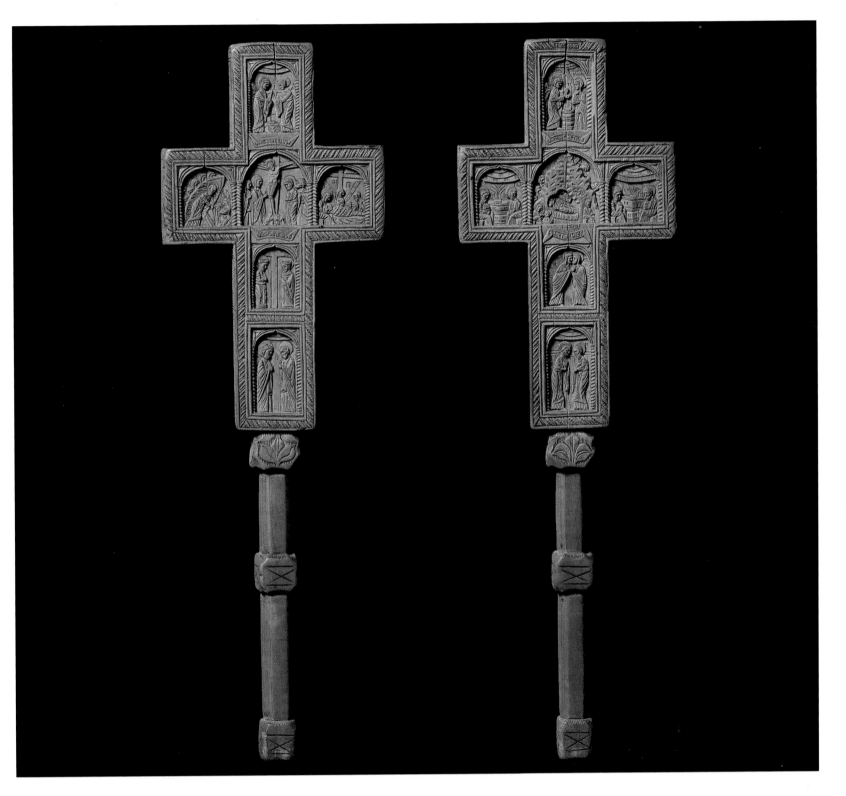

## Byzantine Workshop
Mount Athos(?),
Sixteenth century

**68**

*Benedictional Cross*
Carved wood, gold and silver; enamel,
coral and pearls, semiprecious stones
Assisi, Museo-Tesoro della Basilica
di San Francesco

This benedictional cross, i.e. one used
for blessing the congregation during
services, is one of the most recent objects to have entered the treasury in
Assisi. It was donated to the Sacro
Convento by Loris Capovilla in 1992,
on the occasion of the thirtieth anniversary of Pope John XXIII's visit to
Assisi. In fact, the cross had belonged
to Angelo Giuseppe Roncalli before he
was elected pope, having been given to
him at the time he was apostolic nuncio
in Bulgaria by the king of that country.
In all likelihood it had originally been a
gift from the monks of Mount Athos to
King Boris, perhaps at the time of his
coronation.

A splendid example of the richness of
sixteenth-century Byzantine gold work,
the cross stands on a dome-shaped base,
decorated with motifs of vine shoots
and flowers, to which four medallions
depicting the sun in anthropomorphic
guise are applied. Four semiprecious
stones of a red color are set on top of the
base, ringing the bottom of the hexagonal stem. This is made up of green,
turquoise, blue and violet strips, decorated with vertical shoots of gold fili-
gree. Halfway up the stem is set a knot
of three interwoven bands, each made
up of four golden cords. The stem ends
in the cross proper, made out of carved
wood and surrounded by a casing with
openings that reveal the different
scenes. The case, decorated in the same
manner as the strips on the stem,
terminates at the sides and top in
pointed appendices adorned with semi-
precious stones, to which three small
crosses are attached. Also enameled,
these have three small spheres of coral
fixed to the points of the outward-fac-
ing arms, with the exception of the top-
most one of the upper cross, which ends
in a pearl. Similar beads of coral are
fixed to the edge of the casing of the

cross, alternating, on the lower arm,
with small pearls. Four elaborate and
embossed gold plates, cut out to form
complex phytomorphic motifs, fill the
spaces between the arms of the cross.
The two lower ones have birds sculpted
in full relief and perched on short twigs,
along with two small dragon heads
facing outward and bearing spheres of
coral. The upper ones, on the other
hand, are decorated with two small,
round faces similar to the ones on the
base. In fact, they are not adequately dif-
ferentiated, since they should in reality
represent the sun and the moon, which
in Byzantine iconography allude to time
(the day and night) that comes to a stop,
becomes *present*, at the central *moment*
of History, that of the redeeming death
of the Son of God.

The scenes carved from wood that appear on the front of the cross start, at
the top, with the Annunciation to Mary
(against a rich architectural backdrop).
This marks, through Mary's assent, the
event of the Incarnation of the Lord,
which, right from its incipit, was directed toward His sacrifice on the cross—
and with it His triumph over death.
This image is therefore necessary (almost a premise) for a correct understanding of the mystery of the Cross
within the *Historia Salutis*. The central
scene of the Crucifixion is crowded with
figures and highly effective in spite of its
small dimensions. At the feet of the
*Christus patiens* we see Mary and the
Holy Women on the left and John and
Joseph of Arimathea on the right. Beneath the suppedaneum of the cross an
angel collects the blood flowing from
the Lord's feet in a chalice, while another angel in flight, now lost, once collect-
ed the blood from the wound in His
side: all that is left now is the angel's
hand holding a chalice. Related to the
central scene, but isolated in the open-
ing on the right arm of the cross, we find
the figure of an angel with his hands
veiled. In the left-hand and lower openings two Evangelists are depicted seated
at their desks. They are not individually
characterized and match the two figures
visible on the other side of the cross.

The central scene on the back of the
work depicts the Baptism of Christ in its
canonical iconography. This face was to
be shown on the feast day celebrating
this event, which marks the beginning
of His public life and constitutes, together with the Annunciation on the
front, a prefiguration of things to come.
Against the backdrop of a palm tree, we
see the Baptist entering from the left
and pouring water on Christ's head. The
latter is immersed in the waters of the
Jordan in the middle and attended by an
angel on the right carrying a towel and
by two more angels behind. At the center, above Christ's head, we see the dove
of the Holy Spirit mentioned in the
Gospels (cf. Matt. 3:13–17, along with
parallel passages in the other Gospels),
descending on a ray of light from the
triple divine sphere at the top. In the lateral openings, to the right and left, two
angels with veiled hands (like the one
on the other side of the cross) bow toward the central scene. In the two openings at the top and bottom, finally, are
set portraits of two more Evangelists.
Undifferentiated like the other two on
the front, they are all witnesses to the
surprising mystery of God, who "so
loved the world, that he gave His only
begotten Son" (John 3:16). [UU]

*Bibliography*: Unpublished.

# CERAMICS

## Workshop of Assisi (?)

Late-thirteenth and mid-fourteenth century

*Ceramics*
Assisi, Museo-Tesoro della Basilica di San Francesco

The numerous pieces of pottery found in Assisi over the course of two campaigns of restoration of the monastery constitute the most important discovery of medieval ceramics to have been made in Italy to this date. In fact hundreds of vessels have been brought to light. They probably came from the monastery kitchen as the majority of them are vases, pitchers, two-handled bowls and basins.

The first discovery was made in 1969, when thirteenth-century vaults under the floor that was built in the refectory of San Francesco in the eighteenth century were cleared out. The second dates from 1971–72, when a room was excavated in the north wing of the cloister.

It was a common practice to use pots in filling material to provide room for expansion in case the volume of the earth was increased by damp or infiltration: the resulting pressure and upward thrust was compensated by breakage of the pots, maintaining the stability of the floor. This method of construction was not confined to Assisi and pottery has been discovered under similar circumstances at Todi and Montalcino.

It is likely that the refectory where the first discovery was made was built between 1337 and 1377 and so the pottery must date from the first half of the four-

teenth century. "Archaic" majolica is considered the most valuable pottery produced in Central and Northern Italy toward the end of the Middle Ages. The "archaic" ceramics found at Assisi can be divided into two groups: one is characterized by yellow or green glaze, whose usage is confirmed by the fresco representing the Death of the Knight of Celano (in the cycle of episodes from the life of Saint Francis, 1291–1305) as well as by contemporary documents. The pots in the second group are decorated with purplish-brown glaze made from manganese oxide and green glaze made from copper oxide. Most of the ornamentation consists of geometrical and/or plant motifs, while zoomorphic decorations are based essentially on the representation of birds.

The city of Assisi undoubtedly had kilns for the local production of pottery, as is shown by the discovery of vessels with cracks made by firing. The monastery archives contain a bookkeeping document dating from 1354 which records the importation of a thousand pots from the nearby city of Deruta, an order that should probably be seen in relation to the meeting of the Franciscan chapter general the same year. Thus the crockery found was not all made in Assisi, as some of the vessels came from Deruta. Moreover, there must have been an exchange not just of merchandise but also of artisans between Assisi, Deruta, and Perugia. [PL]

**69**
*Bowl*
Height 5.8 cm; diameter 12.4 cm
Bowl with broad, flattened rim and disc-shaped foot. Yellow glaze.

**70**
*Pitcher*
Height 28.7 cm; diameter 10.4 cm
Pitcher with three-cusped rim, oval body, splayed foot and handle with a circular cross-section. Yellowish-white glaze with zoomorphic decoration representing a bird with its wings spread, painted in copper green and manganese brown. Braid pattern on the neck.

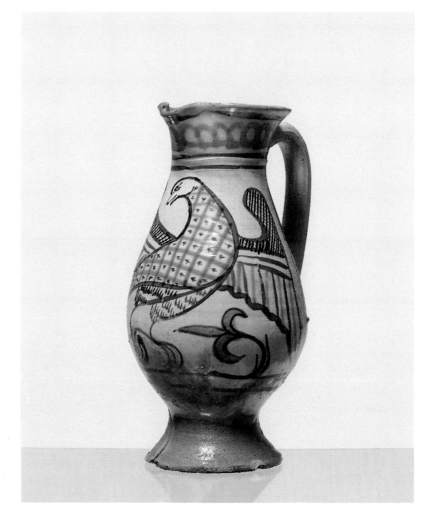

**71**
*Bowl*
Height 6.4 cm; diameter 10.6 cm
Bowl with recessed rim, corrugated lower part, flat base and two handles with a rectangular cross-section. Light-brown clay.

**72**
*Bowl*
Height 5.3 cm; diameter 9 cm
Bowl with flared sides, disc-shaped foot and handle with a circular cross-section. White glaze decorated with a herringbone pattern in copper green and manganese brown.

**73**
*Pitcher*
Height 23.3 cm; diameter 9.9 cm
Pitcher with applied spout, sub-cylindrical neck, spherical body, splayed foot and strip handle. Pinkish-white and yellowish glaze, decorated with leaves on the body, stylized foliage on the neck and an eye-shaped motif on the spout, all in manganese brown.

**74**
*Pitcher*
Height 22.4 cm; diameter 9 cm
Pitcher with profiled rim, cylindrical neck, spherical body, splayed foot and strip handle. Dark green glaze.

# APPENDICES

# Conservation during Transport and Installation
*Rosalia Varoli Piazza*

# The Reasons for a Choice
*Giuseppe Basile*

Nowadays there is rightly great concern over the idea of moving a work of art and subjecting it to changes of micro-climate. This is felt particularly by those whose task it is to study the works of art that chance has brought down to the present and pass them on to posterity. Whether or not this "chance" is to become "mischance" clearly depends on us and whether we are capable of making use of the modern technologies available.

Clearly some objects are simply not suitable for transport, either because of the precarious state of the materials or the size and nature of the objects themselves. On the other hand it is also true that most of these works of art were made to be admired or venerated, and that means to be seen.

We know today that it is possible to take adequate measures so that, for instance, during packing and transport art objects are not subjected to rough handling or variations in micro-climate. So it is important to make use of the information derived from the damage done to art objects, in the recent or distant past, while being transported or exhibited without due care; but it is above all important to know how to make use of the technologies that now make it possible to transport works of art which would have been impossible to move without risk only a few years ago.

The installation of a display is another procedure which requires the greatest care if damage is to be avoided to works of art. Here too new technologies are at hand: for example there are lamps capable of screening out ultra-violet rays (which cause rapid and irreversible damage to all organic materials) while avoiding the emission of infra-red rays. There also exist methods that exclude all stress and strain to items on display and ensure the best possible viewing conditions.

An interesting example of the preventive installation of a work of art is the way that Sixtus IV's splendid altar frontal is displayed at the museum of the treasury in Assisi. It is slightly, indeed imperceptibly, inclined to create the optimal angle for viewing while avoiding subjecting the altarpiece to tensions that would inevitably harm the precious fabric.

Unlike many other countries, Italy has never felt the need to designate works of art that cannot be lent for exhibitons or moved from their present location because of their materials, state of preservation, or their importance. The initiative taken in this regard a decade ago by the Istituto Centrale di Restauro during a conference on the problems involved in transporting works of art ended in stalemate. Actually the project was not explicitly rejected by those attending the conference, but none of them ever took up the proposal, and above all none of them stated their willingness to implement it, even experimentally.

It was only much later, in 1995, that the idea was taken up again by the Soprintendenza per i Beni Artistici e Storici in Milan, which embarked on the difficult task of cataloguing the state of preservation of the works in the storerooms of the Pinacoteca di Brera. This is still under way and should produce, among other things, a list of art works which cannot leave the gallery.

The Istituto di Restauro had already been commissioned by the friars of the Sacro Convento at Assisi to draw up a first list of items to be excluded from loans. The list included the following work: the chalice of Nicolas IV by Guccio di Mannaia (which possessed all the qualities of objects in this class: the importance of the work as the first example of a technique, the intrinsic fragility of the translucid enamels, which are moreover in a rather poor state of preservation and particularly sensitive to vibrations); the two large embroidered silk vestments from Palermo, the altar frontal of Sixtus IV, the Fransciscan Tree, a Processional Cross of the Venetian school, two large panel paintings by Giovanni di Pietro and Tiberio d'Assisi, a fragment of stained glass with the Virgin, the delicate objects of crystal-glass or rock crystal such as an ewer and a large Venetian dish.

This inventory was part of the wide-ranging and complex activitiy of the Istituto di Restauro, which in 1988 embarked on a number of schemes of prevention of damage to works of art, concerning both objects that could not be moved because of their nature or their location (wall paintings, stained glass windows), or moveable objects, which were inventoried in 1996 (paintings on canvas or panel held in the Museo del Tesoro or the Sacro Convento).

Though the earthquake of September 26, 1997 seriously damaged the rooms of the museum it spared the exhibits, which were either moved into the rooms of convent and were unharmed, or placed in special caskets after being inspected, disinfected, and protected by packing. The museum will not be able to exhibit these works until the building is restored. The fact that a selection of these works is today made available to the public of other countries is due solely to the exceptional situation caused by the earthquake.

## Restoration: Bartoli srl "Divisione Restauro"

### Reliquary of Saint Francis' Robe (then of the Companions of Saint Ursula)

*Materials and technique:*
Copper, gilding, carving, enamel, gilt and engraved glass, rock crystal, gemstones.

*Form of restoration:*
Conservational.

*State of preservation:*
The whole surface had a thick protective layer of grease which was impaired, with stains of various kinds and traces of active copper oxides. The gilding on the copper was heavily rubbed. There were numerous dents and scratches. Some stones were missing and the pieces of rock crystal on the front were loose.

*Restoration:*
The reliquary was cleaned with the aid of an appropriate diluent, applied with cotton wool to eliminate the old protective layer of grease and the dirt. The copper oxides were eliminated by a mixture in solution and an appropriate cleaning powder prepared in the workshop, using cotton wool and small soft brushes. The most stubborn oxides were eliminated manually and their corrosive action blocked by an inhibitor. The pins with the missing stones have been fixed by using epoxy glue with two components and the rock crystals were fixed in place by repairing the mountings. After a general examination of the structure and the casing of the glass, a final protective coating was applied.

### Chalice

*Materials and technique:*
Copper, gilding, carving in relief, chasing, silver.

*Form of restoration:*
Conservational.

*State of preservation:*
The surface had a thick protective layer that was badly impaired, with numerous traces of oxidation and some dents. The gilding seemed rubbed in places. The chalice was covered with a layer of dirt.

*Restoration:*
Prelminary cleaning was carried out using a nitrous solution to remove the thick protective layer, which was impaired. Then the chalice was cleaned using a solution and a cleaning powder prepared in the workshop, applied using wooden picks with cotton wool and soft brushes. The most stubborn oxides were eliminated with a scalpel and their action blocked by an inhibiting compound. A final protective coating was applied.

### Reliquary of the Column of the Flagellation and the Stone of the Holy Sepulcher

*Materials and technique:*
Silver, copper, gilding, carving, chasing, engraving, enamel, niello.

*Form of restoration:*
Conservational.

*State of preservation:*
The whole surface was badly stained, with numerous traces of copper and silver oxides. Some small pillars had come unsoldered and were made good with lead. The base was slightly dented. The colors of the opaque and translucent enamels were veiled by a thick layer of dirt and dust.

*Restoration:*
The lead was removed by using a scalpel with a fixed blade. The whole surface was cleaned using a solution applied with cotton wool and soft brushes. The more stubborn oxides were eliminated using a scalpel and the surfaces were treated with a protective substance. The silver oxides were eliminated using a paste prepared in the workshop, applied with wooden picks and soft brushes. The small pillars were replaced using an epoxy glue containing two compounds. The surfaces were given a final protective coating.

**Two Angels**

*Materials and technique*:
Gilt copper carved, chased and engraved.

*Form of restoration*:
Conservational.

*State of preservation*:
The surface was covered with a thick protective coating that had been impaired. The angels were fairly satisfactorily preserved, except for the base of an angel which had come unsoldered. The two bases were soldered with lead. The neck of an angel was dented and cracked.

*Restoration*:
After a preliminary cleaning and the removal of the grease, the lead soldering was removed manually. The inside of the copper figure was cleaned using soft brushes with an appropriate solvent. The base of a small angel was repaired using a wood chisel and reattached using tissue paper and epoxy glue containing two compounds. The scratches and cracks on the neck of one of the angels were made good from inside using an appropriately shaped tool. A final protective layer was applied to the surface.

## Reliquary of Saint Andrew's Finger

*Materials and technique*:
Gilded, engraved and chased silver, rock crystal and red gemstones (garnets?).

*Form of intervention*:
Conservational.

*State of conservation*:
The whole surface was covered with a thick protective coating containing grease and salts. The silver was completely tarnished, and had turned black. A number of gems were missing and the gilding was worn in some places.

*Form of restoration*:
The reliquary was cleaned carefully using appropriate diluents to remove the protective layer, which was impaired, and the salts. The silver oxides—hard to remove—were eliminated by using a paste prepared in the workshop, applied with box-wood picks and soft brushes. Care was taken to ensure that the gemstones and glass were firmly attached and then a final protective layer was applied.

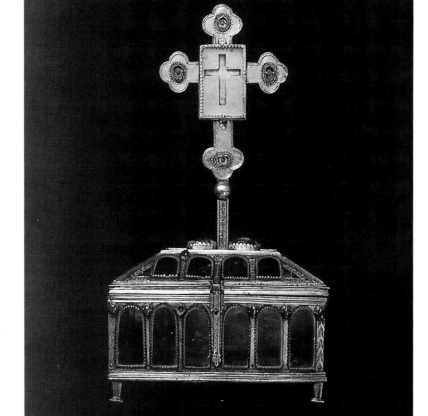

## Processional Cross

*Materials and techniques*:
Copper, gilding, chasing, engraving, wooden support, pin made of iron alloy, moulded pitch.

*Form of restoration*:
Conservational.

*State of conservation*:
The whole surface was covered with a thick protective layer that was impaired and contained traces of salt. There were numerous traces of copper and iron oxides caused by the iron nail (not original). The drapery was badly dented. The cross was also badly scratched, with pieces missing—above all on the legs of the figure of Christ—and the structure was deformed. The gilding was worn in some places. Some pieces on the sides were not original but had been made good using tin. The wooden support had some holes made by woodworm and extensive layers of salt.

*Form of restoration*:
After carefully documenting the state of preservation, the supporting panels were dismantled and the oxides were softened by soaking in a special oil. Where possible the dents were rectified, using a wooden chisel and a leather pad. Then the cross was given a preliminary cleaning with a solution and cleaning powder prepared in the workshop, applied with cotton wool using box-wood picks and brushes. The more stubborn oxides were removed with a scalpel. The interior was protected by applying a solution based on Paraloid B72 with a brush, after preliminary treatment to block the oxidants still active. Some cracks and breaks were made good by applying a lining of tissue paper and using epoxy glue containing two components. Meanwhile the wooden support was restored. The wood was cleaned and treated to protect it from woodworm using permethrine diluted in paraffin applied with a syringe. After making good the holes with wood-paste, a protective coating of Par-

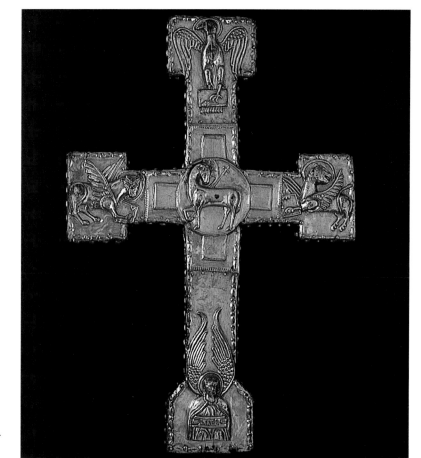

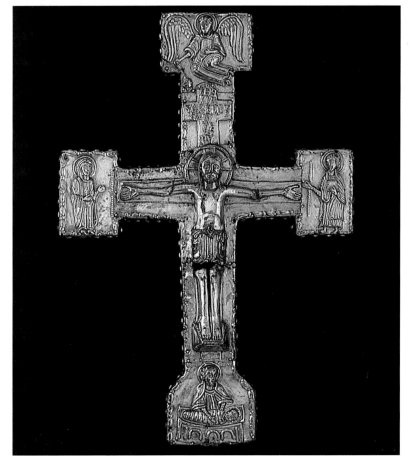

aloid B72 diluted in 3% acetone was then applied. After treatment with a rust-converter, the pieces made of a ferrous alloy were scoured clean of grease, rubbed with cleaning oil and protected with Paraloid. All the panels were then carefully assembled using brass pegs. Some figures moulded in pitch and used in making the cross were found inside it. The fragments found were preserved inside it after being firmly fixed in place.

**Reliquary of Saint Vitus**

*Materials and technique*:
Silver, gilding, carving, chasing, glass.

*Form of restoration*:
Conservational.

*State of preservation*:
The whole silver surface was badly oxidized with deposits of salts. The glass was cracked in several places and some fragments were missing. The gilding was worn in places.

*Form of restoration*:
After preliminary cleaning using acetone, the silver was cleaned using a paste prepared in the workshop, applied with box-wood picks and soft brushes. The glass was restored and reassembled using an appropriate glue. The surfaces were given a final protective coating.

# CHRONOLOGY OF THE MUSEO DEL TESORO AND THE BIBLIOTECA DEL CONVENTO DI SAN FRANCESCO DI ASSISI

**1228**
On July 17 Gregory IX himself laid the first stone of the church consecrated to the body of Saint Francis. At the same time the house and convent of the guardians of the sepulchre were being constructed.

**1230**
Translation of the body of Saint Francis: previously preserved in the church of San Giorgio, it was now laid in the crypt of the new Basilica. Gregory IX donated precious liturgical objects, as did Jean de Brienne, podestà of Perugia (also buried in the church) and later King of Jerusalem and Emperor of Constantinople.
In the bull *Is qui ecclesiam suam* (April 22), Gregory IX withdrew the church and convent he had founded from submission to all authority except that of the pope.

**1236**
Giunta Capitini, known as Pisano, worked at Assisi, where he dated and signed the first work of art placed in the Basilica: a crucifix at the foot of which the donor, the general of the Order, Fra Elia, is shown praying. Pisano was to leave numerous works of art in the Assisi region.

**1253**
During his long sojourn in the Palazzo Gregoriano (on the north side of the church), Innocent IV consecrated the church to god in memory of Saint Francis. With the bull *Dece et expedit* (July 10), he decreed the completion of the architectural complex as well as its embellishment, permitting the friars to keep the "oblationes in pecunia." With the bull *Dignum existiamamus* (July 16), Innocent IV favored the creation of the collection which included not only liturgical items but also goldsmith's work, sacred robes, etc.

**1260–1265**
The pontifical notary Benedetto Caetani (the future Boniface VIII) draws up the first document that records the existence of a collection of books in the convent (the document also mentions the cupboards that contained them).

**1271**
Death of Louis IX of France. A friend to the Minorite friars, the king sent them some important liturgical gifts through his friend Saint Bonaventure (d. 1274). It is probable that the French king had sent to Assisi artists who had worked on his buildings in Paris and, from 1260 on worked in stone and glass in the Upper Church.

**1273–1280**
The Florentine painter Giovanni di Giuseppe, called Cimabue, worked at Assisi. The artist painted numerous frescoes in the Lower and Upper Churches.

**1288–1292**
Brother Girolamo of Ascoli Piceno was elected pope and took the title of Nicholas IV, the first Franciscan pope. During his papacy work continued on the decoration of the Upper Church and the side chapels were added to the crypt (now the Lower Church). Entrusted to the care of noble families and guilds, the chapels were gradually enriched with panel paintings and precious liturgical objects.

**1290 and later**
Artists from Rome (Jacopo Torriti, Pietro Cavallini, Filippo Rusuti), Siena (Duccio di Buoninsegna) and Florence (Arnolfo di Cambio, Gaddo Gaddi (?), Ambrogio Bondone, called Giotto) worked in the Upper Church, decorating the walls of the nave.

**1312 and later**
Simone Martini of Siena decorated the chapel (with frescoes and stained glass windows) of Saint Louis (canonized in 1297) and Louis of Toulouse (canonized in 1317) and the chapel of Saint Martin of Tours.

**1319**
Rise to power of the despotic Ghibelline Muzio di Ser Francesco, who occupied the Basilica of San Francesco. He interrupted work on the decoration of the church and looted the treasure of the cardinals and the pope who were residing in Avignon.

**1322**
An inventory was made of the items remaining in the church and sacristies after the departure of the Ghibelline soldiery.

**1338**
An inventory was made of the objects in the sanctuary. The number and value of the items listed suggests that the sack of the church did not include the treasury but only aimed at the riches that the pope and cardinals had deposited in the Basilica.

**1360**
The constitutions of the general of the Order, Marco da Viterbo, contain the first rule of the "domus librorum": consultation and preservation of the chained books (for visitors to the convent) and unchained books (for the friars, masters and students); hours of consultation, financial arrangements, pens for the friar-librarian, etc.

**1381**
Giovanni Ioli, a friar-librarian trained in Parisian scholasticism, drafted an extremely valuable inventory of the codices in the library.

**1388**
The friars bring a law suit against Niccolò Vannini, a friar who, having been made bishop, refused to return some codices to the convent.

**1429–1448**
Architects and masons from the Como area and joiners from the Marches restore the walls, furniture, and bookcases in the library, which now occupies two floors (now the classrooms of the Istituto Teologico and the chambers of the Postulants).

**1471**
From Venice the general of the order, Giovanni Battista Zanetti, appoints the friar Federico d'Assisi the sacristan and guardian of the treasury.

**1474**
The city of Assisi petitions the pope and general of the Minorite friars to ensure that the relics of Saint Francis should not be exhibited too frequently or without good reason to the general public.

**1479**
Friar Francesco della Rovere is elected pope and takes the name Sixtus IV. He considerably enriched the liturgical furnishings of the sepulchre and undertook imposing works to enlarge, consolidate and restore the church (walls, frescoes, stained glass windows) and the convent. The treasury of the Basilica was by this time housed in the large cloister built by Sixtus IV and named after him.

**1497**
The friars in vain opposed the priors, Count Fiumi and a crowd of citizens who, to meet the expenses of the struggles between the different factions of the town, seized some important sacred objects containing several pounds of silver. The protests of the general of the order Francesco Sansone were followed by a protracted law suit.

**1665–1667**
Twenty-five codices were ceded to the private library of

Pope Alexander VII (and are now in the Biblioteca Apostolica Vaticana).

**1754**
The church of the sepulcher is pronounced a "patriarchal Basilica and papal chapel." This is the only shrine apart from Saint Peter's in Rome to enjoy this jurido-charismatic dignity.

**1798**
The French seize 1,144 pounds of silver and gold in sacred objects and also removed panel paintings and other items of great value.

**1801**
The pope authorizes the friars of the convent, in grave financial straits, to sell 30 pounds of silverware.

**1809**
After a decree of the convent chapter, the friars—again in difficult straits—sell more silver items considered "unusable."

**1810**
Suppression of the convent during the Napoleonic upheavals. The library is emptied to the benefit of the "public libraries" of Spoleto and Città di Castello. In 1814 the convent is reopened and recovers some of its books.

**1860**
The Pepoli decree (December 11) abolishes religious corporations. The library passes to the city of Assisi.

**1862**
A royal decree (April 21) establishes that the books and works of art of the corporations suppressed should be turned over to the communes. The artistic commission of Umbria presents a report on the material held in the "secret sacristy, also called the chamber of the treasury."

**1866**
With the creation of the Kingdom of Italy, attempts are made to seize by violence the sacred obejcts in the convent overlooked by the French.

**1897–1901**
Compilation of a catalogue of precious objects from the Basilica and convent for their exhibition in the rooms which are still the premises of the "Principe di Napoli" hostel.

**1927**
The convent restored to the Franciscans. To enable the public to see the precious objects still in the convent, an exhibition is held in the Salone Papale, on the west of the convent, and in the Sala Rossa, on the north.

**1936**
Inventory of the museum of the treasury made by Emma Zocca.

**1955**
On October 12 the American art critic Frederick Perkins dies at Assisi and bequeathes to the convent of San Francesco fifty-six paintings and one marble bas-relief (Perkins Donation). These works, which date from the fourteenth to the sixteenth centuries, require restoration before being exhibited.

**1977**
The rooms of the Museum-Treasury redesigned by the architects Leone and Marcello di Castro. The precious objects are displayed in the Salone Gotico on the north side of the cloister of Sixtus IV.

**1986**
A contribution from Alitalia enables the fifty-seven works in the Perkins Donation finally to be exhibited in the Sala Rossa. Federico Zeri compiles the scholarly catalogue.

**1997**
On September 26 and the following days, the rooms of the museum are seriously damaged by a series of earthquakes.

# BIBLIOGRAPHY

**Abate, 1960**
G. Abate, "Il primitivo Breviario francescano (1224–1227)," in *Miscellanea francescana*, 60, 1960, pp. 47–227.

**Acidini Luchinat, 1994**
C. Acidini Luchinat, *Benozzo Gozzoli*, Milan, 1994.

**Alessandri, 1906**
L. Alessandri, *Inventario dell'Antica Biblioteca di S. Francesco in Assisi, compilato nel 1381*, Assisi, 1906.

**Alessandri, 1911**
L. Alessandri, "Il Cantorino del card.le di S. Maria in Portico Matteo Rosso Orsini," in *Atti dell'Accademia Properziana del Subasio*, 3, 1911, pp. 245–60

**Alessandri and Pennacchi, 1920**
L. Alessandri and F. Pennacchi, *I più antichi inventari della sacristia del Sacro Convento di Assisi (1338–1473)*, Quaracchi, 1920.

**Alessandri and Pennacchi, 1985**
L. Alessandri and F. Pennacchi, *Inventari della sacristia del Sacro Convento di Assisi*, Quaracchi, 1985.

**Angelini, 1988**
A. Angelini, in L. Bellosi et al., *Umbri e Toscani tra Due e Trecento*, exhibition catalogue, Turin, 1988.

**Angela da Foligno, 1993**
Angela da Foligno, *Complete Works*, translation into English by P. Lachance, with an introduction by the latter and preface by R. Guarnieri, New York, 1993.

**Armstrong, 1988**
*Clare of Assisi: Early documents*, R.J. Armstrong (ed.), preface by V. Namoyo, New York, 1988.

**Assirelli, 1982**
M. Assirelli, "Il movimento francescano e la Francia," in *Francesco d'Assisi. Documenti e Archivi, Codici e Biblioteche, Miniature*, exhibition catalogue (Foligno, 1982), Milan, 1982, pp. 310–18.

**Assirelli, 1988**
M. Assirelli, "I manoscritti francesi e inglesi del Duecento," in M. Assirelli, M. Bernabò, G. Bigalli Luna, with an introduction by M.G. Ciardi Dupré Dal Poggetto, *I Libri miniati di Età romanica e gotica (La Biblioteca del Sacro Convento di Assisi, I)*,
Assisi, 1988, pp. 105–30.

**Assirelli and Sesti, 1990**
M. Assirelli and E. Sesti, *I Libri miniati del XIII e del XIV secolo (La Biblioteca del Sacro Convento di Assisi, II)*, with an introduction by M.G. Ciardi Dupré Dal Poggetto, Assisi, 1990 (with previous bibliography).

**Assisi, 1978**
*Assisi al tempo di San Francesco* (Acts of the V Convegno Internazionale, 1977), Società Internazionale di Studi Francescani, Assisi, 1978.

**Baetjer, 1995**
K. Baetjer, *European Paintings in the Metropolitan Museum of Art, by artists born before 1865*, New York, 1995.

**Banker, 1991**
J. Banker, "The Program for the Sassetta Altarpiece in the Church of S. Francesco in Borgo S. Sepolcro," in *I Tatti Studies*, IV, 1991, pp. 11–58.

**Banti, 1984**
O. Banti, *La chiesa di S. Francesco come luogo di aggregazione civile, culturale e religiosa della società pisana nel medioevo e nell'età moderna*, Pisa, 1984.

**Battisti, 1963**
E. Battisti, *Cimabue*, Milan, 1963.

**Bellosi, 1977**
L. Bellosi, "Moda e cronologia. A) La decorazione della Basilica Inferiore di Assisi," *Prospettiva* 10, 1977, pp. 21–31.

**Bellosi, 1980**
L. Bellosi, "La barba di San Francesco," *Prospettiva* 22, 1980, pp. 11–34.

**Bellosi, 1985**
L. Bellosi, *La pecora di Giotto*, Turin, 1985.

**Bellosi, 1989**
L. Bellosi, *Il pittore oltremontano di Assisi, il Gotico e la formazione di Simone Martini* (Acts of the Conference, Siena, March 27, 28, 29, 1985), Florence, 1989, pp. 39–47.

**Belting, 1977**
H. Belting, *Die Oberkirche von San Francesco in Assisi. Ihre Dekoration als Aufgabe und die Genese einer neuen Wandmalerei*, Berlin, 1977.

**Berenson, 1963**
B. Berenson, *Florentine School*, 1963.

**Berenson, 1968**
B. Berenson, *Italian Pictures of the Renaissance: Central Italian and North Italian Schools*, vol. 3, London, 1968.

**Bertelli, 1969**
C. Bertelli, "L'Enciclopedia delle Tre Fontane," *Paragone*, 235, 1969, pp. 24–49.

**Bigaroni, 1975**
M. Bigaroni, *Compilatio assisiensis dagli scritti di F. Leone e compagni su S. Francesco d'Assisi*, Porziuncola, 1975.

**Bini, 1963**
B. Bini, "Sviluppo delle tecniche orafe. Il Duecento senese," *Antichità Viva*, II, 4, 1963, pp. 57–64.

**Blum, 1983**
D. Blum, *Wandmalerei als Ordenspropaganda: Bildprogramme im Chorbereich franziskanischer Konvente Italiens bis 14. Jahrhunderts*, Worms, 1983.

**Boehmer, 1908**
"Chronica Fratris Jordani," H. Boehmer (ed.), *Collection d'études et de documents*, VI, Paris, 1908.

**Bologna, 1955**
F. Bologna, *Opere d'arte nel Salernitano dal XII al XVII secolo*, Naples, 1955.

**Bologna, 1956**
F. Bologna, "Vetrate del Maestro di Figline," *Bollettino d'Arte*, XLI, 1956, pp. 193–96.

**Bologna, 1960**
F. Bologna, "Ciò che resta di un capolavoro giovanile di Duccio," *Paragone*, 125, 1960, pp. 3–31.

**Bologna, 1962**
F. Bologna, *La pittura italiana delle origini*, Rome and Dresden, 1962.

**Bologna, 1965a**
F. Bologna, *Cimabue*, Milan, 1965.

**Bologna, 1965b**
F. Bologna, *Gli affreschi di Simone Martini ad Assisi*, Milan, 1965.

**Bologna, 1969a**
F. Bologna, "Povertà e umiltà. Il San Ludovico di Simone Martini," *Studi storici*, X, 1969, pp. 231–59.

**Bologna, 1969b**
F. Bologna, *I pittori alla corte angioina di Napoli, 1266–1414 e un riesame dell'arte nell'età fridericiana*, Rome, 1969.

**Bomford, 1989**
D. Bomford et al., *Art in the making: Italian Painting before 1400*, exhibition catalogue, London, 1989.

**Borsook, 1980**
E. Borsook, *The Mural Painters of Tuscany*, Oxford, 1980.

**Boskovits, 1968**
M. Boskovits, "Un pittore 'espressionista' del trecento umbro," in *Storia e arte in Umbria nell'età comunale* (Acts of the VI convegno di studi umbri, 1968), Perugia, 1971, pp. 115–30.

**Boskovits, 1971**
M. Boskovits, "Nuovi studi su Giotto e Assisi," *Paragone*, 261, 1971, pp. 34–56.

**Boskovits, 1973a**
M. Boskovits, "Giunta Pisano: una svolta nella pittura italiana del Duecento," *Arte Illustrata*, VI, 1973, pp. 339–52.

**Boskovits, 1973b**
M. Boskovits, *Pittura umbra e marchigiana fra medioevo e rinascimento*, Florence, 1973.

**Boskovits, 1976a**
M. Boskovits, "Appunti sull'Angelico," *Paragone*, 313, pp. 30–54.

**Boskovits, 1976b**
M. Boskovits, *Cimabue e i precursori di Giotto*, Florence, 1976.

**Boskovits, 1981**
M. Boskovits, "Gli affreschi della Sala dei Notari a Perugia e la pittura in Umbria alla fine del XIII secolo," *Bollettino d'Arte*, LXVI, 9, s. VI, 1981, pp. 1–41.

**Boskovits, 1983a**
M. Boskovits, "Celebrazioni dell'VIII centenario della nascita di San Francesco: Studi recenti sulla Basilica di Assisi," *Arte Cristiana*, LXXI, 1983, pp. 203–14.

**Boskovits, 1983b**
M. Boskovits, "Il gotico senese rivisitato: proposte e commenti su una mostra," *Arte Cristiana*, LXXI, 698, 1983, pp. 259–76.

**Boskovits, 1984**
M. Boskovits, *A Critical and Historical Corpus of Florentine Painting. Sec. III, vol. IX: The Painters of the Miniaturist Tendency*, Florence, 1984.

**Boskovits, 1993**
M. Boskovits, *A Critical and Historical Corpus of Florentine Painting. Sec. I, vol. I: The Origins*

*of Florentine Painting, 1100–1270,* Florence, 1993.

**Boskovits, 1994**
M. Boskovits, *Immagini da meditare. Ricerche su dipinti di tema religioso nei secoli XII–XV,* Milan, 1994.

**Boskovits, 1997**
M. Boskovits, "Jacopo Torriti: un tentativo di bilancio e qualche proposta," in *Scritti per l'Istituto Germanico di Storia dell'Arte di Firenze,* 1997, pp. 5–16.

**Brandi, 1983**
C. Brandi, *Giotto,* Milan, 1983.

**Branner, 1977**
R. Branner, "Manuscript Painting in Paris during the Reign of Saint Louis. A study of Styles," *California Studies in the History of Art,* XVIII, Berkeley, Los Angeles and London, 1977.

**Bredt, 1903**
E.W. Bredt, *Katalog der mittelalterlichen Miniaturen des germanischen Nationalmuseums,* Nuremberg, 1903.

**Bughetti, 1926**
B. Bughetti, "Vita e miracoli di San Francesco nelle tavole istoriate dei secoli XII e XIV," *Archivum Franciscanum Historicum,* XIX, 1926, pp. 636–732.

**Bulgari, 1958**
G.C. Bulgari, *Argentieri, Orafi e Gemmari d'Italia,* I, Rome, 1958.

**Caleca, 1986**
A. Caleca, in *La Pittura in Italia. Il Duecento e il Trecento,* E. Castelnuovo (ed.), 2 vols., Milan, 1986.

**Campagnola, 1971**
S. da Campagnola, *L'angelo del sesto sigillo e l'"alter Christus": Genesi e sviluppo di due temi francescani nei secoli XIII–XIV,* Rome, 1971.

**Campagnola, 1978**
S. da Campagnola, *Le origini francescane come problema storiografico,* Perugia, 1978.

**Campagnola, 1981**
S. da Campagnola, *Francesco d'Assisi negli scritti e nelle biografie dei secoli XII–XIV,* Assisi, 1981.

**Cannatà, 1982**
R. Cannatà, in *Un'antologia di restauri. 50 opere d'arte restaurate dal 1974 al 1981,* exhibition catalogue, Rome, 1982.

**Cannon, 1982**
J. Cannon, "Dating the Frescoes by the Maestro di S. Francesco at Assisi," *The Burlington Magazine,* 124, 1982, pp. 65–69, 947.

**Cardini, 1982**
*Leggenda di santo Galgano confessore: testo volgare inedito del XIV secolo,* F. Cardini (ed.), Sienne, 1982.

**Carità and Mora, 1959**
R. Carità and P. Mora, "Supporti per gli affreschi rimossi," *Bollettino dell'Istituto Centrale del Restauro,* 367, 1959, pp. 149–90.

**Carlettini, 1993**
I. Carlettini, "L'Apocalisse di Cimabue e la meditazione escatologica di S. Bonaventura," *Arte medievale,* VII, 1, 1993, pp. 105–28.

**Carli, 1958**
E. Carli, *Pittura medievale pisana,* Milan, 1958.

**Castelnuovo, 1983**
E. Castelnuovo, "Arte delle città, arte delle corti tra XII e XIV secolo," in *Storia dell'arte italiana,* part II, vol. 1: *Dal Medioevo al Quattrocento,* Turin, 1983.

**Cavallaro, 1992**
A. Cavallaro, *Antoniazzo Romano e gli Antoniazzeschi: Una generazione di pittori nella Roma del Quattrocento,* Udine, 1992.

**Cenci, 1981**
C. Cenci, *Bibliotheca Manuscripta ad Sacrum Conventum Assisiensem,* 2 vols., Assisi, 1981.

**Cenci, 1983**
C. Cenci, "I manoscritti del Sacro Convento d'Assisi catalogati da L. Leoni nel 1862–3," *Miscellanea francescana, Rivista trimestrale di scienze teologiche e di studi francescani,* 83, 1983.

**Cerri, 1992**
F. Cerri, "Le croci reliquiario di Gubbio: tecnica e stile," *Paragone,* XLIII, no. 31, pp. 3–26.

**Chelazzi Dini, 1997**
G. Chelazzi Dini et al., *Pittura senese,* Milan, 1997.

**Chong, 1993**
A. Chong, *European & American Painting in the Cleveland Museum of Art. A Summary Catalogue,* Cleveland, 1993.

**Christiansen, 1982**
K. Christiansen, "Fourteenth-Century Italian Altarpieces," *The Metropolitan Museum of Art Bulletin,* XL, 1, 1982.

**Christiansen, 1988**
K. Christiansen, *Painting in Renaissance Siena, 1420–1500,* exhibition catalogue, New York, 1988.

**Christiansen, 1991**
K. Christiansen, "Sano di Pietro's S. Bernardino Panels," *The Burlington Magazine,* 133, 1991, pp. 451–52.

**Ciardi, 1980**
M.G. Ciardi Dupré Dal Poggetto, "I libri liturgici," in *Il Tesoro della Basilica di San Francesco ad Assisi,* Assisi and Florence, 1980, pp. 63–75.

**Ciardi, 1982a**
M.G. Ciardi Dupré Dal Poggetto, "La nascita dei cicli corali umbri," in *Francesco d'Assisi. Documenti e Archivi, Codici e Biblioteche, Miniature,* exhibition catalogue (Foligno, 1982), Milan, 1982, pp. 349–50.

**Ciardi, 1982b**
M.G. Ciardi Dupré Dal Poggetto, "La miniatura francescana dalle origini alla morte di san Bonaventura," in *Francesco d'Assisi. Documenti e Archivi, Codici e Biblioteche, Miniature,* exhibition catalogue (Foligno, 1982), Milan, 1982, pp. 331, 333–34.

**Ciardi, 1989**
M.G. Ciardi Dupré Dal Poggetto, "La committenza e il mecenatismo artistico di Niccolò IV," in *Niccolò IV; un pontificato tra Oriente e Occidente* (Acts of the Conference, Ascoli Piceno, 1989), Spoleto, 1991, pp. 193–222.

**Cioni, 1987**
E. Cioni, "Per l'oreficeria senese del primo Trecento: il calice di 'Duccio di Donato e soci' a Gualdo Tadino," *Prospettiva,* 51, 1987, pp. 56–66.

**Cioni, 1994**
E. Cioni, "Guccio da Mannaia e l'esperienza del Gotico transalpino," in *Il Gotico europeo in Italia,* Naples, 1994, pp. 311–23.

**Cioni Liserani, 1979**
E. Cioni Liserani, "Alcune ipotesi per Guccio da Mannaia," in *Prospettiva,* 17, 1979, pp. 47–58.

**Coletti, 1949**
L. Coletti, *Gli affreschi della Basilica di Assisi,* Bergamo, 1949.

**Collareta, 1991**
M. Collareta, "Forma Fidei – Il significato dello stile negli arredi liturgici," in *Ori e argenti dei Santi,* Trent, 1991, pp. 23–25, fig. 3.

**Conti, 1981**
A. Conti, *La miniatura bolognese. Scuole e botteghe, 1270–1340,* Bologna, 1981.

**Coor-Achenbach, 1949**
G. Coor-Achenbach, "A New Attribution for the Dugento Crucifixion in the Museum of Fine Arts, Boston," *Bulletin of the Museum of Fine Arts,* 47, 1949, pp. 40–42.

**Crocetti, 1989–90**
G. Crocetti, "Giovanni di Stefano da Montelparo intagliatore marchigiano del secolo XV," *Arte Cristiana,* LXXVIII, 735, pp. 465–74; LXXIX, 736, pp. 15–30.

**Crowe and Cavalcaselle, 1866**
*A New History of Painting in Italy from the Second to the Sixteenth Century,* vol. 3, London, 1866 (facsimile, New York and London, 1980).

**Cuoghi Costantini and Silvestri, 1991**
M. Cuoghi Costantini and J. Silvestri, *Capolavori restaurati dell'arte tessile,* Padua, 1991, pp. 103–5.

**D'Alverny, 1957**
M.T. D'Alverny, "L'explicit du 'De Animalibus' d'Avicenne traduit par Michel Scot," *Bibliothèque de l'Ecole des Chartres* 115, 1957.

**Dabell, 1996**
F. Dabell, in *Gold Backs, 1250–1480,* exhibition catalogue, Matthiesen Fine Art Ltd., London, 1996.

**Dal Poz, 1994**
L. Dal Poz, "Manoscritti francesi ed inglesi del Duecento in Italia dal XIII agl'inizi del XV secolo," in *Il Gotico europeo in Italia,* Naples, 1994.

**Davies and Gordon, 1988**
M. Davies, *National Gallery: Catalogue of the Early Italian Schools, before 1400,* revised by D. Gordon, London, 1988.

**De Marchi, 1990**
A. De Marchi, in L. Bellosi et al., *Pittura di luce: Giovanni di Francesco e l'arte fiorentina di*

*metà Quattrocento*, exhibition catalogue, Milan, 1990.

**De Marchi, 1998**
A. De Marchi, in *Sumptuosa tabula picta: Pittori a Lucca tra gotico e rinascimento*, exhibition catalogue, Livorno, 1998, pp. 266–71, 400–25.

**Di Berardo 1996**
M. Di Berardo, entry "Guccio di Mannaia," in *Enciclopedia dell'arte medievale*, vol. 7, Rome, 1996, pp. 146–50.

**Donnini, 1975**
G. Donnini, "Una Crocifissione umbra del primo Trecento," *Paragone*, 305, 1975, pp. 3–12.

**Eisenberg, 1989**
M. Eisenberg, *Lorenzo Monaco*, Princeton, 1989.

**Farnetani, 1978**
B. Farnetani, *Museo-tesoro della Basilica di S. Francesco*, Assisi, 1978.

**Fattorini, 1997**
G. Fattorini, in *Galleria Nazionale di Parma. Catalogo delle opere dall'Antico al Cinquecento*, L. Fornari Schianchi (ed.), Milan, 1997, pp. 60–62.

**Filieri, 1998**
M.T. Filieri, in *Sumptuosa tabula picta: Pittori a Lucca tra gotico e rinascimento*, exhibition catalogue, Livorno, 1998, pp. 272–73.

***Fontes franciscani*, 1995**
*Fontes franciscani*, E. Menestò and S. Brufani (eds.), Assisi, 1995.

***Francesco d'Assisi*, 1982**
*Francesco d'Assisi: storia e arte*, Milan, 1982.

**Francis, 1945**
H.S. Francis, "A Fifteenth-century Florentine Processional Cross," *Cleveland Museum of Art Bulletin*, XXXII, 1945, pp. 3–5.

**Fratini, 1882**
G. Fratini (ma. A. Cristofani), *Storia della Basilica e del Convento di S. Francesco in Assisi*, Prato, 1882.

**Frenfanelli Cibo, 1872**
S. Frenfanelli Cibo, *Niccolò Alunno e la scuola umbra*, Rome, 1872.

**Freuler, 1994**
G. Freuler, "Sienese Quattrocento Painting in the Service of Spiritual Propaganda," in *Italian Altarpieces, 1250–1550: Function*

*and Design*, E. Borsook and F. Superbi Gioffredi (eds.), Oxford, 1994, pp. 81–100.

**Frinta, 1976**
M.S. Frinta, "Deletions from the Oeuvre of Pietro Lorenzetti and related works by the Master of the Beata Umiltà, Mino Parcis da Siena and Jacopo di Mino del Pelliccaio," *Mitteilungen des Kunsthistorischen Institutes in Florenz*, XX, pp. 271–300.

**Frugoni, 1993**
C. Frugoni, *Francesco e l'invenzione delle stimmate. Una storia per parole e immagini fino a Bonaventura e Giotto*, Turin, 1993.

**Frugoni, 1998**
C. Frugoni, *Francis of Assisi: A Life*, New York, 1998 (first edition, Turin, 1995).

**Fusetti and Virilli, 1994**
S. Fusetti and P. Virilli, in *Dipinti, sculture e ceramiche della Galleria Nazionale dell'Umbria. Studi e restauri*, C. Bon Valsassina and V. Garibaldi (eds.), Florence, 1994.

**Gallavotti Cavallero, 1985**
D. Gallavotti Cavallero, *L'ospedale di Santa Maria della Scala in Siena*, Pisa, 1985.

**Gandolfo, 1988**
F. Gandolfo, *Aggiornamento a G. Matthiae, Pittura romana nel Medioevo. Secoli XI–XIV*, Rome, 1988.

**Gardner, 1975**
J. Gardner, "Some Cardinal's Seals of the Thirteenth century," *Journal of the Warburg and Courtauld Institutes*, XXXVIII, 1975, pp. 72–96.

**Gardner, 1982**
J. Gardner, "The Louvre Stigmatization and the Problem of the Narrative Altarpiece," *Zeitschrift für Kunstgeschichte*, 45, 1982, pp. 220–21.

**Garrison, 1949**
E.B. Garrison, *Italian Romanesque Panel Painting*, Florence, 1949.

**Gauthier, 1972a**
M.-M. Gauthier, "De la palette au style chez les émailleurs du Moyen Âge," in *Evolution générale et développements régionaux en histoire de l'art* (Acts of the XXIIᵉ Congrés international d'histoire de l'art), Budapest, 1972.

**Gauthier, 1972b**
M.-M. Gauthier, *Emaux du Moyen Âge occidental*, Fribourg, 1972.

**Gauthier, 1973**
M.-M. Gauthier, "Incunables des émaux translucides," in *Civiltà delle arti minori in Toscana* (Proceedings of the conference, Arezzo, 1971), Florence, 1973.

**Giglioli, 1906**
O. Giglioli, *Empoli artistica*, Florence, 1906.

***Giotto e i giotteschi*, 1969**
*Giotto e i giotteschi in Assisi*, with an introduction by G. Palumbo, Rome, 1969.

***Giotto e il suo tempo*, 1971**
*Giotto e il suo tempo* (*Atti del Congresso Internazionale per il VII centenario della nascita di Giotto*, 1967), Rome, 1971.

**Gnoli, 1907**
U. Gnoli, "L'oreficeria alla mostra di Perugia," *Emporium*, XX–VII, 1907, pp. 429–56.

**Gnoli, 1911**
U. Gnoli, "Il 'Gonfalone della Peste' di Niccolò Alunno e la più antica veduta di Assisi," *Bollettino d'Arte*, V, 1911, pp. 63–70.

**Gnoli, 1921–22**
U. Gnoli, "Il Tesoro di San Francesco d'Assisi," *Dedalo*, I, 1921, pp. 421–41; and *Dedalo*, II, 1922, pp. 555–79.

**Gnudi, 1958**
C. Gnudi, *Giotto*, Milan, 1958.

**Goffen, 1988**
R. Goffen, *Spirituality in Conflict: Saint Francis and Giotto's Bardi Chapel*, University Park, Pennsylvania, 1988.

**Gordon, 1982**
D. Gordon, "A Perugian Provenance for the Franciscan Double-sided Altarpiece by the Maestro di S. Francesco," *The Burlington Magazine*, 124, 1982, pp. 70–77.

**Gordon, 1984**
D. Gordon, "Un Crucifix du Maître de San Francesco," *La Revue du Louvre*, 34, 1984, pp. 253–61.

**Gordon, 1993**
D. Gordon, "The reconstruction of Sassetta's Altar-Piece for San Francesco, Borgo San Sepolcro. A Postscript," *The Burlington Magazine*, 135, 1993, pp. 620–23.

**Gordon, 1994**
D. Gordon, "The Mass Production of Franciscan Piety: Another Look at Some Umbrian *Verres Englomisés*," *Apollo*, CXL, 394, 1994, pp. 33–42.

**Grégoire, 1967**
R. Grégoire, "Le commentaire du Psautier du moine Odon," *Benedictina*, 14, 1967.

**Guardabassi, 1872**
M. Guardabassi, *Indice-Guida dei Monumenti pagani e cristiani riguardanti l'Istoria e l'Arte esistenti nella provincia dell'Umbria*, Perugia, 1872.

**Habig, 1972**
*St. Francis of Assisi: Writings and Early Biographies. English Omnibus of the Sources for the Life of St. Francis*, M.A. Habig (ed.), Chicago, 1972.

**Haseloff, 1938**
G. Haseloff, *Die Psalterillustration im 13. Jahrunderts*, 1938.

**Hertlein, 1965**
E. Hertlein, "Capolavori francesi in San Francesco di Assisi," *Antichità Viva*, IV, 1965, pp. 54–70.

**Hindman, 1998**
S. Hindman, in *Les Enluminures, Moyen Âge, Renaissance*, cat. 7, Paris, 1998.

**Hoch, 1985**
A.S. Hoch, "A New Document for Simone Martini's Chapel of St. Martin at Assisi," *Gesta*, 24, 1985, pp. 141–46.

**Hoch, 1986**
A.S. Hoch, "The Identity of a Saint in the Chapel of St. Martin at Assisi," *Arte Cristiana*, LXXIV, 1986, pp. 103–5.

**Hoch, 1987**
A.S. Hoch, "St. Martin of Tours: His Transformation into a Chivalric Hero and the Franciscan Ideal," *Zeitschrift für Kunstgeschichte*, L, 1987, pp. 471–82.

**Hoch, 1991**
A.S. Hoch, "The Dedication of the St. Elizabeth Altar at Assisi," *The Burlington Magazine*, CXXXIII, 1991, pp. 36–37.

**Hueck, 1969**
I. Hueck, "Una Crocefissione su marmo del primo Trecento e alcuni smalti senesi," *Antichità Viva*, VIII, 1, 1969, pp. 22–34.

**Hueck, 1979**
I. Hueck, "Le vetrate di Assisi

nelle copie del Rambaux e notizie sul restauro di Giovanni Bertini," *Bollettino d'Arte*, LXIV, 1979, pp. 75–90.

**Hueck, 1981a**
I. Hueck, "Cimabue und das Bildprogramm der Oberkirche von San Francesco in Assisi," *Mitteilungen des Kunsthistorischen Institutes in Florenz*, XXV, 1981, pp. 279–324.

**Hueck, 1981b**
I. Hueck, "La Basilica francescana di Assisi nell'Ottocento; alcuni documenti su restauri progettati ed interventi eseguiti," *Bollettino d'Arte*, LXVI, 1981, pp. 143–52.

**Hueck, 1982a**
I. Hueck, "Pace di Valentino und die Entwicklung des Kelsches im Duecento," *Mitteilungen des Kunsthistorischen Institutes in Florenz*, XXVI, 1982, pp. 258–59.

**Hueck, 1982b**
I. Hueck, "L'oreficeria in Umbria dal secolo XII alla fine del XIII," in *Franceso d'Assisi. Storia e arte*, exhibition catalogue, Milan, 1982.

**Hueck, 1984a**
I. Hueck, "Der Lettner der Unterkirche von San Francesco in Assisi," *Mitteilungen des Kunsthistorischen Institutes in Florenz*, XXVIII, 1984, pp. 173–202.

**Hueck, 1984b**
I. Hueck, "Ein Dokument zur Magdalenenkapelle der Franziskirche von Assisi," in *Scritti di storia dell'arte in onore di Roberto Salvini*, Florence, 1984, pp. 191–96.

**Hueck, 1986**
I. Hueck, "Die Kapellen der Basilika San Francesco in Assisi: die Auftraggeber und die Franziskaner," in *Patronage and Public in the Trecento*, Florence, 1986, pp. 81–104.

**Hueck, 1991**
I. Hueck, "Ein umbrisches Reliquiar in Kunstgewerbemuseum Schloss Köpenick," *Forschungen und Berichte. Staatliche Museen zu Berlin*, 31, 1991, pp. 183–88.

***Il gotico a Siena*, 1982**
*Il gotico a Siena: miniature, oreficerie, pitture, oggetti d'arte*, exhibition catalogue (Siena, 1982), Florence, 1982.

**Il gotico europeo, 1994**
*Il gotico europeo in Italia*, V. Pace, M. Bagnoli and F. Martin (eds.), Milan, 1994.

**Il Maestro di Figline, 1980**
*Il Maestro di Figline: un pittore del trecento*, exhibition catalogue, L. Bellosi (ed.), Florence, 1980.

**Il Tesoro della Basilica, 1980**
*Il Tesoro della Basilica di San Francesco ad Assisi*, Florence, 1980.

**Il Tesoro di San Francesco, 1922**
"Il Tesoro di San Francesco d'Assisi, II," *Dedalo*, 1922, pp. 555–79.

**Inventario di Codici**
*Inventario di Codici Rossiani*, Biblioteca Apostolica Vaticana, Ms. Rosso 399 (1–8), Vatican.

**Inventario dei Manoscritti**
*Inventario dei Manoscritti Chigiani*, Biblioteca Apostolica Vaticana, Ms. Rosso 389 (1–6), Vatican.

**Kanter, 1988**
L.B. Kanter, in K. Christiansen et al., *Painting in Renaissance Siena, 1420–1500*, exhibition catalogue, New York, 1988.

**Kanter, 1994a**
L.B. Kanter, *Italian Paintings in the Museum of Fine Arts Boston*, vol. I: *13th-15th Century*, Boston, 1994.

**Kanter, 1994b**
L.B. Kanter et al., *Painting and Illumination in Early Renaissance Florence, 1300–1450*, exhibition catalogue, New York, 1994.

**Kleinschmidt, 1926**
B. Kleinschmidt (Order of Minor friars), *Die Basilika San Francesco in Assisi*, 3 vols., Berlin, 1915–1928 (especially vol. 2: *Die Wandmalereien der Basilika*, Berlin, 1926).

**Krüger, 1992**
K. Krüger, *Der Frühe Bildkult des Franziskus in Italien: und Funktionswandel des Tafelbildes im 13. und 14. Jahrhundert*, Berlin, 1992.

**Labarte, 1856**
J. Labarte, *Recherches sur la peinture en émail dans l'antiquité et au moyen âge*, Paris, 1856.

**Labriola, 1997**
A. Labriola, in M. Boskovits et al., *Miniature a Brera, 1100–1422. Manoscritti dalla Biblioteca Nazionale Braidense e da Collezioni private*, exhibition catalogue, Milan, 1997.

**Laclotte, 1976**
M. Laclotte, "Un Saint Evêque de Pietro Lorenzetti," *Paragone*, XX–VII, 317–19, 1976, pp. 15–18.

**Laclotte, 1983**
M. Laclotte, in *L'Art gothique siennois*, exhibition catalogue, Florence, 1983.

**Laclotte and Mognetti, 1976**
M. Laclotte and E. Mognetti, *Avignon-Musée du Petit Palais. Peinture Italienne*, Paris, 1976.

**Lancombe, 1955**
G. Lancombe et autres, *Aristoteles Latinus*, 2 vols., Rome, 1955.

**Leone de Castris, 1979**
P.L. Leone de Castris, "Smalti e oreficerie di Guccio da Mannaia al Bargello," *Prospettiva*, 17, 1979, pp. 59–64.

**Leone de Castris, 1984**
P.L. Leone de Castris, "Trasformazione e continuità nel passaggio dello smalto senese da champlevé a traslucido" (Acts of the "I giornata di studio sugli smalti traslucidi," A.R. Calderoni Masetti (ed.), Pisa, 1983) *Annali della Scuola Normale Superiore di Pisa, Classe di lettere e filosofia* XIV, s. III, 1984, pp. 533–56.

**L'Art au temps des rois maudits, 1998**
*L'Art au temps des rois maudits. Philippe le Bel et ses fils, 1285–1328*, Paris, 1998, pp. 193–95.

**"Legendae", 1926–41**
"Legendae S. Francisci Assisiensis saeculis XIII et XIV conscriptae," with introductions by M. Bihl, in *Analecta francescana*, X, 1926–41.

**Les Registres, 1886–1893**
*Les Registres de Nicolas IV*, ed. Langlois (*Bibliothèque des Ecoles françaises d'Athènes et Rome*, V, 1–2, s. II), vol. l, Paris, 1886–93, p. 13, n. 74.

**Lindberg, 1970**
D.C. Lindberg, *John Pecham and the Science of Optics*, Madison, Milwaukee and London, 1970.

**Liscia Bemporad, 1980**
D. Liscia Bemporad, in *Il Tesoro della Basilica di San Francesco ad Assisi*, Assisi and Florence, 1980, entry nos. 22, 49, pp. 96–98, 123–25.

**Lisini, 1904**
A. Lisini, "Notizie di orafi e di oggetti d'oreficeria senesi," *Bollettino senese di storia patria*, XI, 1904, pp. 645–78.

**Lloyd, 1993**
C. Lloyd, *Italian Paintings before 1600 in the Art Institute of Chicago*, Chicago and Princeton, 1993.

**Lochoff, 1937**
L. Lochoff, "Gli affreschi dell'Antico e del Nuovo Testamento nella basilica superiore di Assisi," *Rivista d'Arte*, XIX, 1937, pp. 240–70.

**Longhi, 1927**
R. Longhi, "In favore di Antoniazzo Romano," *Vita Artistica*, II, 11–12, 1927, pp. 226–33 (repr. in *Opere complete di Roberto Longhi - Saggi e ricerche [1925–28]*, Florence, 1967, pp. 245–56).

**Longhi, 1928**
R. Longhi, "Un dipinto dell'Angelico a Livorno," *Pinacotheca*, I, 3, 1928, pp. 153–59.

**Longhi, 1948**
R. Longhi, "Giudizio sul Duecento," *Proporzioni* II, 1948, pp. 5–54.

**Longhi, 1963**
R. Longhi, "In traccia di alcuni anonimi trecentisti," *Paragone*, 167, 1963, pp. 3–16.

**Lunghi, 1982**
E. Lunghi, in *Francesco d'Assisi. Documenti e Archivi, Codici e Biblioteche, Miniature*, exhibition catalogue (Foligno, 1982), Milan, 1982.

**Lunghi, 1986**
E. Lunghi, in *La Pittura in Italia. Il Duecento e il Trecento*, E. Castelnuovo (ed.), 2 vols., Milan, 1986.

**Lunghi, 1993**
E. Lunghi, *Niccolò Alunno in Umbria*, Assisi, 1993.

**Lunghi, 1995**
E. Lunghi, *Il Crocefisso di Giunta Pisano e l'Icona del "Maestro di San Francesco" alla Porziuncola*, Assisi, 1995.

**Lunghi, 1996**
E. Lunghi, *The Basilica of St. Francis at Assisi: The Frescoes by Giotto, his Precursors, and Followers*, translated by C. Evans, London, 1996.

**Luscombe, 1985**
D.E. Luscombe, "'Venezia Biblioteca Nazionale Marziana [*sic*], Latini Classe II, 26 (2473)' and the Dionisian Corpus of the University of Paris in the Thirteenth Century," *Recherches de Théologie Ancienne et Médiévale*, 52, 1985.

**Machetti, 1929**
I. Machetti, "Orafi senesi," *La Diana*, IV, 1929, 1975, pp. 5–110.

**Maginnis, 1975**
H.B.J. Maginnis, "Assisi Revisited. Notes on Recent observations," *The Burlington Magazine*, CXVII, 1975, pp. 511–17.

**Maginnis, 1976**
H.B.J. Maginnis, "The Passion Cycle in the Lower Church of San Francesco, Assisi," *Zeitschrift für Kunstgeschichte*, 39, 1976, pp. 193–208.

**Maginnis, 1980**
H.B.J. Maginnis, "The so-called Dijon Master," *Zeitschrift für Kunstgeschichte*, XLII, pp. 121–38.

**Magro, 1991**
P. Magro, "Il paliotto di Sisto IV ad Assisi," *San Francesco patrono d'Italia*, 11, 1991, pp. 47–53.

**Mallory and Freuler, 1991**
M. Mallory and G. Freuler, "Sano di Pietro's Bernardino Altar-piece for the Compagnia della Vergine in Siena," *The Burlington Magazine*, 133, 1991, pp. 186–92.

**Manuali, 1982**
G. Manuali, "Aspetti della pittura eugubina del Trecento: sulle tracce di Palmerino di Guido e di Angelo di Pietro," *Esercizi*, 5, 1982, pp. 5–19.

**Marchini, 1956**
G. Marchini, *Le Vetrate in Italia*, Milan, 1956.

**Marchini, 1973**
G. Marchini, *Corpus vitrearum Medii Aevii: Italia*, Vol. I, Umbria, Rome, 1973.

**Marinangeli, 1914a**
B. Marinangeli, "Il calice di Niccolò IV," *Miscellanea francescana*, XV, fasc. 1, 1914, pp. 21–26.

**Marinangeli, 1914b**
B. Marinangeli, "Il Messale di San Ludovico," *Miscellanea francescana* XV, fasc. 4, 1914, pp. 121–25.

**Martin, 1993**
F. Martin, "Die Apsisverglasung

des Oberkirche von S. Francesco in Assisi: Ihre Entstehung und Stellung innerhalb der Oberkirchenausstattung," *Manuskripte zur Kunstwissenschaft in der Wernerschen Verlagsgesellschaft* 37, Worms, 1993.

**Martin, 1997**
F. Martin, *Die Glasmalereien von San Francesco in Assisi*, Ratisbon, 1997.

**Martindale, 1988**
A. Martindale, *Simone Martini*, Oxford, 1988.

**Martinelli, 1973**
V. Martinelli, "Un documento per Giotto ad Assisi," *Storia dell'arte*, 19, 1973, pp. 193–208.

**Matthiae [1965-1966]**
G. Matthiae, *Pittura romana nel Medioevo*, 2 vols., Rome, no date [1965–66].

**Meiss, 1960**
M. Meiss, *Giotto and Assisi*, New York, 1960.

**Meiss, 1962**
M. Meiss, "Reflections on Assisi: A Tabernacle and the Cesi Master," in *Scritti di storia dell'arte in onore di Mario Salmi*, Rome, 1962, pp. 74–111.

**Menestò, 1982**
E. Menestò, "La Biblioteca di Matteo d'Acquasparta," in *Francesco d'Assisi. Documenti e Archivi, Codici e Biblioteche, Miniature*, exhibition catalogue (Foligno, 1982), Milan, 1982.

**Mercati, 1924**
G. Mercati, "Codici del Convento di S. Francesco in Assisi nella Biblioteca Vaticana," *Miscellanea Francesco Ehrle*, vol. 5: *Biblioteca ed Archivio Vaticano; Biblioteche diverse* (Studies and Texts, 41), Vatican, 1924.

**Mercati, 1937**
G. Mercati, "*Opere minori raccolte in occasione del settantesimo natalizio sotto gli auspici di S.S. Pio XI*, vol. 4 (Studies and Texts, 79), Vatican, 1937.

**Merzenich, 1995**
C. Merzenich, "'Di dilettanza per un artista' – Der Sammler Antonio Giovanni Ramboux in der Toskana," in *Lust und Verlust. Kölner Sammler Zwischen Trikolore und Preussenadler*, exhibition catalogue, Cologne, 1995, pp. 303–14.

**Moench-Scherer, 1992**
E. Moench-Scherer, *Sienne et Avignon*, exhibition catalogue, Avignon, 1992.

**Molinier, 1891**
E. Molinier, *L'emaillerie*, Paris, 1992.

**Monferini, 1966**
A. Monferini, "L'Apocalisse di Cimabue," *Commentari*, XVIII, 1966, pp. 25–55.

**Mora, Mora and Philippot, 1977**
P. Mora, L. Mora and P. Philippot, *La conservation des peintures murales*, Bologna, 1977.

**Mostra storica, 1953**
*Mostra storica nazionale della miniatura*, exhibition catalogue, G. Muzzioli (ed.), Florence, 1953.

**Munro, 1983**
J.H. Munro, "The Medieval Scarlet and the Economics of Sartorial Splendour," in *Cloth and Clothing in Medieval Europe: Essays in Memory of Professor E.M. Carus-Wilson*, London, 1983, pp. 13–70.

**Neri Lusanna, 1977**
E. Neri Lusanna, "Percorso di Guido Palmerucci," *Paragone*, 325, 1977, p. 12.

**Nessi, 1982**
S. Nessi, *La Basilica di San Francesco in Assisi e la sua documentazione storica*, Assisi, 1982.

**Nicholson, 1930**
A. Nicholson, "The Roman School at Assisi," *The Art Bulletin*, XII, 1930, pp. 270–300.

**Offner, 1933**
R. Offner, "The Mostra del Tesoro di Firenze Sacra - I," *The Burlington Magazine*, 63, 1933, pp. 72–84.

**Offner, 1947**
R. Offner, *A Critical and Historical Corpus of Florentine Painting: Sec. XIII*, vol. 5, New York, 1947.

**Offner, 1956**
R. Offner, *A Critical and Historical Corpus of Florentine Painting: Sec. XIII*, vol. 6, New York, 1956.

**Omelia Ferrata, 1975**
J. Omelia Ferrata , *Niccolò da Foligno and His Frescoes from S. Maria in Campis*, Ph.D. thesis, New York University, 1975 (Ann Arbor, 1978).

**Padoa Rizzo, 1992**
A. Padoa Rizzo, *Benozzo Gozzoli:*

*Catalogo completo*, Florence, 1992.

**Pagano, 1981**
M. Pagano, "Cinquino, Natuccio," in *Dizionario biografico degli italiani*, vol. 25, Rome, 1981, pp. 647–49.

**Paliaga and Renzoni, 1991**
F. Paliaga and S. Renzoni, *Le chiese di Pisa: Guida alla conoscenza del patrimonio artistico*, Pisa, 1991, pp. 39–40.

**Palladino, 1996**
P. Palladino, in *Gold Backs, 1250–1480*, exhibition catalogue, Matthiesen Fine Art Ltd., London, 1996, pp. 77–80.

**Palumbo, 1973**
G. Palumbo, *Collezione Federico Mason Perkins, Sacro Convento di San Francesco, Assisi*, Rome, 1973.

**Parenti, 1994**
D. Parenti, in *Dipinti, sculture e ceramiche della Galleria Nazionale dell'Umbria. Studi e restauri*, C. Bon Valsassina and V. Garibaldi (eds.), Florence, 1994.

**Pavone and Pacelli, 1981**
M. Alberto Pavone and V. Pacelli, *Enciclopedia Bernardiniana*, vol. 2: *Iconografia*, Salerno, 1981.

**Perdrizet, 1908**
P. Perdrizet, *La Vièrge de la Miséricorde*, Paris, 1908.

**Petrucci, 1987**
F. Petrucci, "Bicci di Lorenzo," in *La pittura in Italia. Il Quattrocento*, vol. 2, Milan, 1987, p. 585.

**Pietralunga, 1982**
L. di Pietralunga, *Descrizione della Basilica di S. Francesco e di altri santuari di Assisi*, comments by P. Scarpellini, Treviso, 1982.

**Poeschke, 1985**
J. Poeschke, *Die Kirche von San Francesco in Assisi und ihre Wandmalerein*, Munich, 1985.

**Pope-Hennessy, 1950**
J. Pope-Hennessy, "Matteo di Giovanni's 'Assumption Altarpiece,'" *Proporzioni*, III, 1950, pp. 81–85.

**Pope-Hennessy and Kanter, 1987**
J. Pope-Hennessy and L.B. Kanter, *The Robert Lehman Collection*, vol. 1: *Italian Paintings*, New York, 1987.

**Previtali, 1965**
G. Previtali, *Gli affreschi di Giot-*

*to ad Assisi*, Milan, 1965.

**Previtali, 1967**
G. Previtali, *Giotto e la sua bottega*, Milan, 1967.

**Previtali, 1969**
G. Previtali, "Povertà e umiltà. Il San Ludovico di Simone Martini," *Studi storici* X, 1969, pp. 231–59.

**Ragionieri, 1993**
G. Ragionieri, *Note filologiche*, in H. Thode, *Francesco d'Assisi e le origini dell'arte del Rinascimento in Italia*, L. Bellosi (ed.), Rome, 1993.

**Ranghiasci, 1820**
S. Ranghiasci, in C. Fea, *Descrizione ragionata della Sagrosanta Patriarcal Basilica e Cappella papale di S. Francesco d'Assisi*, Rome, 1820.

**Roma anno 1300, 1983**
*Roma anno 1300* ("Actes de la conférence," May 19–24, 1980), with contributions by L. Bellosi, G. Bonsanti, I. Hueck, and V. Pace, Rome, 1983.

**Romano, 1985**
S. Romano, "Pittura ad Assisi, 1260–1280: Lo stato degli studi," *Arte medievale*, 2, 1985, pp. 109–21.

**Romano, 1994**
S. Romano, in *Dipinti, sculture e ceramiche della Galleria Nazionale dell'Umbria. Studi e restauri*, C. Bon Valsassina and V. Garibaldi (eds.), Florence, 1994.

**Rossi, 1872**
A. Rossi, "I pittori di Foligno nel secolo d'oro delle arti italiane," in *Giornale di erudizione artistica*, I, 1872, pp. 258–80.

**Rossi, 1957**
F. Rossi, *Capolavori di oreficeria italiana dall'XI al XVIII secolo*, Milan, 1957, pp. 258–80.

**Ruf, 1974**
G. Ruf, *S. Francesco e S. Bonaventura: un'interpretazione storico-salvifica degli affreschi della navata nella chiesa superiore di San Francesco in Assisi alla luce della teologia di S. Bonaventura*, Assisi, 1974.

**Ruf, 1981**
G. Ruf, *Das Grab des hl. Franziskus: Die Fresken der Unterkirche von Assisi*, Fribourg, 1981.

**Salmi, 1921**
M. Salmi, "Note sulla Galleria di

Perugia," *L'Arte*, XXIV, 1921, pp. 155–71.

**Sandberg-Vavalà, 1929**
E. Sandberg-Vavalà, *La croce dipinta italiana e l'iconografia della Passione*, Verona, 1929 (reprinted in Rome, 1985).

**Santangelo, 1948**
A. Santangelo, *Museo di Palazzo Venezia*, exhibition catalogue, Rome, 1948.

**Santi, 1969**
F. Santi, *Galleria Nazionale dell'Umbria. Dipinti, sculture e oggetti d'arte di età romanica e gotica*, Rome, 1969.

**Santi, 1976**
F. Santi, *Gonfaloni umbri del rinascimento*, Perugia, 1976.

**Scarpellini, 1969**
P. Scarpellini, *Di alcuni pittori giotteschi nella città e nel territorio di Assisi*, in *Giotto e i giotteschi in Assisi*, Rome, 1969, pp. 225–38.

**Scarpellini, 1980a**
P. Scarpellini, "Il Volto dell'Eterno," in *Il Tesoro della Basilica di San Francesco ad Assisi*, Florence, 1980.

**Scarpellini, 1980b**
P. Scarpellini, "Le pitture," in *Il Tesoro della Basilica di San Francesco ad Assisi*, Florence, 1980.

**Scarpellini, 1982a**
P. Scarpellini, *Commentario a Ludovico da Pietralunga. Descrizione della Basilica di San Francesco e di altri santuari di Assisi*, P. Scarpellini (ed.), Treviso, 1982.

**Scarpellini, 1982b**
P. Scarpellini, *Iconografia francescana nei secoli XIII e XIV*, in *Francesco d'Assisi. Storia e Arte*, exhibition catalogue, Milan, 1982.

**Schenkluhn, 1991**
W. Schenkluhn, *San Francesco in Assisi: Ecclesia Specialis, Die Vision Papst Gregors IX, von einer Erneurung der Kirche*, Darmstadt, 1991 (also published in Italian, *San Francesco di Assisi: Ecclesia Specialis. Fonti e ricerche* 5, Milan, 1991).

**Schultze, 1961**
J. Schultze, "Ein Dugento-Altar aus Assisi? Versuch einer Rekonstruktion," *Mitteilungen des Kunsthistorisches Institutes in Florenz*, X, pp. 59–66.

**Schultze, 1963**
J. Schultze, "Zur Kunst des 'franziskusmeister,'" *Wallraf-Richartz Jahrbuch*, XXV, 1963, pp. 109–50.

**Schwarz, 1993**
M.V. Schwarz, "Zerstört und Wiederhergestellt. Die Ausmalung der Unterkirche von S. Francesco in Assisi," *Mitteilungen des Kunsthistorischen Institutes in Florenz*, XXXVII, 1993, pp. 1–28.

**Seay, 1957**
A. Seay, "Le Manuscrit 695 de la Bibliothèque Comunale d'Assise," in *Revue de Musicologie*, XXXIX, 1957, pp. 10–35.

**Sesti, 1990**
E. Sesti, in M.G. Ciardi Dupré Dal Poggetto et al., *La Biblioteca del Sacro Convento di Assisi*, vol. 2: *I libri miniati del XIII e XIV secolo*, Assisi, 1990.

**Seymour, 1970**
C. Seymour Jr., *Early Italian Paintings in the Yale University Art Gallery*, New Haven and London, 1970.

**Shapley, 1979**
F.R. Shapley, *Catalogue of the Italian Paintings, National Gallery of Art*, 2 vols., Washington, 1979.

**Shorr, 1954**
D.C. Shorr, *The Christ Child in Devotional Images*, New York, 1954.

**Simon, 1976**
R. Simon, "Towards a Relative Chronology of the Frescoes in the Lower Church of San Francesco at Assisi," *The Burlington Magazine*, CXVIII, 1976, pp. 361–66.

**Sirén, 1905**
O. Sirén, *Don Lorenzo Monaco*, Strasbourg, 1905.

**Sirén, 1922**
O. Sirén, *Toskanische Maler im XVIII Jahrhundert*, Berlin, 1922.

**Skaug, 1994**
E.S. Skaug, *Punch Marks from Giotto to Fra Angelico: Attribution, Chronology, and Workshop Relationships in Tuscan Panel Painting*, 2 vols., Oslo, 1994.

**Smart, 1963**
A. Smart, "Ghiberti's '*quasi tutta la parte di sotto*' and Vasari's Attribution to Giotto at Assisi," *Re-naissance and Modern Studies*, VIII, 1963, pp. 5–24.

**Smart, 1971**
A. Smart, *The Assisi Problem and the Art of Giotto*, Oxford, 1971.

**Solberg, 1991**
G.E. Solberg, *Taddeo di Bartolo*, 2 vols., Ph.D. thesis, New York University, 1991 (Ann Arbor, 1995).

**Soldati, 1928**
M. Soldati, "Nota su Jacopo Torriti," *L'Arte*, XXXI, 1928, pp. 247–53.

**Spike, 1996**
J.T. Spike, *Fra Angelico*, New York, 1996.

**Sricchia Santoro, 1976**
F. Sricchia Santoro, "Sul soggiorno spagnolo di Gherardo Starnina e sull'identità del 'Maestro del Bambino Vispo,'" *Prospettiva*, 6, 1976, pp. 11–29.

**Stanislao da Campagnola, 1971**
Stanislao da Campagnola, *L'Angelo del sesto sigillo e l'"alter Christus": Genesi e sviluppo di due temi francescani nei secoli XIII e XIV*, Rome, 1971.

**Stanislao da Campagnola, 1978**
Stanislao da Campagnola, *Le origini francescane come problema storiografico*, Perugia, 1978.

**Stanislao da Campagnola, 1981**
Stanislao da Campagnola, *Francesco d'Assisi negli scritti e nelle biografie dei secoli XIII e XIV*, Assisi, 1981.

**Strehlke, 1987**
C.B. Strehlke, "A Celibate Marriage and Franciscan Poverty Reflected in a Neapolitan Trecento Diptych," *The J. Paul Getty Museum Journal*, 15, 1987, pp. 79–96.

**Strehlke, 1988**
C.B. Strehlke, in K. Christiansen et al., *Painting in Renaissance Siena, 1420–1500*, exhibition catalogue, New York, 1988.

**Strehlke 1994**
C.B. Strehlke, in L.B. Kanter et al., *Painting and Illumination in Early Renaissance Florence, 1300-1450*, exhibition catalogue, New York, 1994.

**Strzygowski, 1888**
J. Strzygowski, *Cimabue und Rom. Funde und Forschungen zur Kunstgeschichte und zur Topographie der Stadt Rom*, Vienna, 1888.

**Stubblebine, 1985**
J. Stubblebine, *Assisi and the Rise of Vernacular Art*, New York, 1985.

**Syre, 1979**
C. Syre, *Studien zum "Maestro del Bambino Vispo" und Starnina*, Bonn, 1979.

**Taburet Delahaye, 1994**
E. Taburet Delahaye, "Lo smalto traslucido a Siena e a Parigi nella prima metà del Trecento," in *Il gotico europeo in Italia*, Naples, 1994, pp. 325–41.

**Tantillo Mignosi, 1975**
A. Tantillo Mignosi, "Osservazioni sul transetto della Basilica Inferiore di Assisi," *Bollettino d'Arte*, LX, 1975, pp. 129–42.

**Tartuferi, 1991**
A. Tartuferi, *Giunta Pisano*, Soncino, 1991.

***Tesori vaticani*, 1993**
*Tesori vaticani – 2000 anni di arte e cultura in Vaticano e in Italia*, exhibition catalogue, G. Morello (ed.), Milan, 1993, p. 287.

**Thode, 1885**
H. Thode, *Franz von Assisi und die Anfänge der Kunst der Renaissance in Italien*, Berlin, 1885 (2nd edition, 1904; Ital. trans. Rome, 1991; *Francesco d'Assisi e le origini dell'arte del Rinascimento in Italia*, L. Bellosi (ed.), Rome, 1993).

**Thode, 1890**
H. Thode, "Studien zur Geschichte der Italienischen Kunst im XIII Jahrhundert," in *Repertorium für Kunstwissenschaft*, 1890, pp. 1–24.

**Tietze, 1911**
H. Tietze, *Illuminierten Handschriften der Rossiana*, Leipzig, 1911.

**Tintori and Meiss, 1962**
L. Tintori and M. Meiss, *The Painting of the Life of St. Francis in Assisi*, with *Notes on the Arena Chapel*, New York, 1962.

**Todini, 1980**
F. Todini, *La Pinacoteca Comunale di Assisi*, Florence, 1980.

**Todini, 1982**
F. Todini, in *Francesco d'Assisi. Documenti e Archivi, Codici e Biblioteche, Miniature*, exhibition catalogue (Foligno, 1982), Milan, 1982.

**Todini, 1985**
F. Todini, "Pittura del Duecento e del Trecento in Umbria e il cantiere di Assisi," in *La pittura in Italia. Le origini*, E. Castelnuovo (ed.), Milan, 1985, pp. 317–56.

**Todini, 1986**
F. Todini, in *La pittura in Italia. Il Duecento e il Trecento*, E. Castelnuovo (ed.), 2 vols., Milan, 1986.

**Todini, 1989**
F. Todini, *La pittura umbra dal duecento al primo quattrocento*, 2 vols., Milan, 1989.

**Toesca, 1927**
P. Toesca, *Storia dell'arte italiana, I. Il Medioevo*, Turin, 1927.

**Toesca, 1948**
P. Toesca, *Artis Monumenta Photographica edita. IV (Gli affreschi del Vecchio e del Nuovo Testamento ad Assisi)*, Florence, 1948.

**Toesca, 1951**
P. Toesca, *Storia dell'arte italiana, Il Trecento*, Turin, 1951.

**Tomei, 1989**
A. Tomei, "Il disegno preparatorio di Jacopo Torriti per il volto del Creatore nella basilica di Assisi," in *Fragmenta picta. Affreschi e mosaici staccati del Medioevo romano*, exhibition catalogue, Rome, 1989, pp. 227–32.

**Tomei, 1990a**
A. Tomei, *Jacobus Torriti pictor. Una vicenda figurativa del tardo Duecento romano*, Rome, 1990.

**Tomei, 1996**
A. Tomei, "Un frammento ritrovato dal mosaico del monumento di Bonifacio VIII in San Pietro," *Arte medievale*, X, 2, 1996, pp. 123–31.

**Tomei, 1997**
A. Tomei, heading "Maestro della Cattura," in *Enciclopedia dell'arte medievale*, vol. 3, Rome, 1997, p. 86.

**Torriti, 1990**
P. Torriti, *La Pinacoteca Nazionale di Siena. I dipinti*, Genoa, 1990.

**Toscano, 1990**
B. Toscano, heading "Giunta Pisano," in *Dizionario della pittura e dei pittori*, vol. 2, Turin, 1990.

**Van Marle, 1919**
R. Van Marle, "Il Maestro di San Francesco," *Rassegna d'Arte*, XIX, 1919, pp. 9–21.

**Van Marle, 1923**
R. Van Marle, *The Development of the Italian School of Painting*, vol. 1, The Hague, 1923.

**Van Marle, 1927**
R. Van Marle, *The Development of the Italian School of Painting*, vol. 9, The Hague, 1927.

**Van Marle, 1929**
R. Van Marle, *The Development of the Italian School of Painting*, vol. 11, The Hague, 1929.

**Varoli Piazza, 1991**
R. Varoli Piazza, *Il paliotto di Sisto IV ad Assisi – Indagini e intervento conservativo*, Assisi, 1991.

**Vasari (ed. Milanesi), 1878–85**
G. Vasari, *Le vite de più eccellenti pittori, scultori ed architettori*, G. Milanesi (ed.), 9 vols., Florence, 1878–85.

**Vattasso and Carusi, 1920**
M. Vattasso and E. Carusi, *Codices Vaticani Latini*, Rome, 1920.

**Venturi, 1907**
A. Venturi, *Storia dell'arte italiana, Vol. 5: La pittura del Trecento e le sue origini*, Milan, 1907.

**Venturoli, 1969**
P. Venturoli, "Giotto," *Storia dell'arte*, 1–2, 1969, pp. 142–58.

**Viale Ferrero, 1982**
M. Viale Ferrero, "Arazzo e pittura," in *Storia dell'arte italiana*, t. XI, Turin, 1982, pp. 125–26.

**Volbach, 1979**
W.F. Volbach, *Catalogo della Pinacoteca Vaticana, Vol. I: I dipinti dal X secolo fino a Giotto*, Vatican, 1979.

**Volpe, 1965**
G. Volpe, *Pietro Lorenzetti ad Assisi*, Milan, 1965.

**Volpe, 1969**
C. Volpe, "La formazione di Giotto nella cultura di Assisi," in *Giotto e i Giotteschi in Assisi*, Rome, 1969, pp. 15–59.

**Volpe, 1989**
C. Volpe, *Pietro Lorenzetti*, Milan, 1989.

**Wagstaff, 1965**
S. Wagstaff Jr., *An Exhibition of Italian Panels and Manuscripts from the Thirteenth & Fourteenth Centuries in Honor of Richard Offner*, exhibition catalogue, Hartford, 1965.

**White, 1956**
J. White, "The Date of the Leg-end of St. Francis at Assisi," *The Burlington Magazine*, XCVIII, 1956, pp. 344–50.

**Winady, 1977**
J. Winady, "La femme: un homme manqué?," *Nouvelle Revue Théologique*, 99, 1977.

**Wixom, 1974**
N.C. Wixom, *The Cleveland Museum of Art: European Paintings Before 1500*, Cleveland, 1974.

**Zaccaria, 1963–64**
G. Zaccaria, "Diario storico della basilica e sacro convento di S. Francesco in Assisi (1220–1927)," *Miscellanea francescana*, 63, 1963, pp. 75–120, 290–361, 495–53; and 64, 1964, pp. 165–210, 433–73.

**Zampetti, 1969**
P. Zampetti, *La pittura marchigiana da Gentile a Raffaello*, Milan, 1969.

**Zanardi, 1996**
B. Zanardi, *Il cantiere di Giotto: le storie di San Francesco ad Assisi*, with an introduction by F. Zeri and essay by C. Frugoni, Milan, 1996.

**Zeri, 1963**
F. Zeri, "Tre argomenti umbri," *Bollettino d'Arte* 48, s. IV, pp. 29–45.

**Zeri, 1964–65**
F. Zeri, "Investigations into the Early Period of Lorenzo Monaco – I and II," *The Burlington Magazine,* 106, 1964, pp. 554–58; and 107, 1965, pp. 3–11.

**Zeri, 1976**
F. Zeri, *Italian Paintings in The Walters Art Gallery*, Baltimore, 1976.

**Zeri, 1987**
F. Zeri, "Ricerche nella Collezione Perkins. Un 'San Paolo' dai molti interrogativi," *Paragone*, XXXVIII, 445, 1987, pp. 20–23.

**Zeri, 1988**
F. Zeri, *La collezione Federico Mason Perkins*, Turin, 1988.

**Zeri, 1992a**
F. Zeri, *Giorno per giorno nella pittura. Scritti sull'arte dell'Italia centrale e meridionale dal trecento al primo cinquecento*, Turin, 1992.

**Zeri, 1992b**
F. Zeri and F. Campagna Cicala, *Messina, Museo Regionale*, Palermo, 1992.

**Zeri and Natale, 1984**
F. Zeri and M. Natale, *Dipinti toscani e oggetti d'arte della Collezione Vittorio Cini*, Vicenza, 1984.

**Zimmermann, 1889**
M. Zimmermann, *Giotto und die Kunst Italiens in Mittelalter. 1. Voraussetzung und erste Entwicklung von Giottos Kunst*, Leipzig, 1889.

**Zocca, 1936**
E. Zocca, *Assisi. Catalogo delle cose d'arte e di antichità d'Italia*, Rome, 1936.